AI Took Your Org Chart

AI Took Your Org Chart

The Rise of Responsive Leadership in the Age of Machines

Ganesh Natarajan
Uma Ganesh
Priyanka Sangani

BLOOMSBURY
NEW DELHI • LONDON • OXFORD • NEW YORK • SYDNEY

BLOOMSBURY INDIA
Bloomsbury Publishing India Pvt. Ltd
Second Floor, LSC Building No. 4, DDA Complex, Pocket C – 6 & 7,
Vasant Kunj, New Delhi, 110070

BLOOMSBURY, BLOOMSBURY INDIA and the Diana logo are trademarks of
Bloomsbury Publishing Plc

First published in India 2026

ISBN: HB: 978-93-61319-89-1; eBook: 978-93-61318-10-8

2 4 6 8 10 9 7 5 3 1

Typeset in Adobe Garamond by Manipal Technologies Limited
Printed and bound in India by Replika Press Pvt. Ltd.

To find out more about our authors and books visit www.bloomsbury.com and sign up for our newsletters

To the spirit of human intelligence and innovation, which has always prevailed in the face of multiple technology shifts

Contents

Tables

Abbreviations

ACES	Autonomous, Connected, Electric and Share Mobility
ADB	Asian Development Bank
AGI	Artificial General Intelligence
AI	Artificial Intelligence
ALICE	Artificial Linguistic Internet Computer Entity
ANI	Artificial Narrow Intelligence
API	Application Programming Interface
AR	Augmented Reality
ASEAN	Association of Southeast Asian Nations
ASHA	Accredited Social Health Activist
ASI	Artificial Super Intelligence
BFSI	Banking, Insurance And Financial Services Industry
BNPL	Buy Now, Pay Later
BYOD	Bring Your Own Device
CBDC	Central Bank Digital Currency
CoE	Centre of Excellence
COiN	Contract Intelligence
CRM	Customer Relationship Management
DARPA	Defense Advanced Research Projects Agency
DAS	Distributed Autonomous System
DeFi	Decentralised Finance
DPDP	Digital Personal Data Protection
DPI	Digital Public Infrastructure
ESG	Environmental, Social and Governance
EV	Electric Vehicle
F&B	Food and Beverage
FMCG	Fast-Moving Consumer Goods
GDP	Gross Domestic Product
GDPR	General Data Protection Regulation
GenAI	Generative AI

GPT	Generative Pre-trained Transformer
GUI	Graphical User Interface
HR	Human Resources
IaaS	Infrastructure as a Service
IIoT	Industrial Internet of Things
IoT	Internet of Things
IPA	Intelligent Process Automation
IT	Information Technology
KYC	Know Your Customer
LaMDA	Language Model for Dialogue Applications
LAN	Local Area Network
LISP	List Processing
LLM	Large Language Model
MSME	Micro-, Small and Medium Enterprise
NBFC	Non-Banking Financial Companies
NLP	Natural Language Processing
OT	Operational Technology
PaaS	Platform as a Service
PDA	Personal Digital Assistant
PLC	Programmable Logic Controller
PLI	Production-Linked Incentives
POS	Point of Sale
QR	Quick Response Code
QSR	Quick Service Restaurants
RaaS	Robotics as a Service
RegTech	Regulatory Technology
RFID	Radio Frequency Identification
ROI	Return on Investments
RPA	Robotic Process Automation
SaaS	Software as a Service
SCADA	Supervisory Control and Data Acquisition
SI	Smart Insights
SLM	Small Language Model
SMAC	Social, Mobile, Analytics and Cloud
SQL	Structured Query Language
TiE	The IndUS Entrepreneurs

UPI	Unified Payments Interface
USSR	Union of Soviet Socialist Republics
UX	User Experience
VR	Virtual Reality
WaaS	Wealth as a Service
XCON	Expert Configurer
XR	Extended Reality

Foreword

What should leaders of organisations believe about artificial intelligence? Are we in entirely new and uncharted territory with regard to this technology? Will it totally transform business, organisations and life as we know it? Will vast numbers of humans be out of work because of it? Will highly intelligent machines dominate less intelligent humans? You would be forgiven if you believed that these hype-laden questions are either entirely correct or entirely wrong. There are elements of truth within each of them, but also substantial exaggeration. But it's likely that the employees of your organisations are taking these questions seriously, and they need your help in addressing them.

AI has, of course, been around for more than half a century, so it shouldn't be viewed as entirely new. But its velocity and visibility have changed dramatically over the last few years since ChatGPT became broadly available in November 2022. Generative AI got everyone's attention because of its (apparent) intelligence, its ability to converse easily with us, and its seemingly effortless content creation. But there have been other technologies that have dramatically changed society and human work—fire, steam engines, electricity, computers, the Internet, etc. We're not in entirely uncharted territory with this new technology. We know that it generally takes a while for people and organisations to adopt it and use it effectively. We know that its successful use requires leadership and change management. We know that it takes too long for governments to produce effective regulation of technologies, so leaders of companies and non-governmental organisations have to find their own way ethically.

The most prominent thing we've learnt from past technologies is surely relevant to AI and at the core of this book. It's the idea that the highest and best use of the technology will be helping humans become more productive and effective. That's the idea behind the 'dual intelligence' concept that's laid out further in this book. The goal of any leader should be to learn how to extract the most value out of smart machines and smart humans working collaboratively. If you are looking at AI as a vehicle for automating jobs and getting rid of lots of your employees, you're looking in the wrong place. You may succeed in the short run at reducing your costs, but your competitors will be doing the same thing. You'll be in a race to the bottom. Much better to combine the intelligence and speed of AI with the creativity and innovation of human workers.

From this book I hope you learn that humans and leadership are critical to success with AI, and that it is part of your job as a leader to persuade employees that they have valuable skills in an AI-centric world and to help them cultivate them. It's not an easy thing to determine exactly what the correct human roles will be in an AI collaboration, so your people will need all the encouragement and help you can provide.

Thomas H. Davenport
Distinguished Professor, Babson College and Research Fellow,
MIT Initiative on the Digital Economy
Author or co-author of seven books on AI, including the
Wall Street Journal bestseller *All In on AI*

Why This Book

IS ARTIFICIAL INTELLIGENCE (AI) just another hype that will become part of the overall technology fabric of an organisation without creating radical disruptions? Will organisations embrace it so completely that the role of people and leadership comes into serious question? And is the horror scenario where super-intelligent machines take over our lives and work and make human capabilities just a pawn in a larger game likely to come true? There are no answers to all this yet, but AI is surely raising many questions in the minds of governments, corporations and social thinkers. Leaders of today and leadership aspirants of the future need to take notice and look for possible answers that will shape their future destiny.

When we look beyond the clichés like 'the only people who will lose their jobs to AI will be those who don't know how to work with AI' and 'the human in the loop will always stay in control of AI', some very real scenarios emerge. Quess Corp, a leader in staffing solutions in a variety of industries from business process outsourcing to manufacturing, has spun off an entity called Digitide Solutions, which already has an employee base of over 50,000. The workforce includes AI agents, and the company is also planning to manage this new kind of labour force that won't call in sick or lose productivity because of external factors.[1] They are one among many companies that view AI as a potential game changer and are prepared to rearchitect the business and redesign around new roles that are part human and part AI agents. Roles like chief listening officer will ensure that performance of the AI agents is optimised and they become an important part of future work design.

While Digitide has focused on the key verticals of insurance, healthcare and financial services, Honeywell Inc., a multibillion dollar global corporation, has designed multiple innovations in its automation businesses. A recent visit to their Process Solutions headquarters in Houston, United States of America, showed us how large process plants can be designed, operated and managed through comprehensive automation with AI at the edge for analysing, predicting, prescribing and optimising the performance of the facility with minimal human intervention. There are many more such examples of organisations that are experiencing and enabling comprehensive transformation in business models and are excited about the future.

What does all this mean for leadership approaches and methods that humans have evolved through the ages? Will we all need to go back to business schools and get reskilled and reoriented in the ways new organisations will need to function and how our roles and, indeed, styles must change? In a recent talk, the historian and author Yuval Noah Harari spoke about the need for human trust to be enhanced lest AI in its super-intelligence avatar ends up exploiting the human divide and takes the opportunity to rule.[2] In the complex world of barriers and geopolitics we live in today, rebuilding trust between humans, which is a prerequisite to retaining command over AI agents, is an agenda that will take some doing. In their book *Genome to Om*, Bhushan Patwardhan and Indu Ramchandani have indicated that true leaders will be able to navigate the entities they lead through a transition from specialised external knowledge that can be vested in AIs that have gone through extensive training by large language models (LLMs) to supreme inner knowledge that does not get swayed by sudden disruptions but continues to design for the future.[3] The comprehensive knowledge that would be desired from true leaders of the future comes from a combination of *anubhava,* which is experiential knowledge derived through observation, experimentation and analysis, and *anubhuti*, the response that comes through intuition and a sense of connection. The authors call this the move from modern science to meta-science. The willingness and ability of next-generation leaders to lead a recalibration in the future progress of society from science to sustainable universal well-being is what the authors call 'genome to Om'! For the leaders who are readers of this book, this is truly an aspirational state of self-actualisation.

If there is so much confusion prevailing about the future of AI, with contradicting views about its future impact on all sides of the disbelief to fear spectrum of responses, why have we written this book for you? In a previous book, also published by Bloomsbury at the peak of the hype on digital transformation, we had presented the various aspects of technology, processes, culture and leadership that lead to true digital success. We have noticed the same hype cycle with all new technologies, from the early days of personal computing to cloud and software as a service (SaaS) to digital transformation and, more recently, augmented reality (AR), virtual reality (VR), mixed reality and metaverse. Many of these have gone through the initial stages of industry hype and mostly perished or become subdued in the trough of disillusionment that follows. A few have stayed the course to ascend the slope of enlightened growth. We believe that AI has the potential to result in enlightened growth for leaders and organisations, and it is wise leaders who will, within a few years, redefine the high impact phase in ways that might well exceed the current frontiers of our imagination.

There is one aspect of the future that we are confident about—the coexistence of leading-edge AI with thoughtful and deliberate human intelligence to create better outcomes by retaining ultimate control for the 'human in the loop'. Your authors have coined a phrase called 'dual intelligence' as the characteristic of all wise and successful organisations of the future, and it is our mission to ensure that thoughtful readers of this book, particularly adopters of AI and leaders of the present and the future, understand how dual intelligence can be developed, honed and practised.

We are not soothsayers, and while we can predict many opportunities and outcomes, we do not attempt to put a stake in the ground to say 'this is what will be'. Instead, this book will take you on a learning journey to enable you to read, reflect, put some ideas into practice and develop comfort and a level of mastery in navigating unexpected incremental and disruptive technology shifts and, in many cases, creating a better future for the organisation and all its stakeholders. We have chosen to stay away from diving too deep into the technology hype that always surrounds AI and its many avatars and inventors—from the multi-trillion-dollar-valued Nvidia to the massively hyped OpenAI and ChatGPT and similar generative AI (GenAI) products to the quiet ascent of DeepSeek and other non-American innovations that have come into the market. Instead, we approach every discussion in the book through a leadership lens so that leaders can absorb what they need to know about the history and current state of the art in technology, applications and impact on work and life and develop their own approach to leadership for the future.

We are hopeful that the future will continue to belong to the human race. As you read on, we invite you to share that confidence!

1

Evolution of Leadership Contours

LEADERSHIP HAS BEEN THE quintessential element for the progress of humanity. Every positive and negative dimension of society has been shaped by leaders who have left their imprints on the sands of time, and the future will also be defined by the leaders of today. In the early days of the evolution of communities, leaders were restricted in their sphere of influence to small territories and were constrained in their ability to transmit their ideas across vast regions due to limited transportation and communication possibilities. However, with the advancement in communication technologies, means of transport and the globalisation phenomenon, leaders can be heard, understood, followed and shaped by forces from around the world. Some inherit the role of a leader, and others achieve it through education, exposure, aspirations, opportunities and, sometimes, unexpected circumstances.

Leaders of businesses and communities are expected to develop their vision, articulate the vision with the immediate communities and work collaboratively with the stakeholders to translate that vision into action. The hallmark of successful leaders is their ability to inspire and influence the stakeholders to achieve the goals. This would require the leader to possess excellent communication skills, charisma and the technical capabilities that are required to make the mission a success. The key metric for leadership success is the rate of achievement of goals. There could be various dimensions in which leadership could be assessed in terms of its effectiveness—scope, scale, complexities addressed, distinctiveness, associated risk-taking ability, cost versus outcomes, impact, growth and longevity, to name a few. Leadership has to be rooted in ethics, empathy and integrity and is judged for its resilience, innovation and ability to adapt and thrive even in the most challenging environment. Leaders should be able to build successful future leaders and are expected to foresee as well as create the future. Use, adoption or invention of the right tools, technologies and processes would be critical ingredients for success for leaders from all walks of life.

A Historical Perspective of Leadership

History is replete with innumerable examples of success as a result of vision coupled with the right action. Warrior kings known for their successful expansionist exploits had to bring together large armies who were loyal and willing to sacrifice their lives for achieving the vision of their masters. While they were also suitably rewarded upon being victorious, it was a huge risk that they were willing to accept while signing up for being part of the warfare. Warrior kings had the tough task of selling their dream, which seemed impossible to realise, and packaging it such that it resonated with the soldiers and the people at large. They often aligned their vision to religious or mythological symbolism to gain the acceptance of their subjects.

In Greek mythology, the gods and kings drew inspiration from divine forces and set up seemingly impossible goals, as described in *The Iliad* and *The Odyssey*.[1] They goaded the people and rallied them around to work towards the achievement of their vision, which was often aligned with avenging insults or such other personal missions. Agamemnon, the hero of the Trojan War, inspired the people and the rival kings of the Greek city states to wage a ten-year war to eventually achieve Greek victory. Similar examples of valour, bravery and heroism to achieve lofty goals can be found in the vision of Odysseus, the king of Ithaca; Theseus, the king of Athens and other heroes from the Greek mythologies.

The Roman Empire had several leaders who had grandiose visions similar to that of the Greek mythological heroes, aimed at Rome transforming from a city state into an empire. Julius

Caesar's famous quote 'Veni, Vidi, Vici'[2] encapsulated his vision and was the thrust to the reforms, the public games and all forms of communication. Augustus's vision was similar, the glorification of Rome, and encouraged the preservation of traditional Roman values, thus creating the gold standard for the Roman rule. Constantine's vision was for Rome to become the seat of religious leadership for Christianity for the entire world, and he led efforts in the conversion of the pagan population to Christianity.

The Indian epics Ramayana[3] and Mahabharata[4] offer valuable lessons on how the visionary leadership of warrior kings enabled them to tackle complex moral dilemmas and accomplish extraordinary feats. They offer useful insights into their decision-making processes and strategies to overcome seemingly insurmountable challenges and achieve their lofty ambitions. Rama's vision for Dharmarajya was demonstrated through his personal conduct—of upholding the promise made by his father to Kaikeyi and rescuing his wife, Sita, from the demon king Ravana despite several odds. Rama was a source of inspiration because of his visionary leadership and the ideals embodied in Maryada Ram for Hanuman, Sugriva and his monkey brigade who supported him in his battle across the ocean with Ravana to free Sita from his clutches. In the Mahabharata, Krishna lifts the veil of confusing principles and guides Arjun to fight the war with clarity and purpose. Krishna propounds his vision of *Svadharma* (one's path) and answers other questions of morality and righteousness through the compendium of his teachings on the battlefront, the Bhagvad Gita, which acts as a guiding light for all, even today.

Alexander the Great created one of the largest empires at the young age of thirty-two in the 4th century BCE and led his army over difficult terrains over a distance of over 22,000 miles to create a vast empire comprising Eastern and Western cultures.[5] In the 13th century, the ruler of Mongolia, Genghis Khan, invaded several countries and created a huge empire stretching from the Pacific Ocean to eastern Europe. He managed to convince the nomadic tribes that were part of his army that he was 'destined by the eternal blue sky' to rule the world.[6] In the 19th century, Napolean Bonaparte inspired his army to commit to his vision to restore French glory by creating a modern European empire under French rule.

In the 17th century, Shivaji Maharaj managed to bring together peasants, warriors and nobles under a unified banner and made them part of his guerrilla warfare to put up a stiff resistance against the Mughals and Europeans to achieve his vision of *Hindavi Swarajya* (Indian self-rule).[7] Simon Bolivar had a similar vision of self-rule in the 19th century and had the vision of freeing Latin America from Spanish colonial rule. His efforts led to the independence of several countries in South America, namely Peru, Venezuela, Colombia, Bolivia and Ecuador, which led to the new trajectory of possibilities for the continent.[8]

Leaders also emerged based on philosophical or religious guidance and influenced kings as well as the masses. The pope, as the head of the Vatican, has wielded enormous power, wealth and influence over many countries whose kings were Catholics and encouraged them to exert influence on the population of countries they conquered to become part of the Christian fraternity. The pope continues to influence over 1.1 billion Catholics around the world, who account for 17 per cent of the global population.[9] Guru Nanak founded Sikhism and challenged ritualistic and caste-based approaches. The ideas of the philosopher Confucius on governance, family and ethics shaped Chinese statecraft for centuries. Religious leaders and social reformers drew strength from their inner self, and their personal vision became the vision for the community or society that they were part of. In many countries, the hereditary leadership or leadership based on the religious order prevalent in the society resisted scientific quests and innovations and suppressed any effort made to change the status quo.

Gautama Buddha, who was born into a princely family in the 6th century BCE, at a time when social inequality and hierarchical rigidity were rampant, gave up all his worldly possessions and went through a journey of personal experimentation and inner transformation. Buddhism, the religion he envisioned on the principles of simplicity and righteous conduct, is thriving and has found millions of followers around the world. His legacy and teachings have influenced later-day leaders such as Ashoka, Ambedkar, Gandhi and others.

In the 7th century, when there was tribal warfare, slavery and lawlessness in Arabia, Prophet Muhammad articulated his vision of universal brotherhood. He founded the new religion Islam, which has almost 25 per cent of the world's population as its followers as of 2025.[10] Promoting a society centred on justice and compassion, Prophet Muhammad's leadership model has continued to influence several countries over the centuries.

During the early part of the 8th century, at a time when a significant part of India's population had embraced Buddhism or Jainism, and Vedic traditions and ritualistic practices of Hinduism were being discarded, Jagatguru Adi Shankaracharya came forward to rejuvenate the religion.[11] He envisioned bringing back people into the fold of Hinduism by getting rid of complex and archaic practices. He succeeded in a short span of time, travelling across the country, addressing people along the length and breadth of the country and emphasising the significance of Vedic philosophy. He set up four *mathas*[12] and appointed four gurus whom the local population could look up to for spiritual guidance and tenets of moral living. His vision, coupled with thoughtful action, has withstood the test of time until now. In addition to the mathas and the successful lineage of the gurus continuing to be the torchbearers of his teachings, the Hindu religion and the traditions are thriving.

Later, in the 10th century, another Hindu philosopher, Ramanuja, advocated for an inclusive and personal relationship with God to counter casteism and rigid practices and worked for the proliferation of Vaishnavism in South India. He expounded his vision for a new branch of spiritual practice through his prolific writings, social reforms, institutional leadership and promotion of vernacular language as the medium for hymns and chants. Ramanuja's vision and Vedanta discourses democratised spiritual life, inspiring large communities to follow his spiritual guidelines and practices. His teachings have also influenced several other spiritual leaders like Swami Vivekananda and Chaitanya Mahaprabhu in the subsequent centuries to follow his principles.[13]

Imbibing the principles of inclusivity and moral righteousness from the spiritual and religious domains into the sociopolitical context, Mahatma Gandhi unveiled his vision for securing the freedom of the country from the clutches of the colonial ruler, Britain. Against the might and wealth of the rulers and their representatives, Gandhi inspired the nation to rise as one and use non-violence or Satyagraha as the method for expression of protest or disagreement, which eventually helped India win its freedom. Gandhi's principled approach influenced other nationalistic leaders such as Nelson Mandela and Martin Luther King to develop their own vision to use the non-violent approach to focus attention towards the problems of inequalities and social injustice and lead their masses towards their transformation journeys.

While there are several examples of vision leading to positive outcomes, there are also some examples of it leading to outcomes that may be of interest to the followers of the particular doctrine for some time and no longer relevant or compelling enough for them to continue to support such leaders at a later stage. In recent decades, the world has seen many leaders who were dictators who suppressed societies with draconian power through totalitarian rule and withdrawal of civil liberties. Adolf Hitler's narratives of Aryan supremacy with the promise of national revival after the defeat in the First World War using Nazi propaganda appealed to the Germans, who started believing that loyalty to Hitler was the same as loyalty to the nation.[14] Aligning himself with Hitler, Mussolini promised Italians a return to Roman imperial glory by promoting anti-Semitism and suppressing the opposition.[15] Joseph Stalin articulated a vision of a utopian future through communist ideology, eliminated political rivals and projected himself as the father of the nation.[16] Mao Zedong's Cultural Revolution, which led to the death of millions of people (estimate ranging from 500,000 to 2 million), was based on the promise of liberation from feudalism and imperialism.[17]

The key takeaways from these examples of leaders from the socio-religious-warrior spheres would be that for a leader to be successful, there has to be a clear vision with ethical intent and inclusive values. The success of the leader lies in the adoption of the vision, as we have seen in the examples cited, where a large number of people have been inspired to become followers. The rate of adoption is based on how the vision is translated into action by the leaders propagating the vision and how they relate to people in solving their problems. When all of these dimensions are aligned and lead to a demonstrable outcome, these individuals who embarked on their missions are recognised as leaders.

For translating vision into action, impactful communication and periodic reinforcement through narration of success stories has been found to be essential. Warrior kings, spiritual leaders, social reformers and business leaders have all understood the importance of this and have found different ways to address their stakeholders. They used the medium of discourses or books or lectures to get people to appreciate and reflect upon their visionary ideas. Often, they have had to set personal examples to inspire the people.

Whether it was leading from the front in the battlefields or spiritual leaders walking the talk or socially conscious leaders demonstrating their conviction through personal acts, creating the appropriate culture and norms have been important for all the leaders to get people to believe in them and imbibe their ideas. This enabled the creation of a bond and identity among the leaders and the followers. Shivaji Maharaj is remembered as the people's king even today for not only fighting for the pride of the people in the battlefields but also treating them as his equals. Mahatma Gandhi's followers, hailing from various religious and socio-economic groups, lived with him in his ashram as he became synonymous with non-violence and simple living.[18] Swami Ramakrishna Paramahamsa lived the life of a Muslim for several days to be able to enunciate the universality of religious themes, and thus, his philosophy found appeal with people from various walks of life in different parts of the world.[19]

Institutionalising the vision was found to be crucial in the proliferation of the central themes for transformation and sustainability over a period of time. The apostles of Jesus Christ are possibly the finest examples of founding a new faith against all odds and inspiring a large number of nations and people to become part of this movement. Today, 1.1 billion people in the world are followers of Christianity, making it one of the most widely practised religions on the planet. It has been possible to build solidarity within this fraternity and reaffirm its beliefs because of the systematic codification of the teachings of Jesus through the Bible and the tireless efforts of the apostles in the initial phase and later on through the institutionalisation efforts of the churches for the spread of Christianity.[20] The simplicity and the impact of messages conveyed with clarity, as found in the example of the Bhagvad Gita, have continued to be the guiding light for people of all walks of life for centuries.[21]

Political leaders also carried out institutionalisation efforts through formal structures and hierarchies and communication channels to effectively implement their vision and policies. These systems and processes were put to use in anti-Semitic activities during the Nazi rule and were also found to be positively beneficial in undertaking large-scale protests against British rule by Gandhian followers through a series of initiatives such as the Swadeshi Movement or the Quit India Movement. The mathas established by Adi Shankaracharya have been following the institutional code for functioning even after hundreds of years as the fountainhead of knowledge dissemination for spiritual quest. Literature, speeches and rituals are the essential tools that have continued to act as the medium for communication of messages aligned with the vision. Warfare, arsenal and ammunitions empowered the people to achieve the goals of the mission as much as literature, poems and various inspirational artefacts. Capture of forts, ships, slaves and precious jewels were symbolic wins that were also considered as booty and part of the mission. Places of worship, communal baths, grandiose statues and other buildings marked significant milestones and acted as reminders for the journeys undertaken. These interim and eventual rewards and milestones were important in motivating the people to remain committed to the vision.

Notably, the vision of the leaders resonated with their target audiences as their messaging and the value propositions were relevant during the specific time periods and were distinctive in addressing the challenges faced. We can draw several examples of how innovation worked for leaders over the centuries. The erstwhile chief minister of Tamil Nadu K. Kamaraj introduced the innovative mid-day meal scheme in schools in the 1950s to encourage children to attend schools, reduce drop-outs and improve nutrition.[22] This was one of the factors that contributed to Tamil Nadu becoming one of the leading states with an educated workforce that attracts investments in new-age sectors such as automobile and electronics.

Gautam Buddha's innovative eightfold path to enlightenment toppled the rigidities of caste-based Vedic rituals. Guru Nanak's vision to spread the principles of equality in the society materialised through innovative methods such as *kar seva* (selfless service) and community kitchens. Swami Vivekananda's unique message of blending modern science and nationalism helped place Indian philosophy on the world stage.

Changing Leadership Landscape

For many centuries, warrior kings and, to some extent, spiritual leaders were the primary movers of the socio-economic structures of countries. The ownership of farms, trades and businesses was small or limited to small geographies and the owners were largely dependent upon the kings to conduct their businesses. Until the middle of the 18th century, agriculture was a predominant occupation in most parts of the world. Governance by kings, nobles or zamindars impacted the produce and income from agriculture. In Europe, religious leaders were held in high esteem and looked upon for guidance. As a result, they had a significant influence on monarchies or other forms of government. Popes, priests, mullahs, gurus, maharajas and emperors were the leaders who shaped the thinking of the society and created frameworks for law and order as well as socio-economic policies. In some parts of the world, sea voyages and the volume of long-distance commerce had increased, largely on the strength of colonisation and human trading. In some locations, guild-based production, training and collective bargaining began to gain momentum. Medieval European guild leaders determined standards for production, defined terms for acceptance of new members and nurtured talent and mastery of craftsmanship through apprenticeships and strict hierarchies rooted in tradition and trade ethics.

Feudal systems and rule by fear were by and large common, and intellectual calibre or merit was not considered an essential prerequisite for leadership. Thus, leadership assumed legitimacy by way of tradition, inheritance or physical force. Tribal and community leaders in Africa, Native America and Asia maintained social order through patriarchal leadership stemming from age and lineage. Kings granted lands to nobles and zamindars who not only safeguarded the interests of their masters but also acted as conduits to the welfare of the citizens. While nobles often acted as warrior leaders, defending territories and maintaining order, in India, we also witnessed warrior leaders like Shivaji who could inspire the masses to be part of his army for the protection and expansion of his territory.

Leadership Patterns in the First Industrial Revolution

The hallmark of the First Industrial Revolution was the transition of the society from an agrarian to an industrial economy. Manual labour was replaced by mechanical manufacturing powered by steam and water, leading to significant improvements in productivity and lower production costs. While the initial impact was felt in Britain, soon, these inventions and methods of manufacturing spread to other parts of Europe and North America. As a result, there was a dramatic shift in how production took place and how people lived and worked. People started migrating to cities from rural areas in large numbers to work in factories. Factories were established by entrepreneur capitalists who centralised production under a single roof with the focus on efficiency and control but with no attention being given to poor working conditions and long working hours of the workers. Leaders were taskmasters focused on maximising productivity, often enforcing child labour as workers had no recourse to legal support.

Most of the businesses were family-run enterprises. The leaders were hands-on and controlled all aspects of their businesses. The businesses were established around inventions, with the focus on taking advantage as first movers with those inventions. The environment was unstable, and leaders had to take huge risks on new technologies, untested markets and large capital investments. Many leaders were inventor-entrepreneurs. James Watt, known for the invention of the steam engine, expanded the use of the steam engine to various domains, including transportation, agriculture and factories, thus making it a hugely successful business proposition. James Watt partnered with Matthew Boulton, a businessman with complementary strengths in sales, finance and business development, and thus created an impactful business model in the energy segment.[23] Richard Arkwright invented the mechanised spinning device and established the first factory system in Cromford Mill, Derbyshire, which became the prototype for future mills.[24] He built a scalable model combining machinery, water power and wage labour that he licensed to others, leading to rapid mechanisation of manufacturing. His innovation helped transform Britain into the world's textile hub, making cotton goods more affordable. George Stephenson was a self-taught engineer working in coal mines when he invented the steam locomotive. He soon realised that railways were not just for mining and collaborated with other engineers to design the railway system for transportation. Stephenson is credited with building Stockton and Darlington Railway, the world's first public railway to use steam locomotives, and developing the Liverpool and Manchester Railway, which was seen as the precursor to an economically viable railroad system.[25]

Thus, the First Industrial Revolution brought to the fore leaders who possessed both technical expertise and business acumen. Since these were the early days of formal industrialisation, top-down control was necessary to ensure quality and maximise production output. The leaders possessed the vision to convert their inventions into solutions beneficial to the society and create the foundation for future innovations. Some of them demonstrated a paternalistic leadership style, believing that they had the moral responsibility to uplift the status of workers through housing, education, healthcare and religious instruction. This phase also witnessed the beginnings of labour unrest due to poor working conditions and low wages creating a class divide. Hence, some of the leaders were mindful of the need to develop strategies to address these concerns and, at the same time, build employee loyalty. Robert Owen was one such industrialist who was a pioneer in blending social reformation with business economics. As a co-owner and manager of New Lanark Mills, a company that employed 2,000 workers, including children, Owen banned child labour and established infant schools and adult evening education, improved worker housing and introduced moral instruction without religious coercion. Owen transformed the industrial village of New Lanark in Scotland, which eventually became the model across Europe for humane factory management.[26] This trend of blending commercial interests with social welfare objectives has been carried forward in subsequent decades, leading to the ESG (environmental, social and governance) framework in the current day being adopted by several organisations worldwide.

Leadership Patterns in the Second Industrial Revolution

The late 18th century to mid-20th century witnessed the industrial revolution during which period efficiency and productivity gained importance and a new definition of economic models emerged.

With the demand for products increasing substantially, large factories began to be set up, which meant hiring a large workforce with minimal education to carry out the work. To get the required output from them, laying down well-defined processes and having a strict control over operations was necessary. Therefore, leadership continued to be centralised and authoritarian, with orders flowing from the top. Henry Ford succeeded with a manufacturing model led by assembly lines due to standardisation and military-style supervision of the factory.[27] Frederick Taylor's work on time and motion studies and optimising labour productivity focuses on maximising output by repeating tasks and processes with predictable quality with low tolerance for deviation or failure and, at the same time, little room for innovation.[28]

The role of the leaders was to supervise large teams by monitoring their productivity and ensuring compliance with the laid-down processes. New ideas and changes were slow and not encouraged, with the focus being on maintaining stability. Leadership positions were largely occupied by men who reinforced the prevalent societal norms of authority and discipline in their conduct of affairs with strict hierarchical organisation structure, centralised decision-making and clear lines of authority, control and responsibility. There was very little delegation, and power was concentrated at the top. Some industrialists such as George Pullman provided housing, education and healthcare support to the workers and expected loyalty in return.[29] While industrialists benefited with large-scale factories and rapid urbanisation, excessive controls on functioning and an authoritative style of leadership led to the emergence of labour unrest and labour rights movements. Industrialists built their businesses, leading their organisations with personal charisma, and were rewarded for their risk-taking ability.

Andrew Carnegie emigrated from Scotland to the United States of America, where he initially worked as a bobbin boy in a textile mill and later as a telegraph operator. He also managed a railroad business.[30] He was known as a steel magnate for foreseeing that steel would become the mainstay for infrastructure projects.

Controlling the complete supply chain, including raw materials, transportation and manufacturing, enabled him to build the successful conglomerate Carnegie Steel. Andrew Carnegie built a successful steel empire through relentless focus on cost control and maximum efficiency. Carnegie Steel was sold to J.P. Morgan for US$480 million in 1901, the largest business deal in history at the time. This led to the formation of US Steel. Carnegie possessed outstanding expertise in putting across his ideas in captivating ways, and he even demonstrated his moral conviction that the rich had a duty to improve society through his investments for social good.

Cornelius Vanderbilt was considered a railroad and shipping tycoon. He wielded fear and respect among his employees and rivals through his larger-than-life personality. He started a ferry service at an early age and set up a steamboat business by offering faster and cheaper services. Vanderbilt bet upon the future of rail transportation and invested in buying and merging railroad businesses. The oil tycoon John D. Rockefeller, with his calm demeanour and frugal lifestyle exuding moral conviction, was well respected by his employees and the industry, despite building a monopoly business. He built an enormously successful oil-refining business through buyouts, price wards, purchase of businesses during downturn at low costs and secret deals with railroad businesses. He was admired for his large-scale philanthropy, including the founding of the University of Chicago and the Rockefeller Foundation.

Successful leaders in the industrial phase drew strength from mastering emerging technologies and supply chains. As regulation was minimal, they exploited opportunities through centralised control and market dominance, often becoming monopolies in their businesses. They could rationalise their ruthless behaviour through philanthropic activities or religious conviction. As pioneers in their businesses, they took full advantage of the lack of rules or restrictions for conducting business affairs and also the limited worker rights and collective bargaining capabilities.

Leadership Patterns in the Information Age

In the aftermath of the Second World War, there were massive investments in rebuilding the infrastructure of nations and technology. The Cold War between the erstwhile Union of Soviet Socialist Republics (USSR) and the United States of America also led to competition in path-breaking innovations, especially in the domains of space, defence and science. This resulted in the expansion of higher education, creating a huge asset bank consisting of talent with skills in engineering and science and later in information technology (IT), not only in the developed world but also in several developing countries. There was a significant rise in the number of women joining the workforce. As per an International Labour Organisation report, in 2000, the labour force participation of women increased to approximately 50 per cent.[31]

Also known as the Third Industrial Revolution or the Digital Age, the Information Age saw a transition from mechanical and analogue technologies to digital systems. This has resulted in the transformation of businesses, functioning of societies and redefinition of the leadership approach. The invention of the transistor and, later, the microchip, the proliferation of computing due to reduced costs of hardware and access to affordable software, and advancement in communication through a combination of developments in satellites, mobiles phones and fibre optics as well as the democratisation of the World Wide Web have resulted in dramatic changes in the way we work, live and communicate. The constraints of time and space have disappeared, and business leaders have become global-minded as they seek to identify and service customers from around the world. Process orientation has become a must for every business for every function.

Management by family members has given way to professional management. The matrix organisation structure adopted by several multinational organisations enables them to address the needs of implementing global strategy but with local action and verticalised business-focused expertise blended with horizontal practices. Globalisation, outsourcing, integration of supply chains and the ability of people to work remotely across the world has led to the creation of knowledge economies. Thus, intellectual capital has become more valuable than the physical assets, and a new category of knowledge-based assets has emerged as a result. Innovations by Bill Gates, Steve Jobs, Larry Page, Sergey Brin and several other entrepreneurial leaders have resulted in the establishment of world-class global businesses. Microsoft, Apple and Google have become household products that are part of everyday life. Leaders have been constantly rethinking the power and the potential of digital logic to create new products and services and scale their businesses. While engineering design and quality in production have remained important, scaling of businesses by creating products and services that deliver human-centred experiences has been the high point of this phase of digital transformation. Design aesthetics and user experience (UX) have driven sales volumes for products such as Apple and have drawn millions of customers to products of Google or Amazon. In this pursuit, the unique capabilities of many of these path-breaking businesses have been in their leaders bringing together technology, design and cognitive sciences, a hitherto unexploited phenomenon. Leaders of these successful corporations also recognised the importance of building talent ecosystems and focussed on fostering culture that would help in attracting and retaining talent to scale their businesses. This is a far cry from the earlier phases of the industrial revolution where an authoritarian top-down approach, including welfare measures at times, was prevalent among leaders to achieve loyalty from employees.

It can be deduced from the analysis of successful leaders across multiple phases of industrialisation that they possessed vision—to change the world order or the business landscape. They remained focused on delivering on this vision and could articulate it well and communicate it to various stakeholders. Their ability to innovate, inspire and ensure positive outcomes has depended largely upon the extent of buy-in they could derive from the stakeholders. Among the various factors that determine the growth trajectory of a business, technology intervention is a key subject that leaders have had to address as it has brought in its wake the responsibility to determine the technology to use or adopt, the timing, change management for successful implementation and the likely outcomes. Choice of technology and sophistication options have been industry-specific and depend on the maturity, the opportunity landscape and the risk-taking ability of leaders.

The Impact of Technology Interventions on Leadership

Interventions and disruptions with technology are not new to humankind. They form the basis for the progress of the society. From the discovery of fire by rubbing stones together to wheels and beyond, technology has played a significant role from time immemorial in the advancement of human civilisation. Leaders understood the importance of technology and tools that were available in each era and their use or enablement in the conduct of their affairs. Technology has been used effectively by successive leaders to communicate, wage wars, govern their kingdoms and build economies. In short, technology has been integral to the successful strategies of leaders. Alexander the Great was able to rapidly conquer most parts of Asia and Egypt by leveraging the innovative Greek military formation, the phalanx. Emperor Ashoka used edicts on stone inscriptions effectively for the spread of Buddhism and for governance across his large empire. Roman aqueducts were the lifelines of the Roman empires and symbolised urban sophistication. These aqueducts influenced the later-day European architects and urban planners to build baths and fountains as part of the urban landscape. The apostles of Jesus Christ used scrolls for the rapid dissemination of Christianity across the Roman Empire. Countries like Spain and France celebrated their successful conquests by building huge statues in honour of their leaders. South Indian rulers built massive temples in India and other parts of South East Asia as symbols of their prosperity and to create awe and loyalty within the communities.

These and several such examples highlight the role technology has played in successful leadership. There are also several instances of nations and businesses languishing with identity crises on account of late adoption of technology. One of the important examples from recent times is how European countries, with their guns and superior warfare techniques, could defeat several Indian kingdoms because the latter did not have access to modern military technologies and continued to practise traditional warfare methods up until the 19th century.[32] Similarly, businesses not in tune with changes in technology trends or other environmental factors in the past have experienced failures and, in many cases, become extinct or struggled for survival. The Indian jute industry was a major global player before and during the Second World War. However, post-Independence and Partition in 1947, the industry's leadership failed to modernise production methods and diversify products. This lack of innovation and foresight, coupled with increased competition from synthetic materials, led to the decline of many jute mills (although lately there has been a revival due to the reversing trend of replacing synthetic materials with natural materials such as jute). The Lancashire textile industry was once the heart of Britain's industrial prowess. However, after the Second World War, the industry faced intense competition from abroad, particularly from countries like India and Japan. The industry's leaders failed to modernise machinery, invest in new technologies or shift production to meet changing market demands, leading to a steep decline.[33] As one of the largest steel producers in the United States, Bethlehem Steel played a crucial role during both World Wars. However, post-war leadership failed to invest in modernising its plants and technologies. Facing increased competition from more efficient global producers and declining demand, Bethlehem Steel filed for bankruptcy in 2001 and dissolved in 2003.[34] HMT Watches is another example of failure emanating from its inability to adapt to changing market dynamics. Founded in 1961, it was known for affordable and durable watches. The business failed to keep pace with the emerging trends of digital and quartz watches, and eventually, in 2016, production of watches was stopped completely.[35]

With the advent of personal computers in the 1980s, thanks to the operating system made available by Microsoft and the user-friendly Apple's Macintoshes, typewriter companies like Underwood and Smith-Corona went out of business. Several traditional stores such as Borders, Sears and Blockbuster went bankrupt, unable to face the competition of tech-savvy online stores of which Amazon was the prime mover. At its peak, Borders had over 1,200 stores and generated more than US$3 billion in revenue. It could not withstand competition from online retailers. Its late entry into e-commerce and digital books in addition to its financial mismanagement led to its downfall. Borders outsourced its online sales to Amazon, which lent a fatal blow to its ability to create an online presence. Finally, Borders ended up filing for bankruptcy in 2011.[36]

Sears failed to adapt to the changing landscape in the retail formats of businesses. Specifically, it could not transform itself to be a part of the e-commerce boom. Originally created as a mail order company in 1898, Sears Roebuck played a crucial role in the rich history of consumer retail in the US market. The company's reach in the rural market was excellent with its catalogue business. Later, after the initial success of its first retail store in Chicago, it spread its wings across the United States. In the 1960s, Sears diversified its offerings with its own credit card and entered various markets, including insurance and financial services. However, with competition creeping in from Target and Walmart in the 1980s and later from e-commerce companies, it was slow to adapt and develop the new DNA needed to survive in the competitive landscape. Ultimately, this led to the demise of the former retail powerhouse and it filed for bankruptcy in 2018.[37]

Dick Smith Electronics is an example of an electronics retail business that expanded rapidly in the 1980s and 1990s with a network of approximately 400 retail outlets across Australia and New Zealand. Due to its inability to deal with competition from online retailers, the business could not be sustained and wound down in 2016.[38] The Canadian retail giant Eaton's, which was known for its retail outlets and catalogue business, faced challenges with dwindling business due to its inability to adapt and lack of technological capabilities to build an online presence, the same as Sears Roebuck. Ultimately, Eaton's also folded in 1999.[39] The case of Comet, a major electronics retailer in the United Kingdom, was similar. Unable to adapt to the changing retail landscape and e-commerce requirements, the business, founded in 1933 by George Hollingbery, went into administration in 2012 and closed all it stores, which accounted for 250 across the United Kingdom at its peak.[40] Zavvi, a major music and entertainment retail brand founded in the United Kingdom in 1971, had at its peak a network of 125 stores across the United Kingdom and Ireland. The company struggled to compete with online players and cope with digital media. All its stores were shut down in 2008, and the business was closed.[41]

Blockbuster is another US company that was prominent in home movie and video game rental services. Founded in 1985, it grew aggressively and soon became the largest video rental chain in the world with 9,000 stores at its peak, well known for stocking a wide variety of movies. In 1994, Viacom acquired Blockbuster for US$8.4 billion to use Blockbuster stores as distribution channels for its films. Soon, digital streaming, online rental services like Netflix and on-demand viewing started posing challenges to Blockbuster. Its attempt at an online rental service was not successful, and despite a split from Viacom to conduct independent business, it ended up filing for bankruptcy in 2010.[42]

Once dominant mobile phone brands, Nokia and Blackberry had to bite the dust with the introduction of low-cost, user-friendly mobile phones from companies like Apple and Samsung. The market value of Nokia dropped from over US$200 billion in 2000 to under US$20 billion around 2010 as it was unable to adapt to the smartphone revolution.[43] Blackberry, too, plummeted from the high of US$80 billion in market value in 2008 to under US$5 billion by the mid-2010s as it, too, failed to adapt to the change.[44]

As the smartphone adoption rate increased across the globe, apart from new versions of Apple and Samsung eagerly awaited in the market every six months or so, markets are also being flooded with Chinese devices that are rich in features and low in cost, thus giving more options to customers.

Kodak is another iconic company that failed to adapt to digital technology in time and ended up filing for bankruptcy in 2012.[45] The market value of Kodak in the 1990s touched US$31 billion, and it dropped to less than US$150 million at the time of filing for bankruptcy. With the steady transition to cloud computing, the physical IT infrastructure business has been impacted. A classic example is that of Sun Microsystems, which was not equipped to provide cloud-based solutions and, hence, ended up being acquired by Oracle for US$7.4 billion in 2020—a far cry from its peak valuation of over US$200 billion.[46]

In recent times, many taxi companies have been struggling to survive because of the digital disruption of offerings by companies such as Uber, Lyft, Ola and others. What is also unique about them is that they do not own a fleet of cars, but by acting as the aggregator and disrupting the transportation service, they have been able to offer superior services to customers, who find them to be cheaper and more convenient.

The businesses in the examples cited earlier lacked the technology firepower and the ability to adapt to the changing market scenario, unlike the newcomer Amazon. Amazon, founded in 1994, has been aggressive in its approach to consumer retail. Amazon first disrupted the retail model for book stores and later went on to become a global e-commerce giant. It has disrupted several other industries. Today, it is counted among the pioneers in the use of AI in customer engagements for business generation.

These and many other such examples indicate the imperative for leaders to be alert and quick to adapt to technological changes, failing which there will be value erosion and decline in market capitalisation of the businesses they run. The continued success of IBM is a classic example of a company that has experienced successive technology disruptions and market turbulences due to World Wars and other factors and yet has managed to sustain and grow its business through several decades. Founded in 1911 by Thomas J. Watson, the company has successfully pivoted several times—from being focused on mechanical tabulating machines to electronic computers to cloud-based services and now the AI-led solutions in the last few years. IBM has been dominating the business computing market for several decades because of its astute leadership and its ability to adapt. However, IBM, too, was too slow to transition from mainframes to personal computers. It was unwilling to take the risk and clung to familiar terrain. It took a while for IBM to recognise the need for change and adopt new ways of doing business to survive and maintain growth. After that, IBM's downward spiral was arrested, and in 2023, it reported a free cash flow of US$11.2 billion, a significant improvement over previous years, and revenues of approximately US$61.9 billion, up 3 per cent growth from the previous year. This achievement is owing to its transformation with the strategic initiatives driven by leaders such as Ginni Rometty and, lately, Arvind Krishna as its CEO.[47] IBM's thrust on the Watsonx AI platform and Red Hat OpenShift for hybrid cloud environments is paying rich dividends.

Leadership That Matters

Why have some businesses thrived while others stagnated and many ceased to exist? The answer lies in the vision and the leadership style of the individuals who are at the helm of affairs. It's the leaders and their strategic thrust that make the difference to the business. Leadership styles depend upon a number of factors, including the environment within which they function, personality traits, background and exposure, values, skills and experience. Leaders adapt their leadership style to suit a given situation, and hence, every leader may possess multiple leadership styles. Their success underscores the importance of leaders identifying the leadership strengths they possess to cultivate them further. Developing the right strategy for their business and motivating the employees for success, therefore, hinges upon this approach to leadership.

Steve Jobs was one such leader who became a cult figure with a fan following among customers, employees and partners whom he inspired to favour high-quality, user-friendly products. He is credited with creating an environment of innovation and creativity at Apple, which has continued to flourish even after his departure. Although over-reliance on a charismatic leader can be a risk and it may be difficult to sustain the transformational changes if the leader leaves, in the case of Apple, under Tim Cook's leadership, innovation has continued to thrive and Apple has managed to remain a dominant player in the technology field. Elon Musk is another such leader who is revolutionising multiple industries, although he has been a controversial figure in recent times. He sowed the seeds of inspiration for people to think and act globally to find solutions for sustainability and interplanetary colonisation. Reed Hastings has led the transformation agenda of Netflix, transitioning from DVD rentals to streaming and now customised options for entertainment at one's fingertips. Hastings has created a corporate culture that encourages employees to take risks and innovate, which has made Netflix a leading platform for global programme content.

Such leaders possess the innate capability to foresee the future, take the right bets and get their teams to buy into their vision to go after lofty goals year after year. The job of the leaders in technology companies is even harder than those who run domain businesses as they are in the driving seat of technology innovation and possess the power to reshape the future and sell this vision to the businesses and consumers of technology. They need to be mindful of the dangers of falling short of fulfilling the promises of the products and creating a harmful impact—to not only their shareholders and employees but also their customers and the society at large.

Samsung Galaxy Note 7, released in 2016, had problems with its battery causing explosions and fires, which led to costly recalls and damage to Samsung's reputation.[48] Theranos, the health technology company, promised revolutionary blood testing technology, but it was later revealed that its technology was flawed and its results unreliable, leading to its collapse and legal consequences for its founder, Elizabeth Holmes.[49] Then there are businesses that have collapsed due to technology deployed in their functional areas. For example, Target Canada had to withdraw in 2015 from the Canadian market within two years of its entry due to major problems with IT and supply chain.[50] India's Aakash Tablet, launched in 2011 as an affordable tablet for students, failed due to its poor performance, delays in delivery and failure to meet its educational goals.[51] The electric tricycle designed by Clive Sinclair's inventions in the United Kingdom failed due to safety concerns, limited range and poor weather conditions.[52] Even if the product or technology is superior, ultimately, the success lies in meticulous implementation. The larger the organisation, the more complex would be the alignment of all stakeholders to the vision and the mission of the organisation. In technology-driven companies, change management is a continuous process.

In the context of an AI-driven era, conceptualising what AI means for the business and getting it integrated with the business calls for a special calibre of leadership. There are several dimensions of leadership that are going to be vastly different from the past generations of leaders. We are now fully immersed and engulfed in technology in our daily life as well as our business conduct. With the AI component added, we need to factor in the methods of engagement with this new dimension. Further, for every action, the counter-action or response would emerge in an AI-driven environment. Hence, leaders would be required to be bolder and smarter to deal with the fuzziness at every step.

2

Increasing Role of Technologies

FOR A LARGE PART of the 2010 decade, you would be hard-pressed to meet someone running a business who was not talking about digital transformation. The size of the enterprise did not matter. From small mom-and-pop enterprises to start-ups to global conglomerates, if you weren't digitally transforming your business in some manner, you were a labelled a laggard who was not likely to survive the transition into the next decade.[1] Or at least that's what consultants and technology experts had everyone believe. What exactly digital transformation meant varied depending on the nature and size of the business, but at its heart, it was about using new and emerging technology to fundamentally transform how core processes were being run and operated. This was also a culmination of the changes that had been triggered by the entry and gradual spread of computers in the workplace, a shift that had started a few decades earlier.

For the longest time, computing was synonymous with mainframe computers: large machines that took up the entire room and were inaccessible to all but a select few. That started changing in the 1980s with the advent of the personal computer. Cheaper microprocessors and improvements in hardware and software resulted in computers becoming compact and cheaper, opening up a whole new market for companies manufacturing them. In addition to home buyers who started buying computers for their personal use, companies started investing more in computers and making them available to different functions within the business to see how they could be used effectively by different departments.

The first steps towards digital transformation of business were taken in the 1980s and 1990s as traditional enterprises started adopting personal computers in the workplace. In the early days, computers were restricted to the accounts and finance sections with software being used to better manage employee payroll systems and accounting. Over time, the IT industry took shape in India in the late 1980s, which is when things started changing. Suddenly, students were learning how to code in college or at dedicated coaching classes, aspiring for a software job. Computers started making an entry into people's homes, increasing their familiarity with how to use these in the workplace. The biggest factor driving the shift towards digitisation in the 1990s was the drop in prices of personal computers.[2] This shift was triggered with the launch of Intel's Pentium chip in 1993, which paved the way for this transformation. At the same time, there was an improvement in the graphical user interfaces (GUIs), most notably, Microsoft Windows with Windows 95. This made computers more accessible for non-technical users, resulting in widespread adoption across offices. Affordability and ease of use together made people start exploring other uses for computers in areas like finance, documentation and human resources (HR). As people became familiar with the Office suite of products like word processing and spreadsheets, computers started spreading into other departments across the organisation. This spread was further compounded by the launch of dedicated software solutions from companies like Adobe or Autodesk, which provided customised solutions for specific needs like accounts or design management.

Snowball Effect

The 1990s were a bridge between computers making their way into enterprises and becoming ubiquitous across sectors in the 2000s. At the start of the 1990s, companies had started adopting computers, albeit in a phased manner. As hardware costs reduced and software got better, the size and the cost of computers also began to reduce, putting them within reach of a much larger section of society. Microsoft had launched its now iconic MS Word program as far back as 1983. Labelled Word 1.0, this program was made for the MS-DOS and Xenix systems and was soon followed by versions for other operating systems before launching a Windows version in 1989.[3] Computers were now being used as a productivity tool—digitising core information and processes and reducing the use of paper. In some cases, companies were also using the entire set of tools from the productivity suite to speed up and automate core processes. Over time, almost all these companies that were providing early software or hardware solutions have gone on to become giants in their fields. Notably, the main growth driver was computers becoming more compact and affordable.

Email systems, which were still very niche in the 1980s, burst on to the mainstream in the 1990s. It's hard to say whether the adoption of email by people in their personal lives drove companies to switch their workplace communication to a digital format, but this was among the early examples of people wanting to replicate the tech tools they were using in their personal life in the workplace, a movement that really gained momentum in the next decade.

While these developments may have been small, they had a snowball effect on how companies and offices functioned. The emergence of tools like spreadsheets and, eventually, email drastically reduced the time spent on manual processes. Employees were now free to do more value-added tasks instead of manual data entry and processing. The use of technology also enabled better interaction and collaboration between teams and helped boost productivity. While all these tools were more focused on the individual user, companies also started implementing data management systems and databases to better manage the growing stacks of information they now had access to. Supply chain management and customer relationship management were the big buzzwords then, with large enterprises rushing to adopt these systems. As they did so, they encountered issues around making information available in the required format and making sure people had the discipline to enter and upload the data as per a set schedule. This marked a fundamental shift in how organisations handled and managed data and set the base for the sharp uptick in digitisation of data and analytics that was to follow. Over time, these systems helped with driving better decision-making and efficiency, freeing up people by automating repetitive tasks.[4]

As the adoption of technology in the workplace became more widespread, companies started to introduce local area networks (LANs), which helped boost workplace productivity by allowing employees to streamline tasks like file sharing, having a common email server and common information database. This has now come to be a standard feature in all offices irrespective of their size as a key collaboration and productivity driver, leading to resource optimisation. It's easy to forget that it was a rarity about three decades ago, and the impact it had on boosting collaboration in the workplace cannot be overlooked.

It was not all smooth sailing. Like every decade, the 1990s had a unique set of challenges. The biggest perhaps was the resistance to change leaders faced while trying to introduce new technologies. Employees were resistant to adopting these, mostly due to concerns around job losses—something that has accompanied every major technology introduction and shift and continues to do so. It was also difficult for leaders at times to convince employees that this technology was a good thing. Computers were still running on fairly basic operating systems and were not as powerful as they were to become in subsequent years. They were glitchy and prone to crashing, often causing users to lose valuable data and effort. It was the early days of dial-up internet connections, which again were unsteady and slow, effectively curtailing how much users could actually benefit from going online.

Automation Enters Offices

The other significant impact of all these changes was that it led to a new wave of automation in workplaces. Up until then, automation in the workplace was synonymous with factory automation. However, the advent of computers in offices changed that.[5] From data entry and processing to analysing spreadsheets and generating digital invoices, there were suddenly several new avenues where businesses could automate processes and speed up time to completion, freeing up labour hours in the process. Over time, this switch towards automation in offices resulted in reduced operational costs, which were then ploughed into other parts of the business. While all these factors had their benefits, it wasn't a seamless transition. Computers were still expensive, and there was a steep adoption curve, coupled with some resistance to the introduction of computers in the workplace. Added to this was the cost of training the workforce, which was considerable at that time. Parallelly, the workforce stared undergoing a major transformation. The kind of jobs that were respected and in demand started changing. With simple tasks now being done by software, there was demand for more value-added skills. Anyone who was comfortable using computers was at an immediate advantage in a traditional business. The biggest shift was in the rise of a whole new workforce that was trained in computer software, which led to the birth of the IT industry. This nascent industry in the 1990s eventually catapulted India to the global services stage and set the foundation for the subsequent waves of digital transformation that were to follow. The 1990s were crucial for the foundation of the digital economy by making personal computing a critical part of business operations and management. It enhanced efficiency, sparked innovation and shaped modern business practices as we know them today, opening up global markets to businesses all around the world.[6]

By the turn of the century, IT was a hot commodity in India. The fears around the Y2K bug (concerns that computers would not be able to handle the transition from 1999 to 2000 and would reset, causing chaos all around the world) resulted in the rapid rise of Indian software firms, and with it, Indian software engineers. When the world managed to seamlessly transition from 1999 to 2000 without any notable systems crash, enterprises across the world took note of India's software prowess. Suddenly, IT companies were in demand with entire batches of college students pursuing software engineering. These were the most coveted jobs of the early 2000s, and this phase also birthed several start-ups in India and abroad, all riding the first wave of the internet or Web 1.0.[7]

The other significant thing that happened at the turn of the millennium was that the world was in the midst of what came to be called the dot-com bubble. The spread of the internet coupled with the massive adoption of personal computers and the affordability of sending and storing information resulted in a slew of start-ups that were trying to bring different services to the web.[8]

While several businesses did not survive the crash, there were also companies that were fundamentally strong enough to make it through the lull that followed. Notable among these are Amazon, Adobe, IBM and Intuit, among several others. All these companies were operating in areas that were not gimmicky—they had established paying customers, and most had a path to profitability. All of these companies also went on to deeply impact how the technology and business world changed over the course of the next two decades and are behemoths in their own right.

The Rise of Social Media and the SMAC Stack

Several factors came together at the start of the 2000s to eventually result in the kind of boom we saw closer to 2010. Key among these were the emergence of social media platforms like Facebook, YouTube and Twitter, the launch of 3G networks, improvements in mobile phones and phone technology and the emergence of cloud computing through platforms like Microsoft Azure and Amazon Web Services, coupled with analytics tools. If there was one key theme defining the tech progress that was made in the early 2000s, it would be the focus on making tools and technology more user-friendly and accessible to a wider audience.

This was also a time characterised by technological breakthroughs and massive slumps, like the dot-com crash and the subsequent correction in the market that followed. The key themes that started to emerge were the coming of age and eventual coming together of technologies like social, mobile, analytics and cloud (SMAC) computing, which resulted in the establishment of the SMAC stack in the next decade.[9]

Several factors laid the groundwork for this to happen across varied areas of the technology spectrum. On the networking front, 3G was launched in 2001, which made it possible to offer mobile internet on phones. Smartphones became a reality with people addicted to their Blackberry or PDA (personal digital assistant). This was the first stage of smartphones and mobile computing, which underwent a second coming with the launch of the Apple iPhone in 2007. Websites transitioned from basic static sites (Web 1.0) to more interactive and dynamic ones (Web 2.0), shaping how companies and people interacted with them and used them. The early 2000s were also characterised by individual users finding their voice on the internet, whether through the rise of blogging platforms or early social networking sites. LinkedIn, Myspace, Facebook, Reddit, YouTube and Twitter were all launched between 2003 and 2006, followed by Instagram and Pinterest in 2010.

These two factors demonstrated how powerful individual users could be if provided a voice and a platform. The growth of mobile internet also demonstrated what a powerful tool the handheld device could be, setting the stage for the eventual emergence of the mobile phone at the centre of all corporate tools and communication strategies.

Simultaneously, companies like Microsoft and Amazon launched their cloud computing offerings. Amazon Web Services was among the pioneers in this space, offering a pay-as-you-go cloud storage service in 2006, followed by the launch of Microsoft Azure in 2010.[10] These innovations provided scalable, flexible and cost-effective computing infrastructure, making the Cloud accessible to businesses of all sizes. This also brought about an explosion of digital data that was now available to enterprises. Companies started offering specialised tools to slice and dice and make sense of this data to use it effectively. Early analytics solutions allowed organisations to derive actionable insights from data, laying the groundwork for the analytics piece in SMAC.

Another development, while not directly associated with the SMAC stack, had a major impact on it—the growing dominance of Google and online search and advertising. As search engine optimisation started to gain traction, companies started relying on data to target their advertising and communication to cater to user queries. The emergence of this kind of data-driven and targeted advertising was the early stage of the use of analytics within social media to target messaging to specific users.[11]

Businesses turned to scalable, efficient technologies like SaaS (Software as a Service), cloud computing and data analytics to reduce costs and improve return on investments (ROI). [12] While the widespread adoption of cloud computing resulted in an abundance of data availability, it also brought with it early concerns about data privacy, which led to the introduction of regulations that emphasised transparency and accountability in digital systems.[13] These measures helped build trust in digital technologies, encouraging businesses to adopt cloud computing and analytics solutions, and were the foundation for several of the newer data privacy measures that followed in subsequent decades.

The emergence of SMAC resulted in what came to be known as the consumerisation of IT and set the framework for the massive digital adoption that was to follow. It built upon a keenly held belief that technology innovation normally happens on the back of already existing infrastructure and architecture, building upon what were seen as innovations a few years ago rather than entirely dismantling an existing system. The biggest change, perhaps, was the ability of employees to use their own devices for office work. Bring your own device (BYOD) quickly became a selling point for companies trying to attract a younger workforce. These employees were digital natives and had grown up using technology in its myriad forms in their day-to-day lives. When these people entered the workforce, they were stunned by the obsolete tech that was in use in some pockets and industries. Companies that were smart enough to realise that allowing these employees to use their personal devices under certain conditions would help hold on to them were among the first to launch BYOD programmes. Employees accustomed to seamless, mobile-first experiences in their personal lives began demanding similar flexibility at work.

Up until the start of the decade, enterprise computing was synonymous with software and hardware that lived on the premises or within the physical boundaries of the workplace. The launch of services like Amazon Web Services and Azure changed that. Coupled with the improvements made in mobile devices, the traditional computing model changed significantly over the course of the decade. According to Gartner, it was a 'nexus of forces' (social media, mobile technology, cloud computing and information), which laid the groundwork for digital businesses, defining new business models that blur the physical and digital worlds.[14] The research firm IDC termed SMAC the third platform—mainframes and the client-server networking model being the first two. This was as big a paradigm shift as the first two developments.[15] The evolution of the SMAC stack led to the transformation of several aspects of how an enterprise functions, from daily operations, employee engagement, management of its data and security and several others. This decade was also when younger millennials started entering the workforce. Collaboration, social connectivity and mobile accessibility were essential to them to be able to work in a manner that made sense to them, leaving companies with no choice but to adapt. Tools like Slack and Microsoft Teams exemplify this shift, bringing social-style collaboration into enterprise settings. They brought in commonly used elements like instant messaging, social feeds and a cleaner interface to employee communication tools, which was more in line with what people were used to in their personal lives. In addition to using social media to facilitate smoother employee interactions, companies also started experimenting with the use of platforms like Facebook and Instagram to communicate with their customers. These platforms transitioned from being personal networking sites to business and marketing tools in the 2010s.[16] LinkedIn especially emerged as the centre point for a company's recruitment and brand-building activities. This is one of the ways in which the emergence of the SMAC stack has had a far-reaching impact on how businesses operate. Consumers, too, started taking to social media platforms like Facebook and Twitter (now X) to voice any grievances they had with companies or brands. This direct line of communication with companies suddenly gave consumers a strong voice and made companies realise that they needed to keep a close watch on social platforms. Companies started investing in teams to monitor social media, cognizant of the brand impact of any negative chatter online. Over the next decade, this emerged as a separate marketing and communications channel. Enterprises now spend a sizeable part of their budget on maintaining their presence and collecting consumer data from these online channels, gaining better insights into the consumer's mind.

For consumer-focused companies like Amazon and Netflix, this boom in data availability had a direct impact on their business models and plans.[17] These companies could now analyse and use this data to provide personalised recommendations to consumers on what they should buy next or watch, leading to increased engagement and revenues. The same customer who was being served personalised insights at home realised the power these insights could have at work. Analytics platforms started getting integrated into existing data systems and providing actionable insights to employees. There was democratisation of data within the organisation, leading to faster and more efficient decision-making processes. Over the course of the next decade, this would become a critical part of how companies planned their overall strategy. It was still early enough for the average consumer to not be too paranoid about how their data was being used and willingly share personal information because they loved the experience of having recommendations and suggestions personalised just for them. We were still a few years away from concerns around data privacy and sovereignty.

The growth and evolution of these four factors—social, mobile, analytics and cloud computing or SMAC—has been interconnected, with the growth of one spurring the growth of the others. Over time, there was an emergence of partnerships across providers and the emergence of a larger ecosystem beyond just the individual companies. Application programming interface (API) and platform-driven models started to emerge and became a defining feature of the new business models.

The financial crisis of 2008 further sped up the adoption of technologies like cloud computing as economic and financial pressures necessitated the adoption of cost-saving measures while maintaining the rate of growth.[18] Cloud computing promised lower upfront investments in traditional IT infrastructure and servers and allowed companies to pay for storage as per their requirements. This marked a significant shift in how they had been operating up until then. It also democratised access to cloud storage for several mid- and small-size companies for whom the cost of IT infrastructure had been a barrier until then.

What this also resulted in was a convergence between consumer and enterprise offerings. Tools like WhatsApp and Zoom, originally consumer-oriented, found widespread use in businesses, while enterprise technologies adopted consumer-like functionality. This integration further entrenched consumerisation in workplace IT. The single biggest defining characteristic of this era was how end-user needs and requirements finally became a linchpin of enterprise technology. It fundamentally altered the relationships between consumers and service providers/enterprises and between employees and their bosses, and reshaped how people communicate and collaborate at work. The other long-term impact, further heightened by the Covid-19 pandemic, was the reshaping of power dynamics at work and the emergence of remote work.

Adopting a cloud-based system for data management and allowing employees to use their own devices meant that they did not necessarily need to be in their office to work. While these cases were few and far between till 2020, there were instances where employees, especially sales and service personnel, no longer needed to clock in every day.

This was the first phase of decentralised communication with employees and partners, which was further enhanced with the introduction of AI-based chatbots in recent years.

Cloud Impact

While the emergence of SMAC had wide-reaching consequences collectively, cloud computing perhaps had the single most transformative impact on enterprises. The shift from investing in on-premises IT infrastructure, which required accurate business and requirement forecasting and massive capital expenses upfront, to an operational expenditure model where companies could opt for a pay-as-you-use model gave businesses the ability to scale their IT infrastructure up or down as per their demand without having to plan too far ahead. It also opened up access to enterprise-grade IT resources for small and medium businesses as it democratised access to infrastructure. Outsourcing their IT infrastructure management allowed companies to focus on their core business rather than managing servers and their networking needs. Further, it fundamentally transformed business models in several industries. Some of the biggest companies to emerge during this time were Netflix, Airbnb, Spotify and Uber. All of them could rapidly scale globally by leveraging cloud infrastructure and not having to invest in their own data centres. They combined this with the direct consumer reach they had through social media and mobile phones and the use of analytics to give consumers exactly what they wanted and when and how they wanted it, turning them into some of the biggest success stories of that decade.[19]

In other industries, too, the intersection of data analytics coupled with cloud computing resulted in far-reaching innovations and changes. Banks and financial institutions started using data analytics to help with risk management and fraud detection. They also invested in mobile banking applications, bringing a massive change in how people banked and accessed their banking information. Within the healthcare space, it opened up new avenues like telemedicine as well as AI-enabled diagnostics, leading to an improvement in the quality of treatment and diagnosis available. This, in turn, led to the emergence of several new business models, which would have a transformative impact on how companies and industries evolved. As cloud adoption grew, technology companies switched from selling software stacks to offering everything 'as a service'. The first off the block were software companies with SaaS providers emerging as a whole new wave of companies.[20] The availability of cloud-based software applications did away with the need for on-premises software installations and made high-end software stacks accessible to larger groups of companies. The same shift happened with infrastructure and platform providers, with terms like 'infrastructure as a service' (IaaS) and 'platform as a service' (PaaS) entering the business vocabulary.

Internet of Things

While cloud computing was rapidly making strides worldwide, companies realised that there were certain applications that needed data to be processed right then and there. These applications were on the edge of the organisation's network and weren't always able to be connected to the company's computing network. This led to the emergence of edge computing, which allowed organisations to capture, process and analyse data at the 'edge' of the enterprise's network. This found use in situations where the data had to be rapidly processed for things to continue functioning, like an oil rig drilling in the middle of the ocean.[21]

The idea with edge computing was to make data processing capabilities available right where they were needed, especially in critical applications. Over time, this has found takers across sectors like healthcare (to process wearable device information) to autonomous vehicles and smart city projects.

An offshoot of the Internet of Things (IoT) was the emergence of the Industrial Internet of Things (IIoT). It refers to the use of this capability specifically in factory and industrial settings where equipment is enabled with sensors for real-time processing of data. IIoT is a convergence of sensors, internet-connected devices and advanced analytics in industrial operations. The main aim of using IIoT-enabled devices is to boost productivity and efficiency in fields like manufacturing, energy, transportation and healthcare, among others. Used primarily to drive operational efficiencies, IIoT has found application in functions like supply chain optimisation, predictive maintenance and automation. By using data collected by the sensors, the system processes and analyses it immediately to enable real-time decision-making.[22]

More recently though, there have been rising concerns about the potential for causing harm through internet-enabled devices. Instances of a city's power grid or utilities network being shut down by cyber criminals have become increasingly common in the last few years. As more and more of the world goes digital, this has emerged as an important area of concern for individuals, enterprises and governments alike. Most of us live our lives online and store anything remotely important in the Cloud. What happens when the service provider is under threat or gets attacked is something many of us have experienced first-hand. What this requires now is greater investments and innovation in security architecture and awareness among users on common traps and how to bypass them.

During the Covid-19 pandemic, once the world started coming out of the lockdown, companies started investing more in IIoT devices for automation and remote monitoring of their assets. The increased investments in this space also generated a lot more data on machine health and usage, which companies have used to further boost efficiency. Another recent use case for technology in manufacturing has been the emergence of digital twins. These are virtual replicas of physical assets that are created to simulate actual operations to help with strategic decision-making. Digital twins are adept at predicting failures and breakdowns and also provide an accurate projection on the likely efficacy of an asset.[23]

Data Boom

The widespread adoption of IIoT devices has translated into a surge in availability of high-quality actionable data, leading to the further evolution of predictive analytics. From being used primarily as a statistical modelling tool in the early 2000s by the finance and insurance industries, predictive analytics has evolved into a mainstream practice. The surge of data that became available to enterprises over the last decade with the boom in big data and machine learning meant that systems and tools had to get smarter to be able to leverage this data for critical insights. The coming together of multiple forces—cloud computing, IoT, distributed computing and the growth of the open-source ecosystem—all collectively contributed to creating an environment where the world had access to more data than it knew what to do with. Technology companies doubled down on creating newer, smarter algorithms and tools to harness this data. The evolution of AI-based tools and the integration of AI into these analytics systems in the later part of the 2010 decade gave a huge boost to the efficacy and accuracy of these predictive systems. Developments in neural networks led to the evolution of tools like natural language processing (NLP) and image recognition software, opening up a whole new area for analytics. Companies could now parse through data across different formats and different platforms and still gain insights from it. Earlier, this data had to be in a specific format for companies to be able to segregate and analyse it. NLP made it possible to glean insights from unstructured data sources like newspaper articles and social media posts and even images, something that analytics systems could not use earlier. It allowed companies to tap into a vast source of information on what consumers were talking about and how they felt, not only about the company or product but other matters as well, enabling them to cater their brand messaging and communication to make it more appealing to their target audience. Enterprises also started experimenting with chatbots since it was easier for consumers to interact with them using conversational language.

On the enterprise side, predictive and prescriptive analytics became a part of larger enterprise functions with better collaboration and insights across departments.[24] Financial firms and banks started using analytics to analyse transaction patterns and used these to create fraud detection systems, while retailers used it to improve their demand forecasting and inventory management. Infrastructure firms could now use equipment running data to predict equipment failure, resulting in the emergence of predictive maintenance for power grids and other large infrastructure resources. This scale of growth came with a whole new set of challenges. All around the world, consumer groups and governments woke up to the risks that unfiltered access to personal data could pose. There were also concerns around data manipulation and use of the generated data to influence outcomes, often with serious consequences. These were the early days of data privacy regulations, which were led by lawmakers in Europe. Talks around the need for a strict security framework governing the collection and use of personal data by enterprises gained strength. By 2016, Europe had put a clear structure in place that eventually became the General Data Protection Regulation (GDPR).[25] Over the years, this has gone on to serve as a base model for several other countries that have wanted to adopt a data security framework. Concerns around ensuring compliance and data security came to the forefront with tech firms and enterprises who were using these tools both doubling down on improving their cybersecurity frameworks and pledging to improve data security. Conversations around the role of bias and ethics in AI models also entered the mainstream. The start of the 2020 decade saw the world grappling with the Covid-19 pandemic, which brought normal life to a virtual standstill for large parts of 2020 and 2021. This, however, translated into a steep uptick in demand for technologies of all kinds as everything, from workplaces to education to shopping and socialising, went online. IT companies doubled down on finding newer and more efficient ways for people to live their lives online. There was a boom in collaboration tools like Microsoft Teams and Zoom, while companies also tried to find efficient ways to remotely manage their people as well as infrastructure resources. Investment in AI increased, and AI-based applications started finding use across an ever-increasing number of categories. For marketers, this meant the opportunity to provide hyper-personalised experiences and recommendations for each specific customer, often resulting in a bump up in sales and demand. Alongside, advances in IoT and edge computing also led to the mainstreaming of platforms like OpenAI's GPT or ChatGPT and Google's Gemini. The high quality of data insights available found great use during the pandemic, speeding up the vaccine development process, mapping disease spread, modelling disease outbreak and predicting future disease hotspots. It also helped identify markers of high-risk individuals, helping prioritise their care and optimising the use of stretched medical resources.[26] AI-based modelling has since been implemented in several other areas as well, like supply chain management and logistics, helping companies plan and track their supply chains more efficiently.

AI Challenges

Ever since the early days of what we now know as AI, there have been concerns over how this will impact humanity and the world at large. While great strides have been made in integrating and analysing unstructured data, there's still more that needs to be done. Researchers are currently working on how to balance model complexity with interpretability in their data models while maintaining ethical guidelines. None of the AI or GPT models in use right now are anywhere close to perfect. There have been several instances of the system hallucinating or making up information and responding to queries based on this made-up information. There have also been instances of the AI system generating biased or ethically inappropriate information based on information that was fed into it as part of the training data. Even as companies work to contain these issues, these factors are compelling enough for governments to introduce restrictions around the use of these GenAI engines.[27]

It's a lot smoother sailing with predictive analytics. The integration of AI with predictive analytics is creating self-learning models that can update themselves as new information is made available and based on responses to earlier outputs. In the next few years, the tech experts predict that AI as we know it will improve in leaps and bounds, driven by improvements in data usage and efficiency, model architectures and real-world applications. With better data and better algorithms, AI models will become more precise and reliable, resulting in adoption across several other industries. There will also be a push towards explainability to get more transparency on how the AI system is using the information to arrive at its predictions. There are already some steps being taken on the regulatory side in the European Union region to make this happen. The coming together of text, video, image and other data will drive multimodal AI, which will translate into better insights and outcomes. There is also likely to be a convergence of predictive and GenAI models, which could be used by businesses to further boost scenario planning and predictions on important parameters like customer churn and journey. While the focus has been largely on big data and LLMs so far, we are also seeing the emergence of small data models that will use less data to make more specific and accurate predictions. These models could be industry- or sector-focused or customised for a specific enterprise and will work on lesser volumes of more relevant data to base their predictions. Given the scale of change that that could bring about in the world at large, companies and individuals must remain cognizant of the dangers it can pose and build safeguards into the AI guard rails to ensure that we continue to optimise the benefits that AI has to offer.

3

Rise of the AI Phenomenon

FOR A LOT OF people, their first recollection of the possibility of computers being smarter than humans harks back to 1997 when IBM supercomputer Deep Blue beat then reigning world chess champion Garry Kasparov. Up until then, the idea that computers would excel at tasks that required strategic and analytical thinking had mostly been the stuff of science fiction—or academic research. Deep Blue's victory over the Russian grandmaster changed that. Suddenly, the idea that humans could train computers to undertake tasks to an extent where they could then outperform humans was no longer a nebulous concept but reality. What most people don't realise is that this victory was decades in the making. Deep Blue was a result of a college project that started in 1985, which then underwent several iterations. The earlier versions of the program were good but not good enough to outplay a human being. Kasparov defeated an earlier iteration of Deep Blue as late as 1996, less than a year before he lost to the computer program.[1]

This event firmly established the notion that it was possible to train machines to perform tasks that went beyond simple automation and instruction and required strategic thinking and analysis. Deep Blue's triumph built upon decades of work that went into a broad field of research that has come to be known as AI, the earliest seeds of which were sown in the 1950s.

Before going any further, it is important to be clear on what AI means. In simple terms, AI is a simulation of the human intelligence process by computer systems and machines. The Oxford English Dictionary defines it as 'the theory and development of computer systems able to perform tasks normally requiring human intelligence, such as visual perception, speech recognition, decision-making, and translation between languages'.[2] Harvard University's Marvin Minsky, who is known as one of the fathers of AI, defines it as 'the science of making machines do things that would require intelligence if done by men'.[3] Practically, this translates into the ability of computer systems to carry out tasks that normally require human cognition and understanding. This can mean helping a person buy the appropriate insurance plan for their specific needs or speeding up the early stages of new drug development.

The genesis of AI can be traced back to 1950. Noted British computer scientist and mathematician Alan Turing published a paper in 1950, *Computing Machinery and Intelligence*, where he introduced the world to the Turing Test or what was then called the Imitation Game. This is the ability of a machine to exhibit intelligent behaviour similar to a human being without being found out. The way to test this is if a computer program can hold a conversation with a human being without the person realising that they are talking to a computer.[4] This test, in many ways, has come to be symbolic of the first time AI entered the broader scientific discourse. Over the years, only a handful of supercomputers have come close to passing this test.

A lot of the foundational work in the field of AI can be traced back to the early 1950s in the United States of America, a time before AI was a recognised term or a field of study. At Carnegie Mellon University, Marvin Minsky and Dean Edwards went on to develop the world's first artificial neural network. This is a system of artificial neurons that mimics the neurons in the human brain. The development and use of an artificial neural network paved the way for the introduction of a type of machine learning process called deep learning. Over the next few decades, this was fundamental to the advances made in the field of AI and how machines could be taught to train themselves.[5] Building upon this same line of reasoning, Arthur Samuel created the Samuel Checkers-Playing Program at IBM, which was the world's first self-learning program to play games. The system was designed such that it could learn how to play checkers based on the results of games that had already been played. Over time, this ability of the machine to learn from experience rather than explicitly fed in data came to be known as machine learning, and Samuel is credited with coming up with this system of training. All these were scattered instances of experiments that were building up towards the establishment of AI as a separate, stand-alone field of scientific research. Notably, in the early 1950s, all this development was still being referred to as synthetic intelligence.[6]

The pivotal moment for AI came in 1956 at Dartmouth College in New Hampshire, United States of America. It was the Dartmouth Summer Research Project on AI that led to the birth of this field of research. The project was the brainchild of John McCarthy, who was then a mathematics professor at the college and who later went on to set up the AI Lab at Stanford University and at Massachusetts Institute of Technology. The foundation for this project was laid by McCarthy and Minsky, along with Nathaniel Rochester of IBM and Claude Shannon of Bell Telephone Laboratories, all of whom were among the pioneers in the AI movement and came to be known as the fathers of AI. This is the first time the term *artificial intelligence* was used, and McCarthy has been credited with naming the then nascent stream of science. The summer of 1956 is also recognised as the formal birth of this stream of science and research.[7]

Around this same time, parallel advances were being made in what would come to be known as automation, which would deeply impact the manufacturing industry. Automation, at its most basic level, has been core to any kind of industrial development in the past century. Even as it is currently understood, automation is not a new concept. In the simplest of terms, automation is the use of any kind of technology that enables a process to happen with minimal human assistance or inputs. This, in turn, is supposed to result in improved efficiency, productivity and the ability for machines to perform increasingly complicated tasks. In the current context, the term *automation* is most often used in two instances: the use of machines on the shop floor and robotic process automation (RPA), which is using software to perform repetitive tasks. There is also business process automation, which uses software to automate end-to-end processes within the organisation.[8] However, all of this only gained steam in the 1980s and 1990s as computers and software programs became more ubiquitous in offices. Up until then, automation almost exclusively referred to the use of technology and machines in the manufacturing sector.

The mid-1950s marked the start of a period of high excitement and exuberance in the AI research community. Fresh off the success of the conference, John McCarthy went on to develop LISP, the first AI programming language. LISP (list processing) became the foundation of AI research and continues to remain in use till date among AI researchers. Through the decade, scientists across the US were working on different projects to demonstrate how computers could be trained to think and process information like humans. Two standout examples are ELIZA, the world's first chatbot, and Shakey, the world's first intelligent mobile robot. Unlike other robots that were in use at that time that needed step-by-step directions on how to undertake a large task, Shakey had the 'intelligence' to analyse and assess for itself the series of steps needed to complete a larger task. It used a combination of NLP and robotics and was a rare example of bringing together logical processing and physical action.

Then expert systems were created. Expert systems were designed to replicate human behaviour, to the extent that it was possible, and were modelled on human knowledge. Such a system could, hypothetically, analyse a person's medical history and reports and suggest a diagnosis to a physician.[9]

For the first few decades, all the work being done in developing the field of AI was restricted to research laboratories. It still hadn't reached a stage where it had real-world applications and remained a 'promising area of research' for several years. Progress in AI research coincided with a period where computers were gradually getting better, faster and more accessible. Government interest in AI solutions was also increasing, leading to more research and development in the field. Scientists were optimistic that within the next decade, they could build a machine with the general intelligence of an average human being. Computers were still prohibitively expensive, and while storage capacity was improving, it still had to get a lot better for machine learning algorithms to work in the way scientists envisaged they would.

An AI Winter

In 1973, the United States and United Kingdom governments decided to withdraw funding from AI projects. The result was an AI winter, where new development largely came to a slow crawl. An AI winter is a period where general interest in the AI space tends to wane, both in terms of research and funding, often as a result of disenchantment in what the community expected it to achieve as compared to the actual progress that was made.[10]

In hindsight, people attribute this slump more to unrealistic expectations rather than an actual lack of progress.[11] Buoyed by the early wins over the course of the decade, scientists had come to expect that a lot more could be achieved in the next few years than what was actually possible given the resources and technology available at that time. For instance, in 1970, some researchers were talking about creating a machine with the same level of general intelligence as the average human being by the end of the decade—something the world's best minds are still working on five decades later. Once investors started to realise that this was not feasible, interest started waning, and so did the funds available for research.[12]

Lack of computing power was one of the biggest hurdles to pursuing deeper research within AI. Teaching computers how to learn required them to be able to handle a large volume of data, which simply wasn't possible for the machines of that time. In the 1970s, computers were not powerful enough or fast enough to store and process all the information they needed to complete these tasks. Despite advancements being made in computing and computer science, the late 1970s were slow when it came to new developments in the field of AI. While processors and storage systems kept getting better and more powerful, research focus had shifted away from AI as researchers failed to achieve the lofty, and possibly unreasonable, targets they had set themselves. However, this period saw the focus shift to other technologies, which ultimately resulted in the development of new software systems and RPA. RPA allows companies to automate low-value mundane tasks, which frees up employees to work on more value-added activities. Data entry, invoice processing, basic customer service tasks and repetitive tasks like payroll processing were among the earliest tasks that were automated. A large proportion of mid- and small-sized organisations have automated these tasks, showing just how widespread process automation has become. In addition to speeding up the process, the use of automation has also improved efficiency to an unprecedented level, dropping error rates to near zero. This was among the earliest instances of technology doing a human's work, and not surprisingly, there was a great deal of consternation among employees about their jobs being taken away by machines.

The 1970s and the 1980s saw the advent of programmable logic computers in industrial automation, further enhancing the role of technology on the shop floor. Industrial robots made an appearance in Europe and the United States of America. In 1969, Victor Scheinman invented the 'Stanford Arm', which could be used to carry out basic tasks, eventually paving the way for robots to perform more complex tasks like assembly and welding.[13] European firms like ABB Robotics started producing industrial robots, leading to a further spread of industrial automation. This was the start of an era of significant productivity gains and efficiency on the shop floor as companies started doing more with less and speeding up production. Assembly lines started getting automated, and people started getting trained on how to use the machines effectively to do their jobs better. Parallelly, researchers kept making incremental progress in AI, with the period between 1980 and 1987 being another boom era for AI.

The early 1980s saw the first commercial deployment of an expert system, which brought a lot more attention to what they were capable of. This was the R1 or XCON, which was developed at the Carnegie Mellon University by John McDermott. XCON, or expert configurer, was introduced by the Digital Equipment Corporation in 1982 to configure computer orders and improve their accuracy based on customer orders. Four years later, Digital Equipment said that it had saved US$40 million a year through the use of the R1 system.[14]

What struck a final death blow to the exuberance around AI in the 1980s was the decision of Defense Advanced Research Projects Agency (DARPA) to stop funding AI research in 1987. Prior to that, the government agency had been among the biggest funders of AI in the United States, having invested significantly in research—US$100 million in 1985 alone. However, by the late 1980s, DARPA started slashing funding for this project after failing to see any significant progress. The withdrawal of support from DARPA eventually resulted in the start of the second AI winter, which lasted well into the mid-1990s.[15] At around the same time, the Japanese government shut down its Fifth Generation Computer Systems initiative. Japan had been among the biggest investors towards commercial use cases of AI and expert systems. However, the heavy costs associated with the project coupled with the results not matching up to expectations resulted in the Japanese government pulling the plug on the initiative after a decade. This marked the end and failure of the parallel processing approach to AI.[16]

Computing devices from companies like Apple and IBM were starting to hit the market with far better processing capabilities than the specialised LISP systems. As these desktop computers began gaining market share, it resulted in interest rapidly declining in the LISP systems for AI.

As with the first AI winter, this period, too, saw a lull in funding and a drop in broader interest in AI projects, even as researchers continued to make progress on some key parameters. One among these was the development of probabilistic reasoning, which led to a revival of interest in AI projects, opening up a new approach towards AI. Meanwhile, industrial automation continued to make deep inroads into all areas of the manufacturing process across industry sectors and geographies. The drop in microprocessor prices and spread of personal computers helped this spread further, leading to the advent of RPA. The evolution of RPA meant that automation was now impacting office workers and not just the shop floor. So far, automation had been synonymous with the use of machines to automate processes. The progress made in computing, coupled with the basics of automation, resulted in RPA, where over time, bots could be programmed to carry out repetitive and routine tasks. In addition to cost and time savings, this also freed up people to work on more value-creating tasks. The way these bots have evolved, it is now possible to program the same bot to carry out multiple tasks as well. These bots are trained to interact with the IT systems or applications in the same way a human would and are increasingly learning to respond better to natural language inputs. They continue to get better, with AI systems now being integrated into them.[17]

Meanwhile, for researchers working on AI, the shift towards probabilistic reasoning marked a fundamental shift in how AI systems addressed problems. This now allowed the AI system to handle uncertainty and ambiguity in decision-making, something that had been missing in the past. Taking off from the work done by Joseph Weizenbaum with ELIZA in the 1960s, Richard Wallace, a computer scientist, created a chatbot called ALICE (Artificial Linguistic Internet Computer Entity). ALICE had been programmed with sufficient basic knowledge to be able to converse with another human. One significant difference was that it had also been fed a sample data collection of natural language, which allowed it to elaborate the meaning of a phrase through specific terms.[18]

The most significant development in the 1990s towards the growth of AI was the development of NLP capabilities. This, in turn, led to progress across various areas of AI development. This growth was fairly widespread and not just restricted to a few universities or AI Labs. In 1997, Dragon Systems in Massachusetts, United States of America, released NaturallySpeaking 1.0, a speech recognition software prototype.[19] This software included standard natural language and was the first truly accessible computer dictation software. Microsoft's Windows integrated this into its offerings, allowing users to dictate rather than type their inputs. The biggest win for AI in the 1990s came from IBM, with then world champion Kasparov walking off from his match with the Deep Blue supercomputer in 1997. While this might seem trivial in the context of what computers and supercomputers can do today, in the 1990s, this was a massive event.

Renewed Interest and Big Wins

The turn of the century brought with it a renewed interest in AI and possible applications of this technology. The early wins of the late 1990s had once again started to generate interest in AI the world over. Apart from researchers and academics, companies, too, were getting curious about how they could use this new technology to their advantage.

The early 2000s also saw a huge spike in interest in automation software as companies, flush from beating the Y2K bug, were keen on continuing to invest in software that could boost productivity and efficiency. The focus shifted from industrial automation, which was largely focused on bringing in efficiencies in manufacturing, to intelligent automation. While the two terms, *automation* and *AI*, are increasingly being used interchangeably, it is incorrect to do so. An automation system does not necessarily have to use AI or machine learning to function. Similarly, not all AI tools are used to automate a process. No doubt there are overlaps, but by and large, the two are separate kinds of technology. When a service provider like Amazon or Netflix starts to provide personalised suggestions based on your personal history, it is an instance of automation using AI to work effectively. Amazon using machine learning to automatically tag key characteristics in an item on the website once again is a combination of AI and automation.

AI programs started getting better in the early 2000s and had enough intelligence to respond to basic questions. The development that really made the world sit up and take notice was Apple introducing its voice chat assistant Siri in 2011.[20] Suddenly, AI-based conversations and assistance were accessible to pretty much anyone who had an iPhone, which was a reasonable share of the population, especially in the United States of America. AI moved from being something researchers talked about in academic journals to something a layperson had in his or her pocket.

Advent of Machine Learning

The biggest boom around AI development happened after 2010. With the widespread use of the internet all over the world, people began generating massive amounts of data, which, in turn, were available to researchers to train these neural networks. Algorithms could be trained on more accurate image classification and recognition based on the thousands, if not millions, of training samples available. Even as these developments gained pace, some researchers started looking beyond just the tech progress that was being made. Most notable among these was Margaret Boden, a professor of cognitive science at the University of Sussex, who started exploring the philosophical aspects of AI. Her work delved into the nature of creativity in machines and the boundaries of AI.[21] Around the same time, hardware development picked up pace. The launch of very-high-efficiency graphics cards and processers helped in the acceleration of learning algorithms. Computers that would earlier take weeks to process certain data samples could now do it within minutes. This was unheard of in the history of computing. In 2012, Google Search Labs (Google X) could train its AI system to recognise cats on a video. Carrying out what today seems like a simple task, what with cell phones accurately recognising and tagging different members of your family in your photo album, took over 16,000 processers back in 2012. It was still a giant step when it came to the progress made by AI systems, with a machine being smart enough to recognise something and distinguish it from other similar samples.[22] All this was what was happening behind the scenes. What consumers and the average person saw was Watson, a computer answering system created by IBM, beating two of the greatest Jeopardy champions in 2011. Jeopardy is a US quiz-based game show, where contestants are provided answers and have to guess the questions. Soon after, AlphaGo, Google's AI system that specialised in Go Games, beat Fan Hui, the then European champion, and Lee Sedol, the world champion, in 2016. If that wasn't enough, it beat itself—AlphaGo Zero.[23]

All these advancements can be traced back to one core development—a complete shift in how AI systems were being trained. The early 2000s saw a huge improvement in machine learning systems, which further distilled into deep learning systems over time. Fundamentally, a shift from expert systems to deep learning is a shift from creating coding rules for computers to allowing computers to learn and draw inferences through correlation and classification on the basis of substantial amounts of data. Deep learning techniques have since been refined and enhanced, especially with increased amounts of data at our disposal.

In 2003, Geoffrey Hinton at the University of Toronto, Ontario; Yoshua Bengio at the University of Montreal, Quebec; and Yann LeCun at the New York University, New York City, started a research programme to bring neural networks up to date. Simultaneous experiments were conducted at Microsoft, Google and IBM to show that these deep learning techniques resulted in halving the error rates for speech recognition.[24] The experiments done on the impact on image recognition showed similar results, further validating the need to shift from expert systems to deep learning techniques. The challenges with text recognition and understanding are harder, as we have seen with some of the issues with GenAI tools even in 2024. While the AI system may be smart enough to understand the instructions being issued, it often struggles with contextualising them.

The broader field of AI can now further be refined into artificial narrow intelligence (ANI), artificial general intelligence (AGI), artificial super intelligence (ASI) and GenAI.[25] ANI is the use of AI for a fixed, specific task. Among the best examples of ANI is Deep Blue, IBM's chess-playing computer, which was capable of playing chess extremely well but was unable to do anything else. ANI systems are designed to specifically solve a given task or problem and will be able to do so with a very high level of precision. The early stages of autonomous vehicles could be considered ANIs since they were only trained to drive and not have any other features like self-learning based on traffic rules. This is another feature of an ANI system: they tend to be incapable of self-learning and will be unable to use their training to perform another task, even if it is very similar to what they have been trained for. These systems are finding rapid deployment across the world as they are the easiest entry point for enterprises that want to adopt AI-based systems. Some common use cases include scanning and analysing medical reports to come to an initial diagnosis or analysing data to predict demand. AGI systems are designed to be self-learning, such that they can then apply their knowledge to a range of evolving tasks and situations. Most experts believe that we are at an early stage of AGI, and it remains to be seen just how far machines can go with AGI. A truly effective AGI would be akin to a fully functional human being, able to learn, understand and react appropriately in different situations based on its training. Unlike an ANI system, which can scan medical reports and summarise and perhaps even provide a diagnosis, an AGI would then go on to prescribe a preferred line of treatment tailored to the individual patient based on their history and other parameters specific to that person. Currently, AI systems are still not capable of doing this and, at best, are being used by doctors to provide an initial diagnosis, which they then go on to validate based on their experience and then prescribe the way forward for the patient. ASI refers to an AI system more intelligent than a human being. This is one area where experts are currently split down the middle on whether the evolution of an ASI will be good for humanity or an unmitigated disaster. Generative AI, or

GenAI, refers to AI systems that can analyse existing data and create new data based on this. This includes image generation systems like Dall-E 2 and text generation systems like GPT-3 and GPT-4, apart from audio, video and code generation.

What we are seeing at present is a coming together of AI and automation at an unprecedented scale. With RPA, once a developer or programmer defines a specific set of instructions for the robot or bot to perform, it can then perform this repetitive action at high speed and in high volumes in an almost completely error-free manner. There are different kinds of automation from the basic automating of tasks through RPA and business management tools to process automation where software is used to automate entire workflows or processes and even provide business insights and solutions. In AI automation, which is what we see in chatbots and virtual assistants, the system integrates the AI system with the chatbots, which allows them to understand generic questions and trawl through the available data to provide the appropriate responses.[26] At present, most enterprises have adopted some form of basic process automation in their day-to-day operations. Enterprises operating in service-oriented fields like financial services, hospitality, retail and healthcare have been among the early adopters of AI automation, introducing dedicated chatbots and customer service assistants. Several companies now allow you to complete entire transactions without having to ever directly interact with a human being. For instance, if you want to return a pair of jeans you bought online, a series of clicks will take you through the process, and your return request will be filed. Even buying insurance online can be done with zero human interaction. If a customer wants to buy insurance, the system will use GenAI to understand the request and extract the relevant information and then use RPA to generate the quote. This will then be sent to the customer, and if they accept it, another system will create a customer profile and generate the insurance and send it back to them. All this is done without any human interaction on the insurance firm's side.

Combining AI with automation closes the loop on the progress made in the respective fields over the last few decades. The efficiency that's being brought about by combining automation and AI will only increase going forward. The applications could cover a much wider range of tasks than what is currently possible, and all of this, in turn, will have a positive impact on worker productivity and overall efficiency. Setting aside the doomsday scenarios of machines completely taking over the world, most experts believe that this will not cause mass unemployment. Automation has slowly become more prevalent over the last few decades, and each time, there have been concerns over the impact this would have on employment. It was once believed that the introduction of automated teller machines or ATMs in banks would render the bank staff jobless, but five decades on, we can see that that isn't the case. While it does render some specific tasks and roles irrelevant, what automation primarily does is transform jobs. This is apart from the new jobs that automation would create. Leaders, or aspiring leaders, would do well to keep this in mind as they craft their people strategies.[27]

GenAI and the Way Forward

When Elon Musk announced a project called OpenAI along with a group of other people, notably Sam Altman, Greg Brockman, LinkedIn co-founder Reid Hoffman, Jessica Livingston, Peter Thiel along with Amazon Web Services, Infosys and YC Research, people initially took notice largely because of the high-profile Tesla chief's involvement. In the years that followed, OpenAI has come to be synonymous with AI for the layperson. Set up in 2015, OpenAI operated largely under the radar for the first five years of its existence as far as the general public was concerned. It did create a large enough buzz within tech circles to attract early investments from companies as varied as tech giant Microsoft and Indian IT services firm Infosys. OpenAI's mission statement has been to create a safe and ethical path towards AGI.[28] In 2018, the organisation introduced the world to a generative pre-trained transformer (GPT)—a neural network designed to function like a human brain and trained on large data sets to provide relevant responses. Interest in what OpenAI was doing was still largely confined to technology firms. It was only in 2021, when it announced the launch of Dall-E, an image generation engine, that people outside tech circles started hearing about it and paying attention. Dall-E is an AI-based image generation engine that produces visuals based on text inputs provided by users. What made it unique is that the inputs were provided in natural language, which meant that the engine was accessible to anyone, not just a software engineer with coding capabilities. A user could ask it to create an image of '18th century Paris but with skyscrapers' using exactly those words, and it would provide an image that matched these specifications. This was a game changer as it opened up the world of tech development to people with no tech or coding skills. An updated version, Dall-E 2, was launched the next year, and a few months later, OpenAI made its chatbot ChatGPT available to the world on 30 November 2022.[29]

Within the first two months, the program had 100 million users, making it the fastest growing consumer application ever. This is when the non-tech world sat up and took notice of this Silicon Valley start-up, which until then had largely been unheard of outside Valley circles. The internet was abuzz with people sharing what prompts they had put into the app and what it threw back at times, often with unintentionally hilarious consequences. Some were amazed at its ability to provide code to carry out simple functions based on requests entered in conversational English. Others were mildly horrified that it stumbled over simple word problems that a first grader should have been able to solve.[30] One way or another, GenAI and the potential it had to simplify our quest for information had caught the world's collective imagination. Enterprises, too, sat up and took notice. Tech firms wasted no time in announcing their intent to integrate GPT into their existing offerings. Unsurprisingly, perhaps, Microsoft, which is a significant investor in OpenAI, was the first off the block. The company announced that ChatGPT would be integrated into its search engine and browser, with ChatGPT-generated responses being marked out from the regular search results to prevent any confusion for the users.[31] Meta introduced Llama, its own open-source LLM, which has since been integrated into its offerings like WhatsApp.[32] At almost the same time as Microsoft announced this collaboration with OpenAI, rival Google announced the launch of Bard, its GenAI chatbot that was later renamed Gemini. Bard was built on Google's Language Model for Dialogue Applications (LaMDA), which it had launched two years earlier. Bard was launched as an experimental conversational AI offering powered by LaMDA and was largely seen as Google's response to ChatGPT. In 2025, Google said that it was offering an AI mode on its Search function.[33]

These companies and their AI offerings have captured and dominated the wider public consciousness because of their massive user bases. However, the credit for rolling out the first GenAI system that was accessible outside a closed user group goes to Stability AI. While Google, OpenAI and others were working on closed group versions of their GenAI products, Stability AI was the first who made it available for the larger population with the launch of Stable Diffusion, an image-generating tool, in 2022. The company believed that more people using AI tools would help make them better, at a faster pace.[34]

Hype or Game-Changing Tech?

Even in an industry that has come to be known for its hype cycles, the buzz created by GenAI has been unprecedented. It's telling that as recently as mid-2022, there was almost no awareness around GenAI, which then skyrocketed to the top of all emerging technologies and 'technologies to watch' lists the coming year, before companies started to get disillusioned by the lack of tangible results in 2023. This typically happens when everyone is keen to make the most of a new tech and jump onto the bandwagon—often without really evaluating whether they would actually benefit from it or not. Very often, the technology itself is at a very nascent stage, as in the case of GenAI, and not everyone can harness it to its full potential. Companies that get past this stage are likely to derive some long-term benefits from adopting the technology and will continue to work with it till it plateaus and becomes ingrained into their way of working. These companies need to parallelly work on how implementing AI-based tools will impact different aspects of their business, from people to processes. These leaders should ideally be spending an equal amount of time, if not more, on understanding the actual impact of this technology on their company and people and what steps they need to individually take to be able to manage this transition smoothly.[35]

While the hype around GenAI started only towards the end of 2022, AI-based tools were in the spotlight since 2020, largely due to the Covid-19 pandemic. The pandemic-induced global lockdowns accelerated the adoption and implementation of AI tools across industries and functions. Even vaccine development for Covid-19, which was done in record time, relied largely on these tools analysing huge swathes of data, something that hadn't ever been done before.[36] Manufacturing firms turned to AI to boost their supply chain effectiveness and rejig their production patterns as they worked with an additional shortcoming of global transportation systems being hit, impacting raw material availability. Some researchers have compared the AI wars to the space wars of the previous millennium, when nations were competing to see who would be the first to make it into space. With AI, too, they argue, it isn't very different as countries explore how these tools can be used to improve military prowess, alongside manufacturing and other economic capabilities. Experts believe that countries will start making advances in areas where they already have an advantage or a superior position by integrating AI into them.[37]

For India then, there is a lot of focus on how AI can be used to improve its digital and software services. Multiple government departments are working on pilot projects to integrate AI into their offerings under the Government of India's AI Mission.[38]

The potential impact of this scale of AI adoption, especially GenAI, may be likened to the smartphone revolution in India.[39] One reason perhaps is that not since the advent of cheaper smartphones has any tech really had the potential to have an impact at as large a scale as this one, especially in India. Access to affordable smartphones and cheap, even free internet, ensured its rapid adoption even in smaller towns and villages, connecting people irrespective of their location and backgrounds. It also opened up access to goods and services as well as information and entertainment in a way that was previously unimaginable.

What's striking this time around is that leaders are now attributing the need for fewer workers to the adoption of new technologies like GenAI.[40] In the past, automation had not had a significant impact on jobs outside the manufacturing sector. As leaders grapple with this new, ever-changing world, they also need to focus on how to manage employee and investor concerns around the rapidly evolving impact of this technology.

Microsoft chief Satya Nadella has repeatedly drawn parallels between GenAI and other major tech shifts in the last few decades—search, mobile and cloud.[41] Even then, the potential AI can have on industries or on individuals is likely to far outstrip the impact of any of these. While the advent of search primarily changed the lives of individual internet users and cloud had an impact on enterprises, GenAI has the potential to significantly impact individuals, enterprises and governments alike. Sundar Pichai, Google chief executive, has gone on to say that GenAI is the biggest technology shift in our lifetimes and could be bigger than the internet itself. 'It's a fundamental rewiring of technology and an incredible accelerant of human ingenuity,' he wrote in a blogpost on the search giant's 25th anniversary.[42] At the same time, the likelihood of this technology being misused and creating ethical and moral dilemmas far outweighs anything companies or individuals have had to grapple with in the past. Deepfake proliferation has already resulted in scams across the board and presents a never-seen-before potential to create social unrest. Social media platforms and aggregators have ramped up the size of their fact-checking teams to try and minimise the impact and reach of these doctored or AI-generated videos and images.[43] People who have worked closely on AI development over the last few years, decades even, are split down the middle on whether AI will overpower and overshadow humans. Geoffrey Hinton, who also won the Nobel Prize for Physics in 2024, has often been called a godfather in the field of AI, given the decades of AI research under his belt. He said that he is worried about the increasingly powerful machines' ability to outperform human beings in ways that are not in the best interests of humanity.[44] However, not everyone is as worried. Some experts suggest that it is important to have these guard rails and safeguards built into the very foundational layers of the technology to ensure that it doesn't run rogue.[45] Going ahead, it is perhaps important to remember that AI is just another technology, albeit one that has the potential to significantly alter our world unlike anything seen before. What we see happening around us at present is a re-imagining of the way we work and how businesses operate. Pharma, for example, is one industry where there is likely to be a large disruption, especially in the drug discovery process. Though still in the early stages, GenAI can bring down the drug design and discovery process, as well as predicting likely outcomes and side effects, to a few months instead of the few years that it normally takes. This was one reason why companies like Pfizer could quickly design and launch a Covid-19 vaccine in a record period of time.[46] This can also change how products are designed and developed, especially electronic components in devices. Industrial design is another area where GenAI is already being used fairly extensively, as is chip design and material design.[47]

We already see some early implementations in areas like customer service, with the use of advanced chatbots that have almost completely eliminated the need for human interaction. In the future, the customer service industry will be further transformed, with the potential to make a customer service agent much more productive through the use of AI tools.[48] While companies are currently experimenting with using AI tools to generate code, it's quite likely that the AI tool will be able to create a whole new app or payment ecosystem based on a well-worded prompt.

More recently, companies have started adopting agentic AI, replacing repetitive software jobs like quality assurance and testing with AI. This is expected to have a significant impact on entry-level jobs and has set alarm bells ringing for employees.[49] At the same time, companies like Klarna, which had shifted almost their entire customer service function to AI, are now going back to hiring people after seeing significantly higher levels of dissatisfaction among customers.[50] While there is no doubt that the volume of work being done by AI will only increase going forward, it remains to be seen exactly how this will impact jobs in the long run.

Experts caution that while changes in how we work are inevitable, adoption of GenAI is unlikely to result in mass lay-offs or massive waves of specific jobs or roles becoming obsolete. What is more likely over the next few years is that white-collar professionals especially will start to use GenAI tools to augment their work. The more mundane parts of the job will be replaced by AI and automation tools, leaving the humans free to do the more complex aspects of the job. As with any new technology, while some roles become obsolete, AI is also creating new jobs, prompt engineers being the foremost one. Indian-language AI models are likely to power a lot of the new development in this field in India, which again will result in increased demand for trained professionals. For leaders, this is an important time to ensure that their existing workforce is suitably equipped to deal with the changes that are coming in the next few years, even months. Given that this is an evolving skill, it may not be possible to directly hire from the market or from competition to fill the job roles. A better approach would be to invest in training the existing workforce. Identifying high-potential employees and providing further specialised training to them is one way of ensuring that the company doesn't fall behind in the AI race.

Irrespective of the industry, it's still early days when it comes to AI adoption. Most organisations are using open-source models and existing data sets to run pilot projects, but this is likely to change in the next few years. Once organisations start working with their own proprietary data, they are likely to drive more synergies from using AI, and this is the shift that will truly impact jobs going forward. More roles will be done with greater augmentation from AI tools, which will result in a fundamental shift in how leaders need to view jobs—both the ones that will be obliterated by AI and the new ones that will come into play. It's not hard to imagine a situation five years down the line when the entire organisational structure will have to be re-imagined and rethought of to incorporate the tech changes that have taken place. Also, outside of pure play technology companies, other industries, too, are ramping up their hiring of tech talent. There is no doubt, though, that the job and labour market and the workplace as we know it will change significantly in the next five years.

In a conversation with Microsoft founder Bill Gates in 2024, OpenAI CEO Sam Altman said that the AI systems we have currently are set up to do tasks, not jobs. Over the next few years, these will evolve, and people will be able to do more with them. People will be able to use their data and connect it to outside sources to use it more gainfully. 'The speed with which society has to adapt and how the labour market will change is the scary part (with GenAI) compared to other technologies,' said Altman.[51] It is expected that over the next five to ten years, AI systems will be fully equipped to deliver precise results, often with minimal prompts. Software developers are already working with AI tools to speed up the software development process, and over time, coding copilots are expected to become the norm.

Another study of over 2,700 AI researchers done at the University of California, Berkeley, has found that with the widespread adoption of GenAI, there is a possibility that all human tasks will become highly automatable by 2116.[52] While this is still a while away, this prediction has been moved up by half a century from the original estimate of 2164, which was made in 2022. More immediately, these changes are likely to start reflecting in how tech and non-tech corporate jobs evolve in the next decade. This will have implications for not only how companies are run but also how people skill and train themselves.

For aspiring CEOs who are in senior or mid-management roles at present, understanding how these changes will shape the future of their industries and organisations could be crucial when making a bid for the top job. Understanding how the technology landscape is evolving and what it means practically is a skill that will help set potential leaders apart from other contenders.

Despite the rapid progress that's been made in the last few years, it's useful to step back and take stock of what this is likely to be leading up to. Companies are just about starting to introduce multimodal AI capabilities with mixed results. Multimodal AI is a machine learning model that can process information across different formats or modalities, such as text, images and videos. In real terms, this means that a user can upload a picture of a chocolate cake and have the AI generate a recipe for it—or vice versa. While GenAI is a larger, umbrella term for different types of machine learning models that can be used to create new content from a prompt, multimodal AI capabilities expand the possibilities, and users are no longer restricted to only one type of input/output.

Small Is Better

What has tech industry watchers and experts most concerned is the possible advent of AGI. At the same time, there's no clear consensus on what exactly AGI means. Nvidia's Jensen Huang said in March 2024 that AGI could soon become reality.[53] Vested interests in furthering the already massive craze for AI (which has resulted in never-seen-before demand for the company's semiconductor chips) aside, he clarified that he defined AGI as a machine being able to do something 8 per cent better than most people. This could be acing an exam or a logic-based game. However, there's no clear consensus on what qualifies as AGI. In broad terms, it would be when machines reach a stage where they can do something with as much or more competence than a human being. Mustafa Suleyman, head of Microsoft AI and founder of DeepMind, said that artificial capable intelligence would be when a machine is given US$100,000 and it can turn that into US$1 million without any assistance.[54] The company believes—as of May 2024—that current AI models are equivalent to unskilled human beings if it were to map them on a six-level scale of AGI. Meta chief AI scientist Yann LeCun said in an interview with *Time* magazine in 2024 that the current LLMs that power AI chatbots are not on a path towards human-level intelligence. He said that these LLMs work only based on how they have been trained and are incapable of doing anything else beyond that.[55]

While there are reports of Big Tech saying that AGI could be a reality within the next decade, it is important to keep in mind exactly where we are at currently in the AI development cycle. GenAI, while a large step forward in what AI systems can comprehend and achieve, is still predictive at best. It can provide responses only based on the information it has available and cannot think for itself. Even while experts disagree over the exact definition of AGI, there is some consensus that it would need to meet some basic criteria, namely being able to outperform or match humans at a range of tasks and not just a single specific one. OpenAI goes on to add that to be considered an AGI, an AI system must also add economic value of some sort.[56] At present, we do not have systems that are capable of general intelligence or intelligence across multiple fields. While DeepMind may be able to beat the world's best players at a game of chess, it will fail miserably if asked to navigate a self-driving car—or even if asked to play another board game. ChatGPT or other LLMs can provide responses only within the boundaries of the information they have access to and the specific questions asked. There's no adaptability or the ability to adjust their responses on their own unless they receive explicit instructions to do so. These instructions, or prompts, are still being provided by humans.

Given this, leaders need to spend more time focusing on how they can harness the existing AI systems to benefit their business and customers instead of getting caught up in concerns about whether it will replace their entire workforce overnight. One area that is showing scope for significant and more widespread impact is the development of small language models (SLMs). These SLMs are a more streamlined version of LLMs like ChatGPT or Gemini. These are focused on a smaller dataset or application, requiring less infrastructure and architecture, making them cheaper and quicker to run. SLMs currently comprise fewer parameters—a few million at best, compared to LLMs where it runs into billions and even trillions of parameters. This makes them quicker and more efficient to operate and makes them adaptable to applications like personalised chatbots or assistants. These can also be deployed relatively quickly and are more agile than their larger counterparts. At present, enterprises are experimenting with SLMs using their proprietary data, customising them for their specific needs. However, the small size also brings certain constraints, particularly the risk of producing inaccurate or less nuanced responses as compared to an LLM.

While the size of the LLMs enables them to cover a wider range of prompts, it also makes them unwieldy. Technology companies are increasingly working on creating effective SLMs that are easier to implement and monetise. These models are aimed at carrying out simpler tasks and are easier to fine-tune to meet specific customer needs. Big Tech is currently focusing a large part of its energies on shrinking these models to make them quicker and easier to scale.[57] This will make GenAI much more accessible to a larger audience and will also make it easier for companies to adhere to ethical AI guidelines. Another reason for the rapid speed with which GenAI is scaling up is the primarily open-source model that several companies like Meta and Elon Musk's xAI have adopted.

The rapid rise of automation and AI makes it critical for individuals and enterprises alike to focus on upskilling and adapting themselves to the new reality. One advantage that existing employees have over any possible external hire is the latent knowledge they possess about the industry, specific company and role. Because AI is still an evolving field, companies are struggling to find highly skilled specialised talent. They are realising that if they can upskill and retrain their employees, especially the high performers, then they would be in a far better position to take advantage of the automation and AI boom. This is something leaders will have to drive top down and make it a C-suite imperative to train not only themselves but also their top employees. This is a critical time in the transition of the organisational landscape, and it would help leaders to take a more long-term view of how humans and machines can work together, rather than thinking of it as one over another. It's important to start thinking of how machines can be used to further augment human capability and find a way where this can work to the benefit of the enterprise and even society at large. Companies who effectively manage this transition will be well placed to take advantage of the changes and benefits this will drive in the next few years.

Re-imagining the workplace for a world in which humans and machines work together will require a lot more than just thinking about what parts of a task/job can be automated. It will require coming up with an entirely new approach to thinking of how the workplace of the future will look and redesigning it to enable optimal human–machine interaction. Given how widespread the adoption of GenAI is expected to be in the next few years, companies who are creating these AI models and those who are adopting them will have to work hard to mitigate the possible risks and security concerns. The possibility of a widespread cyber-attack driven through a chatbot is no longer the stuff of science fiction. The ability to create malicious code using natural language has made it extremely easy for a person to launch a cyber-attack. This could impact individuals, enterprises and nations, all in varying degrees of severity.

4

Generative AI and the New Frontiers

WORK IS AN INTEGRAL part of human civilisation and has evolved significantly across history. Availability of resources, development of technology, emergence of social structures, division of labour, and cultural values of different societies have shaped the way humans work. In the modern age, work is about innovation. Humans create and apply knowledge and information, design and develop new technologies and solve complex problems and challenges. They work in diverse and dynamic settings, collaborating across boundaries and leveraging the opportunities of the digital world. They work flexibly, autonomously and creatively, adjusting to the changing demands and expectations of society. The nature of work has undergone a significant transformation, especially in the wake of the digital acceleration triggered by the Covid-19 pandemic. As we embark into the AI age, work is undergoing yet another paradigm shift.

The adoption of AI in the workplace is enabling organisations and societies to solve problems that were hitherto impossible or unimaginable—from healthcare to education, from sustainability to accessibility. However, each worker will also get impacted, and for society, there will be unprecedented upheavals. Policy makers and governments around the world have both opportunities and challenges ahead to navigate this period of economic potential and societal transition. Leadership and organisations will undergo transformative changes in this age of GenAI. Leaders will need to adopt AI-driven decision-making, fostering a culture of continuous learning to leverage AI capabilities. They'll need to ensure ethical

AI use, addressing concerns like data privacy, algorithmic bias and safety. Organisations will see structural changes with AI automating routine tasks, necessitating a shift towards roles requiring human creativity and empathy. The workforce will need reskilling to work alongside AI. The advent of GenAI will necessitate a reimagining of leadership styles and organisational structures, emphasising adaptability, lifelong learning and ethical considerations.

Why Are We in the Middle of a Major Paradigm Shift at Work?

One of the characteristics of work is its relationship with time and place. In the industrial age, work was tied to a specific location and a fixed schedule. Workers had to be physically present at their workplaces, whether factories, offices or shops, and follow the same routine every day. Work was organised around the availability and needs of machines and resources, rather than human preferences and potentials.

In the modern age, work has become more flexible and adaptable in terms of time and place. Workers in many industries and functions can choose when and where they want to work, according to their personal and professional goals and circumstances. Work is organised around the availability and needs of information and knowledge, rather than machines and resources. Technology enables workers to access and share information anytime and anywhere as well as to collaborate and communicate with people across different locations and time zones. Work is no longer constrained by the physical boundaries of space and time; rather, it is liberated by intelligence. AI is already triggering a major paradigm shift in work and will increasingly continue to do so in the coming years. A lot of the changes that were set in motion over the past decade with the increase in digital transformation projects in the workplace have been accelerated with the increased adoption of AI. Digital transformation generates data, and data is crucial for AI, which learns and improves through exposure to vast amounts of data. AI identifies patterns and relationships in the data, enabling more nuanced and sophisticated analysis, leading to decisions and action, with or without the involvement of a human being. This is where a positive feedback loop comes into play.

The feedback loop works as follows: AI systems are initially trained on existing datasets to perform a specific task. Once deployed, these systems begin to interact with the real world, where they might encounter scenarios not covered in their training data. The system's responses to these scenarios generate new data, which can be collected and used to retrain the AI, improving its performance. The interplay between digital transformation and AI creates a dynamic ecosystem where data is both the input and output of AI systems. This continuous cycle of data generation and retraining leads to AI systems that are increasingly sophisticated and capable of tackling complex problems. The positive feedback loop also has implications for AI ethics and governance, a topic we shall discuss towards the end of this chapter.

GenAI and Copilots

AI has been through several iterations before arriving at the current system of machine learning and deep learning to train systems. GenAI, the most recent milestone in the advancement of AI, has transformative capabilities that are reshaping the landscape of technology and business. It is characterised by at least three significant attributes that are relevant here: reasoning and planning capability, natural language interface and multimodal interaction. The reasoning and planning capability of GenAI, especially with agentic workflows, has the potential to revolutionise strategic planning and decision-making. By synthesising vast amounts of data and identifying patterns beyond human capacity, it can provide unprecedented insights and foresight. This enables businesses to make informed decisions, anticipate market trends, consider multiple scenarios and devise robust strategies with a level of precision and speed previously unattainable. The natural language interface of GenAI enables interfaces to understand

and interpret natural language input from users. This reduces the learning curve by allowing users to interact with the system using conversational language instead of specific commands or predefined options. OpenAI Codex, for instance, is an AI system that translates natural language to code. It can interpret simple commands in natural language and execute them on the user's behalf, making it possible to build a natural language interface to existing applications.

Finally, multimodal GenAI models are capable of processing and generating content across multiple modalities, including text, audio, image and video. This allows the AI model to create a multifaceted description of reality, meaning they can understand a text description, generate an image, convert speech to text or even generate a video from a script. For instance, in a customer service scenario, a multimodal AI could analyse a customer's email (text), listen to their voicemail (audio) and review any attached images or videos. It could then generate a comprehensive response addressing all the customer's concerns across all these modalities. This ability to seamlessly integrate across modalities opens new avenues for data analysis and decision-making, as insights can be drawn from a much wider range of data sources. A copilot, underpinned by GenAI, is a revolutionary idea that brings together the three attributes mentioned earlier: reasoning and planning capability, a natural language interface and multimodal functionality.

A GenAI copilot is essentially an AI assistant that augments human ingenuity. The reasoning and planning capability allows the copilot to understand context, make logical inferences and plan responses, thereby enabling it to assist users in complex tasks. The natural language interface ensures that interactions with the copilot are intuitive and user-friendly, akin to conversing with a human. The multimodal functionality signifies the copilot's ability to comprehend and generate content in various forms, such as text, code or even images or video. This amalgamation of capabilities, especially when combined with agentic AI workflows, makes the copilot a versatile and powerful assistant, capable of aiding users in a wide array of tasks, from coding to creative writing. This can be a game changer for businesses, enhancing productivity, fostering collaboration and fuelling innovation. GenAI copilots aren't just tools; they are a digital companion that's reshaping how we interact with technology and indeed how we work.

How Copilots Enabled by GenAI Are Changing Work

GenAI copilots are revolutionising the workplace across industries and functions by enhancing efficiency, re-imagining business processes and fuelling unprecedented innovation. Companies across different industries are leveraging GenAI, augmented with agentic workflows, to transform their existing ways of working and are seeing results across these three dimensions with potentially increasing degrees of impact. GenAI copilots are adept at handling mundane and repetitive tasks, which allows employees to focus on more strategic and creative aspects of their jobs, resulting in enhancing efficiency even without any significant changes in business processes or disruptive innovations. For example, in software development, GitHub Copilot suggests code snippets and entire functions, enabling developers to write code more efficiently and with fewer errors. This not only speeds up the development process but also allows developers to allocate more time to complex problem-solving tasks while reducing the inefficiencies of context switching.

Business processes can be re-imagined with AI for better decision-making and collaboration across the organisation. AI can analyse vast amounts of data to identify trends, predict outcomes and recommend actions. AI copilots can facilitate cross-functional collaboration if these trends, outcomes and actions are accessible across the organisation via a unified platform. For instance, in customer service, AI copilots can predict the types of calls and parts needed for home servicing, streamlining the dispatch process and enabling collaboration between field service agents and an AI-based agent or with remotely located experts.

The innovative power of GenAI can be truly disruptive in sectors where AI is enabling solutions to problems that have hitherto been intractable. In healthcare, AI copilots can facilitate access to critical healthcare services for communities that remain underserved and enable an ageing population in many parts of the world to live a productive and fulfilling life. In the legal profession, copilots are democratising access to legal assistance and unlocking new avenues for legal analysis and innovation. Legal firms are now able to process vast amounts of data at unprecedented speeds, allowing lawyers to focus on helping clients.

GenAI and Healthcare

The healthcare industry has perhaps one of the highest potentials for gains in efficiency, collaboration and innovation using GenAI copilots.

Enhancing Efficiency

A prime example of enhancing efficiency is the application of GenAI in patient–clinician interactions. GenAI technology, for example, can convert patient–doctor interactions into clinician notes in real time. Here's how it works: a clinician records a patient's visit using the AI platform's mobile app. The platform adds the patient's information in real time, identifying any gaps and prompting the clinician to fill them in, effectively turning the dictation into a structured note with conversational language. This process significantly reduces the manual and time-consuming note-taking and administrative work that a clinician must complete for every patient interaction, enhancing operational efficiency and addressing challenges of workforce burnout and staffing shortages in the healthcare industry.

Re-imagining Business Processes

The application of GenAI in patient–clinician interactions also has significant implications for healthcare processes and, ultimately, the quality of patient care. The potential for breakthrough comes from the wealth of unstructured data such as clinical notes, diagnostic images, medical charts and recordings available to a clinician in seconds. The impact could be in the form of comprehensive suggestions to a clinician or by redefining how healthcare professionals work and collaborate. For example, AI-powered platforms can facilitate communication and information sharing among healthcare providers anywhere in the world, re-imagining business processes in healthcare and ensuring a unified approach to patient care.

Fuelling Innovation

GenAI augmented with agentic workflows is driving a paradigm shift in drug discovery, offering a new approach to the creation of novel molecular structures and drug candidates. A specific example of this innovation is IBM's Accelerated Discovery[1] initiative that leverages GenAI combined with agentic workflows to significantly compress the timeline and cost of developing new drugs. The AI system uses vast datasets representing the structure of molecules to make predictions of new molecular designs based on specific requirements. This process, akin to reverse engineering, generates novel hypotheses for exploration and creates new molecules that domain experts may not have come up with on their own, potentially unlocking billions of dollars in value.

GenAI and Manufacturing

The manufacturing industry is witnessing significant advancements across various facets of the industry, driven by GenAI copilots.

Enhancing Efficiency

GenAI is transforming the manufacturing sector, offering efficiency and productivity gains. A notable example of this is in predictive maintenance. Predictive maintenance is about identifying and rectifying potential equipment failures before they occur. GenAI can help by interpreting telemetry from equipment and machines and, if a problem is identified, by recommending potential solutions and a service plan to help maintenance teams rectify the issue. This can reduce potential downtime and realise cost savings by streamlining production lines.

Re-imagining Business Processes

GenAI copilots are enabling AI-assisted redesigning of business processes, leading to more outcome-focused operations. One example is the realm of knowledge management. In the manufacturing sector, you often have vast repositories of operating manuals, standard operating procedures, logbooks and past incidents. However, retrieving the correct information quickly and effectively from these repositories can be a daunting task. GenAI can assist in this process by summarising the relevant information, thereby enabling operators to focus more on their tasks without unnecessary delays. This also fosters collaboration among different teams by providing them with the right information at the right time.

Fuelling Innovation

Product development in the manufacturing industry is being impacted by GenAI, enabling a level of innovation and efficiency that was previously unattainable. A compelling example of this is in the automotive industry where companies like Toyota[2] are leveraging GenAI to create more efficient and aerodynamic vehicle designs. Technology allows them to optimise the shapes and structures of vehicle components, leading to significant improvements in fuel efficiency and performance. This level of optimisation was not possible with traditional design methods, which were often time-consuming and lacked the ability to fully explore the vast design space. GenAI and agentic workflows, on the other hand, can quickly generate and evaluate a multitude of design options, identifying solutions that human designers might overlook. Moreover, GenAI can adapt to changing requirements and constraints, making it a powerful tool for agile product development.

GenAI and Banking and Financial Services

Banking and financial services industries have always been among the first adopters of any new technology. So, it's not surprising that when it comes to GenAI, the financial services sector is among the biggest adopters of the technology, using it to improve operations and customer experience.

Enhancing Efficiency

Back-office processes are one area where GenAI is being used to enhance efficiency. Traditionally, tasks such as classifying documents, processing applications, verifying accounts and opening accounts were manual and time-consuming. However, with the advent of GenAI, these repetitive tasks are now automated. GenAI models are trained to understand and process unstructured data in documents with varied formats. This not only speeds up the process but also reduces the chances of human error, thereby enhancing efficiency and accuracy. Moreover, the automation of these back-office processes allows banking professionals to focus on more complex tasks, thereby increasing overall productivity.

Re-imagining Business Processes

A prime example of how GenAI copilots are re-imagining business processes is in insurance underwriting. Underwriting, a critical function in the insurance industry, involves evaluating potential risks and determining appropriate coverage levels. Traditionally, this process was manual and time-consuming and required extensive expertise. However, with the advent of GenAI, underwriters are now assisted by AI copilots that can analyse vast amounts of data, including historical claims, customer information and external factors. These AI models generate risk profiles and recommend appropriate coverage levels, enabling underwriters to make more informed decisions quickly.

Fuelling Innovation

GenAI is helping the financial services industry innovate to promote financial inclusion. For example, the Asian Development Bank (ADB) leverages GenAI to lower the barriers to entry for the unbanked and underbanked in Asia and the Pacific, enabling them to become part of the formal financial system.[3] The AI system extracts data from potential customers to create a lending profile. This innovative use of AI allows ADB to extend financial services to individuals who may lack traditional identification or credit history. This not only expands ADB's customer base but also promotes financial literacy and inclusion among traditionally underserved communities.

GenAI Copilots in the HR Business Function

GenAI is revolutionising the HR function, making it more human-centric by automating repetitive tasks and enabling personalised employee experiences.

A compelling example of this is the use of a GenAI-based avatar in the recruitment process by a large automotive player. This avatar, powered by advanced algorithms, interacts with each applicant, providing personalised feedback on their application process. It can answer queries, provide updates and even offer tips for improvement, thereby enhancing the candidate experience. The avatar also streamlines the recruitment process by automating tasks such as screening résumés and scheduling interviews. This not only increases efficiency but also potentially reduces the risk of human bias, ensuring a fair and objective selection process. It is important, however, to ensure that the AI system is itself fair and free from bias. By taking over these routine tasks, the avatar allows HR professionals to focus on candidate engagement and people development.

GenAI Copilots in the Customer Service Function

An AI copilot has the potential to improve customer experience by helping the customer service function become more efficient and effective. A prime example of this is the implementation of a GenAI model by a technology company, designed to understand customer intent, which is central to many customer service use cases. It operates by first comprehending the customer's query and then searching through various knowledge sources for the answer. These sources can include web links, the knowledge base, customer relationship management (CRM) systems and various other customer databases, which also enable personalisation. The process involves the AI system trawling through these sources to automate a relevant customer response. The generated response is then evaluated by a human or an AI agent, who can edit it, if necessary, before forwarding it to the customer.

This application of GenAI in customer service has several benefits: significant reduction in the time taken to respond to customer queries, thereby improving service efficiency; allowing customer service agents to focus on more complex tasks as the AI handles routine queries and, lastly, providing personalised responses, thereby enhancing customer experience.

GenAI and Marketing

The marketing function is benefiting from GenAI through innovation in product, creative and experience development. An Asian beverage company was looking to enter the EU market and turned to GenAI to help answer two questions: What kinds of new beverages might appeal to European customers and drive growth, and what innovative methods might speed up the product innovation process from end to end?

The beverage company used ChatGPT to provide user insights by feeding it aggregate, non-confidential customer information and then asked questions about flavour trends to generate a baseline understanding of beverage consumption and consumer behaviour in the EU market. Product designers also turned to GenAI to refine concepts. Using a text-to-image generative AI tool, the company was able to produce high-fidelity beverage concepts with detailed imagery. Marketers then took these concepts into the field to perform rapid testing with customers, ultimately helping the company complete a year-long process in just one month.[4]

GenAI for Societal Impact

Beyond the realm of business, GenAI has the potential to enable countries and societies to address challenges that were previously insurmountable in sectors spanning from healthcare to education, from sustainability to accessibility, and beyond.

In the realm of education, AI tools like Khan Academy's Khan Migo are revolutionising the way we learn. Khan Migo uses AI to generate custom learning paths for students, thereby enhancing educational outcomes. This personalised approach to learning ensures that each student receives instruction tailored to their unique needs and learning style. As a result, students are more engaged in their education and are more likely to succeed academically.

One of the challenges in sustainability is optimising resource allocation. GenAI and agentic workflows can address this in real time, reducing waste and enhancing efficiency. For instance, AI can optimise energy usage in smart grids, contributing to a more sustainable future. This application of GenAI could play a crucial role in combating climate change and preserving our planet for future generations.

In terms of accessibility, AI is surging ahead in making digital content more accessible to individuals with disabilities. For example, AI can generate real-time captions for individuals with hearing impairments. Making digital content more accessible ensures that everyone, regardless of their abilities, can fully participate in the digital economy. GenAI can be a tool for societal transformation, unlocking possibilities in healthcare, education, sustainability and accessibility, enabling us to solve problems that were previously thought to be impossible. As we continue to explore and develop this technology, we can look forward to a future where GenAI plays a crucial role in shaping our society for the better.

Ethics, Safety and Responsibility in AI

GenAI copilots are a testament to the potential of AI to transform work across functions and industries. They are not replacements for human workers but enablers that augment human capabilities. However, the opportunities presented by GenAI copilots also present risks, especially with increasingly autonomous agentic AI workflows. As we continue to integrate these AI systems into our work, it is essential to thoughtfully navigate the risks and challenges they present and ensure they are used in ways that are ethical, safe and beneficial for all stakeholders involved.

Ethics, safety and responsibility in AI involve adherence to principles of fairness, inclusion, security and privacy, safety and reliability, transparency and accountability. GenAI introduces additional risks such as harmful content and deepfakes, intellectual property rights and copyright infringement, automation containment, ungrounded outputs or hallucinations and manipulation with human-like behaviour. To harness the full potential of GenAI copilots, while understanding and managing risks, organisations need to use a combination of awareness and training, tools and standards, and policy and governance.

One of the key steps towards awareness and training around the risks of GenAI is to tighten up data practices across the organisation. This not only reduces the risk of inappropriate use and cyber threats but also addresses privacy concerns. By empowering employees with regular training on the ethical implications and risks of GenAI, organisations can ensure responsible use of this technology. Finally, given the dynamic nature of AI, it's important to invest in continuous learning on the latest research and trends in the field.

Managing the risks of GenAI requires a strategic blend of tools and standards. AI tools, such as those for measuring and auditing, can help identify and rectify biases in AI models, thereby preventing discriminatory outcomes. They can also detect anomalies and potential misuse of AI systems, enabling timely intervention. Incorporating diverse human perspectives can help in mitigating the risks of AI. Being aware of individual biases and asking questions in a neutral, open-minded way can lead to more balanced and fair outcomes. Tools for identity and authorisation controls, continuous monitoring and telemetry, layered guard rails and fail-safes as well as human oversight and intervention are required as AI systems are built with increasingly autonomous workflows. Evaluation approaches such as red teaming and adversarial testing are essential even before AI systems are released for general use. Robust data governance tools have become important to implement policies and procedures for data management, quality and privacy. Content provenance technologies can help in combating challenges posed by deepfakes. These technologies work by establishing a verifiable trail of the content's origin and subsequent modifications, thereby providing a reliable method to authenticate digital media.

Standards provide guidelines for the development and use of AI, such as the National Institute of Standards and Technology AI Risk Management Framework.[5] They promote best practices in areas such as data privacy, security and transparency. Compliance with these standards and frameworks ensures that AI systems respect user rights and operate within legal, safety and ethical boundaries.

Creating an AI ethics policy can serve as a guiding light for the responsible and safe use of GenAI, ensuring that its deployment aligns with the organisation's values and ethical standards. In addition to internal mechanisms, organisations should also engage with external regulatory bodies and adhere to relevant laws and regulations pertaining to AI. This includes data protection regulations, intellectual property rights and specific laws governing the use of AI in certain sectors.

Governance of AI is among the top priorities for governments around the world. For example, the European Union's Artificial Intelligence Act is a groundbreaking legal framework that aims to regulate AI applications. It categorises AI systems based on risk levels, with stringent regulations for high-risk systems. The act mandates transparency obligations, ensuring AI systems are understandable and explainable, and seeks to foster development and use of AI that respects fundamental rights, safety and ethical principles. A significant step towards establishing standards for AI, the EU AI act aims to boost user trust and facilitate AI's positive impact on society, underscoring the EU's commitment to shaping global norms for AI governance.[6]

While GenAI holds immense potential, we must develop robust ethical frameworks and regulations to ensure that it is used for the benefit of all. Let us remember to consider the ethical and safety implications of AI and our responsibilities as its creators and users.

Leadership for the Age of Copilots

Given the scale of the changes that GenAI, agentic AI workflows and copilots are already bringing about in the workplace, it would be naïve to assume that it will continue to be business as usual, especially when it comes to managing people. The *2025 Work Trend Annual Report* from Microsoft[7] suggests that every organisation has the opportunity to apply AI technology to drive better decision-making, collaboration and, ultimately, business outcomes. However, the transition from individual impact to applying AI to drive the bottom line requires a clear vision and plan. The rise of AI in the workplace is inevitable, and organisations that can effectively leverage AI will have a competitive advantage.

The advent of GenAI and copilots is ushering in a new era that necessitates a paradigm shift in organisational leadership. As we stand on the cusp of this transformative age, leaders must adapt their strategies to harness the potential of these technologies and drive their organisations towards a future defined by innovation, agility and continuous learning.

Leaders must not only understand the capabilities and limitations of AI but also be able to articulate a clear vision for its strategic application within their organisations. They need to demystify the technology for their teams, helping them understand how AI can augment their work and enhance their creativity.

At the same time, leaders must also address the emotional issues affecting their teams and stakeholders as they navigate the changes brought about by AI. AI has profound implications for the very fabric of our organisations, influencing everything from strategy to the very ethos that shapes our workplaces, making adaptability a paramount skill. The age of AI demands a new model of leadership—one that is less about command and control and more about fostering a culture of innovation and continuous learning. Leaders must be able to manage the complexities of this new landscape, balancing the need for efficiency and productivity with the need for creativity and human-centricity.

The future of work is not about humans versus machines but humans and machines working together to achieve greater efficiency, collaboration and innovation. As we move forward into this exciting new era, the leaders who succeed will be those who can effectively leverage the power of AI to enhance human potential and transform their organisations.

With inputs from Rohini Srivathsa, ex-Chief Technology Officer, Microsoft India & South Asia

5

AI Reshaping the Services Industry

THE SWEEPING CHANGES TAKING place on account of AI are already being recognised by some industries, and the early starters have already realised the benefits too. On the other hand, those who are slow to adapt to the changes have either been left behind or have had to go belly up. The advantages for businesses on account of digital and AI spend have resulted in retention or expansion of customer base, thus reflecting on income generation, or in operational efficiencies resulting in cost optimisation. We have witnessed several examples of those who have been hesitant with their digital and AI strategy failing in their businesses, leading to loss of market share and increased costs, including established businesses such as Toys R Us[1],Sears[2], Bed Bath& Beyond[3], Thomas Cook[4] and several others.

Leveraging AI would not only mean the right investment at the right time. It starts with the foresight on how the business landscape will change in the coming years, shadowing the constantly evolving changes in AI technologies, identifying those technologies that could bring about quantum benefits to the business, understanding the implications of alignment with AI in every function across the organisation and bringing about the required changes in the functioning of the organisation and the roles and the processes of engagements. All of this would be possible only with the right leadership with an excellent ability to steer the business in the right direction and inspire the teams to be flexible to adapt to change on an ongoing basis.

The future of business in every sector is going to be largely centred on its capabilities and timing for absorption of AI technologies in the business. Several established businesses in the services sector have struggled to adapt to the digital changes, which impacted their competitiveness and led to loss of market share or, in some cases, even to bankruptcy. We shall examine the implications for leaders in this context with some examples drawn from the service industry—hospitality, retail and banking, insurance and financial services businesses—that are centred on operational excellence or customer intimacy, resulting in cost optimisation or revenue enhancement or both.

Hospitality Industry

The hospitality industry is primarily built around customer relationships and personalised experiences. Several businesses in this industry were slow to embrace digital and AI technologies, and they failed to read the swiftness with which customers were shifting their preference to digitally served options. This shift in preferences resulted in the galloping progress in customer acquisition that new upstarts such as Expedia and Airbnb achieved relatively quickly. Thomas Cook, which had built a successful travel business through its brick-and-mortar model over 178 years, for instance, could no longer meet the expectations of a large section of their customers who started expecting the same advantages others were offering in terms of dynamic pricing, personalised recommendations and ease of online bookings. After struggling to deal with the new competitors, the business eventually declared bankruptcy in 2019.[5]

On the other hand, hotel chains like the Holiday Inn, the Marriott, Howard Johnson and others owning mighty physical assets faced challenges with the onslaught of born-on-the-web players like Expedia and Amazon offering flexibility with booking and pricing options and new players like Airbnb not owning any assets but zooming to US$83 billion.[6] Although they have managed to subsequently recoup by investing in digital and AI assets, they have let new players enter their territories and allowed them to chip away what could have been their business otherwise.

The changes in customer expectations are here to stay, and the players in the hospitality business have come to recognise that their offerings have to be further tailored around these expectations, resulting in more granular personalisation in automated room bookings, selections, check-in options, food and beverages (F&B) and convenience factors. Further implementation of AI in streamlining operations and enhancing decision-making could result in enormous benefits for the hospitality industry, which has historically been human-driven. The processes, too, have not kept pace with technological advancements in most cases. Hotels or resorts consume a lot of water and energy. With their rising costs and the need to conserve natural resources as a sustainability objective, AI could play an important role in the planning, consumption and conservation of resources to bring down costs and, thereby, offer unique value propositions to customers. Revenue optimisation for hotels would be through AI-driven dynamic pricing models, loyalty programmes built across online and in-person experiences and AI-powered digital concierge services. Thus, blending efficiency with personalisation would enable the hospitality businesses to build differentiation and create customer stickiness through enhanced customer delight.

Let's take a look at the examples of AI interventions that the hospitality business, including several leading Indian hotels like Taj Hotels, Oyo, ITC Hotels and Trident Hotels, has prioritised based on the necessity and feasibility for their businesses.

AI Interventions in the Hospitality Industry

Virtual Assistants

AI-powered virtual assistants are able to interact with customers 24/7 in several ways without any wait time—for bookings, feedback, instant responses about facilities, check-in/checkout details, nearby tourist attractions and customer requests. These chatbots offer convenience to customers, particularly the modern young travellers who prefer to be serviced and get personalised attention without human intervention, especially in the aftermath of Covid. Some hotels have been using Siri or Alexa in their hotel rooms to welcome guests and help them with voice-activated support service to customise their preferences.

Predictive Analytics

Predictive analytics is being used in several areas related to hospitality. Hotel occupancy, design of loyalty programmes, planning of special events and discounts, staff turnover, inventory management and energy consumption optimisation are a few examples of areas that are benefiting the most from the analysis of purchase behaviour, competition trends and buyer preferences through predictive analytics. Predictive analytics and machine learning would continue to play key roles in decision-making, for which data collection, organisation and cleaning up of the data would be essential to build robust models that have to be regularly trained to come up with relevant recommendations.

Dynamic Pricing Models

In earlier times, the hotel industry and customers were used to seasonal or weekend pricing. Digital service providers born on the internet and intermediaries have set the new trend of dynamic pricing, which has become the accepted norm for the industry. Dynamic pricing not only allows customers the advantage of booking as convenient but also enables the hotels to maximise revenues by allowing the algorithms to periodically determine the prices dynamically based on the factors driving the supply-and-demand status, including competitor data and the historic data of increase or decrease in tariffs. Decision making on tariffs also becomes much easier with the forecasting of revenues the models could provide at different price points for different scenarios.

AI-led Resource Management

Hotels consume large amounts of water, electricity and gas. AI could be helpful in managing such resources based on past usage and could specifically create patterns that allow the management to efficiently conserve use of such resources, thus reducing costs. Wastage also occurs in consumption and inventory of food items, laundry and housekeeping, and the spend in such cases could also be optimised.

Robotics for Routine Tasks

As human costs keep increasing and costs of technology dropping, it is inevitable that AI-powered robots would become more affordable for carrying out routine tasks in the days to come. Some hotels are already deploying robots to clean rooms or for basic customer service. This trend is likely to intensify for deployment in seemingly routine or mundane tasks in maintenance, gardening or inventory management, thus cutting down the guest waiting time and enhancing satisfaction. Some hotels in Japan have introduced robots to welcome and interact with the guests.[7] In India, several restaurants are using robots to deliver food to the table and enhance the dining experience. Examples include Moti Mahal, Robot Biriyani and Buhari (Chennai), Yesss Barbecue (Coimbatore), Chitti in Town (Visakhapatnam) and Indian Grill Room (Gurugram).[8]

Facial Recognition for Security and Guest Service

At times, we are pleasantly surprised to hear the gardener or the housekeeping staff call out our names in hotels that have hundreds of guests and which we may or may not frequent. While this may have been more of an exception than routine in some of the properties of the Taj Hotel where the recall is through personal interest or memory and planned human interventions for select customers, personalising guest experiences for a large customer base has become more feasible with analytics. Apart from name and face recall through face recognition techniques, based on the data models built around guest preferences and past interactions, it is possible to offer personalised options for stay or sightseeing or dining, thus maximising customer delight and revenue generation.

Facial recognition for enhanced security and avoidance of human errors is being utilised in several airports. This technology could be used in hotels as part of the check-in/checkout processes, which would not only minimise the time involved but also ensure security and safety for the hotel guests. This would also mean convenience for the customers at various points of interaction at the hotel premises.

AR and VR for Immersive Experiences

AR and VR technologies would help customers to have interactive experiences with the hotel facilities well before they decide to make their bookings. Such immersive experiences are enabling hotels to differentiate themselves from competitors by being transparent and enabling customers to make informed decisions about the hotel and the surroundings. It would be possible to glean data about their preferences from these interactions, and the hotel staff could be well prepared to customise their in-person experiences when they arrive on their premises.

AI-led Operations Management

Integrating AI applications in the core operations of hotels or resorts would help in enhancing operations efficiency. This could include interventions in several areas such as housekeeping needs based on real-time updates and forecast of room occupancy trends, scheduling of maintenance based on predictive analytics, unique experiences for guests based on their profiles through CRM systems, better inventory control based on trends of consumption and bookings made to help optimise inventory, creation of a seamless supply chain to ensure no stock run-outs and optimised staffing plans to meet with the projected occupancy rates.

AI-led Cybersecurity

Cybersecurity has become essential for all businesses to protect their data and that of their customers. In the hospitality industry, since both the businesses and their customers are vulnerable to online fraudsters and thefts, AI-driven systems can help detect patterns and forewarn of transactions that may ring alarm bells in time for the business to take immediate action.

The Future of AI in the Hospitality Business

The several path-breaking possibilities led by AI in the hospitality business are exciting. One of the major departures from the past would be fully autonomous hotels where instead of humans, AI would handle all operations—check-in/checkout, housekeeping, entertainment, dining and requests for any information. Aided by robotic concierges, it would be possible to anticipate the needs of the guests and seamlessly cater to them. Smart rooms will control all the parameters of the room, namely lighting, temperature, entertainment and AI-generated in-room menus and dining options.

To achieve sustainability goals and be sensitive to the environment, AI would support hotels in the optimisation of energy and water consumption, effectively manage waste and support the circular economy concept.

AR and VR would no longer be deployed as independent stand-alone applications but would become integral to the data feeds that would enable the hotel in identifying the preferences of customers and proactively ready these experiences or choices for their customers, servicing them from their own locations or when they visit the hotels.

Events being held at the hotel venues would be elevated to higher levels of immersive experiences with the help of AR and VR tools. AI-led integrated event management systems should be able to manage crowd flows, carry out autonomous identification and security checks and offer networking options based on profiles of participants. Biometric tools would enable hotels to offer hyper-personalisation and unique experiences. They would be able to monitor the health of guests and offer personalised dietary plans or relaxation options.

Prerequisites of People to Succeed in the AI-Driven Hospitality Sector

The tumultuous changes taking place in the hospitality industry in the context of AI intervention in the business call for recognition of the new realities for managing the business and, therefore, steering the business with great acumen and sharp focus. It is not an easy task to have AI engaged at every level in the business. As the industry is traditionally being managed by multitudes of grey-collared personnel, it would be required for the first time to learn to cope and co-exist with AI as its permanent guest. If leaders can get the human–AI partnership to work for all, it could be a game-changing phenomenon for the business.

Changing Roles and Tasks in the Hospitality Industry

Having examined how the hospitality industry is being shaped by AI and the resultant changes in the business functioning, leaders need to ready the organisations with the right talent and organisation structure to prepare the ground for transformation. Let us examine what changes are likely to take place in the traditional roles in the industry. This would also help in reskilling/upskilling of talent in the organisation as required to expedite the AI induction process.

The hospitality industry accounts for a significant part of the global workforce. According to the World Travel & Tourism Council, in 2023, hospitality and tourism contributed to around 330 million jobs globally, which accounts for 10 per cent of the jobs worldwide.[9] This includes roles in hotels, restaurants, travel agencies, airlines and other tourism-related businesses. Hence, it is important to study the future of jobs with increasing AI-led interventions in this industry. Some roles would still be relevant, but the tasks performed may get modified (Tables 5.1 and 5.2).

TABLE 5.1 Evolving Roles in the Hospitality Industry

Functional Area	Roles Likely to Disappear / Evolve	Drivers of Change	New / Emerging Roles	Description
Front office & guest experience	Manual front-desk clerks; Private branch exchange/telephone operators	Mobile check-in, GenAI chatbots, vernacular voice assistants, UPI (Unified Payments Interface)-based payments	Guest experience orchestrator (GenAI-enabled)	• Designs hyper-personalised guest journeys via AI tools • Skilled in omnichannel communication, issue resolution and sentiment analytics
	Night auditors (manual reconciliation)	Cloud property management software, real-time folio/ledger automation	Revenue & guest operations analyst	• Oversees automated reconciliations, guest journey data, fraud/chargeback alerts • Requires data literacy and hospitality finance basics
Housekeeping & facilities	Manual room inspectors; Paper-checklist supervisors	IoT occupancy & cleanliness sensors, robotics for cleaning & bed linen movement	IoT housekeeping operations lead	• Manages sensor data dashboards, robotic fleets & service-level agreements–driven room turnaround • Skills in IoT monitoring, safety & workflow optimisation
	Uniform roles focused only on manual tasks (room attendants without tech enablement)	Automation & exoskeleton/assistive devices	Smart housekeeping technician	• Operates automation aids, uses mobile apps for tasks, conducts quick diagnostics • Requires tech comfort & ergonomics knowledge

F&B	Traditional captains/ waitstaff without digital ordering skills	QR (quick response code) menus, table-side digital ordering, kitchen automation	Digital F&B experience specialist	• Manages AI-assisted upselling, menu personalisation, guest dietary preferences & allergen mapping • Skilled in point of sale (POS), CRM & upselling
	Manual kitchen line operators	Smart kitchens, hazard analysis and critical control points sensors, semi-automatic cooking systems	Smart-kitchen automation engineer	• Oversees automated kitchen equipment, food-safety IoT and energy optimisation • Requires basic coding/product lifecycle knowledge & hazard analysis and critical control points expertise
Revenue, sales & marketing	Traditional revenue managers (spreadsheet-heavy)	AI-driven dynamic pricing, media-to-revenue attribution	AI-powered revenue & distribution strategist	• Uses demand forecasting, online travel agent vs direct pricing models, and attribution analytics • Skilled in channel management, GenAI prompts
	Field sales reps doing only property visits	Digital sales enablement, virtual property tours	Omnichannel hospitality sales manager	• Integrates WhatsApp/WeChat/ LinkedIn, virtual tours & CRM automations • Needs digital selling & business-to-business contracting skills
	Print-focused marketing coordinators	Performance marketing, influencer & creator economy	Creator & community partnerships lead	• Designs influencer collabs, user-generated content strategy, social commerce • Must know brand storytelling, contracts & community engagement

Functional Area	Roles Likely to Disappear / Evolve	Drivers of Change	New / Emerging Roles	Description
Events, banquets & guest engagement	Traditional event coordinators	Hybrid events, immersive experiences, AR/VR	Hybrid events technologist	• Manages streaming, AR/VR guest engagement, sponsor analytics & accessibility compliance for meetings, incentives, conferences and exhibitions
	Activity managers (generic programming)	Experience-driven tourism; wellness & culture demand	Experience & local partnerships curator	• Builds curated city/local experiences (culture, wellness, culinary, sports) • Skills in vendor partnerships, safety & guest profiling
Security & risk management	Physical-only security teams	Keyless entry, camera analytics, cyber threats	Cyber-physical security & privacy manager	• Integrates cybersecurity with on-premises safety • Skilled in video analytics, data privacy (digital personal data protection [DPDP]) and incident response
Sustainability & ESG	Green officers with only reporting focus	Heatwaves, water stress, ESG procurement mandates	ESG & climate resilience lead (hospitality)	• Builds carbon, water & waste reduction road maps • Manages ESG audits, sustainability certifications & crisis-resilience plans
	Waste-handling staff	Circular F&B, zero-waste mandates	Waste-to-value manager (F&B)	• Converts waste into biogas/compost • Tracks food waste key performance indicators • Runs supplier sustainability feedback loops

Technology & digital transformation	Manual IT support (reactive)	PropTech integration, IoT-enabled buildings, app-based journeys	PropTech systems integrator	• Connects property management systems/POS/building management system/IoT/locks/payments • Requires API, cybersecurity & vendor-management knowledge
	Data-entry roles in operations	Automation, AI workflow assistants	Hospitality data & AI product analyst	• Designs AI-enabled service flows • Analyses guest data for upsell/personalisation • Needs Structured Query Language (SQL), dashboards & domain knowledge
Supply chain & procurement	Manual procurement coordinators	Smart contracts, traceability, ESG sourcing	Hospitality supply chain intelligence manager	• Manages AI-driven sourcing, vendor scoring, farm-to-fork traceability, QR provenance & ESG compliance
HR, training & workforce development	Paper-based HR generalists	AI-driven gig staffing, learning analytics	Hospitality workforce architect	• Builds future skill pathways • Manages gig-mix talent • Drives AI upskilling & culture transformation
	Static training coordinators	AR/VR, microlearning, skill-based certifications	Immersive hospitality learning and development designer	• Designs AR/VR simulations for guest scenarios, compliance training and cross-cultural service skills
Mobility, payments & ancillary revenue	Cashiers, billing desk roles	UPI/BNPL (Buy Now Pay Later), cashless, cross-border wallets	Payments & fintech liaison (hospitality)	• Manages UPI cross-border integration, reconciliations, chargeback analytics & anti-fraud protocols
	Traditional concierge transport desks	Electric vehicles (EV), multimodal mobility	EV & mobility experience manager	• Manages EV charging ops, dynamic pricing, tourist mobility tie-ups • Requires fleet & partner-management skills

Source: Curated with inputs from ChatGPT

Table 5.2 Understanding the New Roles in the Hospitality Industry

New Role	Why This Role Is Emerging (Drivers)	Where It Will Exist	Key Skills Needed
Guest experience orchestrator (GenAI-powered)	Personalised stays, AI-curated itineraries, multilingual digital concierge	Hotels, resorts, cruises, co-living	• AI prompting • Guest profiling • Empathy • Journey design
Robot & automation fleet supervisor	Service robots for delivery, cleaning & concierge; labour shortage	Hotels, quick service restaurants (QSRs), resorts, theme parks, cruises	• Robot ops • Safety protocols • Vendor management • RPA basics
Experience & local partnerships curator	Rise of experience economy & hyperlocal cultural tourism	Hotels, resorts, co-living, cruises	• Partnership building • Destination curation • Contracting
Climate & disaster resilience officer	Heatwaves, floods, coastal climate risks; business continuity	Hotels, resorts, cruises, theme parks	• Risk mapping, • Emergency planning • ESG • Drills
UPI & global payments liaison (hospitality)	UPI globalisation, cross-border wallets, BNPL travel	Hotels, cruises, theme parks, serviced apartments	• Payment systems • Fintech risk • Chargeback management
Digital accessibility experience auditor	Accessible travel demand, kiosk/app self-service	Hotels, cruises, airports, theme parks	• Web Content Accessibility Guidelines • Accessibility testing • Inclusive user interface review

Creator collaboration & social commerce manager	Travel influenced by creators; user-generated content drives bookings	Resorts, boutique hotels, theme parks, cruises	• Influencer management • User-generated content strategy • Content governance
Wellness & longevity programme designer	Health tourism, biohacking, sleep tech, Ayurveda and med-wellness	Resorts, luxury hotels, cruises	• Wellness science • Programme design • Health protocols
Sustainable F&B—waste-to-value manager	Zero-waste mandates, circular food practices	Hotels, QSR, resorts, theme parks	• Food waste analytics • Compost/biogas management • ESG
PropTech systems integrator	IoT, smart rooms, keyless, property management systems-building management systems-POS integrations	Hotels, co-living, serviced apartments	• APIs • Integration • Cybersecurity • Vendor orchestration
Digital twin & smart facilities analyst	Predictive maintenance, energy optimisation with digital twins	Hotels, resorts, theme parks, cruises	• Digital twin modelling • IoT data • Computerised maintenance management system
EV & mobility experience manager	EV tourism, charging infra as revenue, multimodal travel	Hotels, highways resorts, theme parks	• EV infra management • Pricing • Fleet partnerships
Medical/recovery hospitality liaison	Medical tourism, post-procedure recovery stays	Hotels near hospitals, resorts, cruises	• Medical protocols • Privacy • Hospital partnerships
Community experience host (co-living)	Shared living requires curated community building	Co-living	• Community management • Events • Conflict resolution

New Role	Why This Role Is Emerging (Drivers)	Where It Will Exist	Key Skills Needed
Hybrid entertainment experience designer	Demand for immersive, AR/VR gamified guest entertainment	Theme parks, cruises, resorts	• AR/VR • Storytelling • Experience design
Pet experience manager	Pet-inclusive travel, specialised amenities	Hotels, resorts, serviced apartments	• Pet care • Safety protocols • Partnerships with vets
Faith-aligned guest experience designer	Pilgrimage tourism, dietary & spiritual experience alignment	Hotels, resorts, serviced apartments	• Cultural sensitivity • Religious protocols • F&B alignment
Sleep experience curator	Sleep tourism, circadian rooms, tech-enabled sleep wellness	Resorts, luxury hotels	• Sleep science • Ambience design • Device integration
Data & consent privacy officer (hospitality)	DPDP Act & privacy for guest data	Chains, cruises, co-living	• Data privacy • Data protection impact assessment • Consent UX • Audits
Immersive brand storytelling producer	4D lobbies, interactive brand experiences	Luxury hotels, theme parks, cruises	• Experiential design • Multimedia • Extended reality (XR)

Source: Curated with inputs from ChatGPT

Retail Industry

The retail industry has evolved over the decades with several changes in the business models and customer servicing. Disruptions in the industry have been both from within as well as due to external factors. For several centuries, local shops and markets were predominantly the source of buying and selling of generic and specialised goods based on the requirements of specific geographies. For a long time, producers were also sellers of the products they created, and this was mostly in local markets based on local needs. Over a period of time, merchants started selling locally produced products through intermediaries or directly to other markets and started sourcing the products in demand from other places to sell to the local community.

With urbanisation, in the late 1800s and early 1900s, supermarkets and department stores started gaining traction. Department stores such as Harrods in London and Macy's in the United States started to bring multiple products under the same roof, offering a plethora of options to their customers and thus creating a new shopping experience. They could offer a variety of products at attractive prices as departmental stores could source in bulk and negotiate good prices that they could pass on to their customers. Stores offered flexibility and free access to customers to select products they prefer from the shelves, thus resulting in reduction in labour costs too. Discount stores and exclusive stores for luxury brand–conscious customers started to be set up. Store-branded products began to get rolled out, and stores started advertising themselves to create a distinctive presence in the market.[10]

With vast improvements in roads and infrastructure and simultaneous increase in automobile sales, people could travel around for shopping with much more ease. As a result, companies like Target and Walmart started setting up a vast network of retail outlets not only in the cities but also in the close proximity of where people resided, making weekend shopping a part of the family outing. This enabled customers to see, touch and feel the products before they decided to buy. The number of options and the lower cost advantage that the retail stores offered were very attractive, which was also instrumental in the slowing down of the mail order business. While companies like Sears set up their own stores to be close to the customers, they could never compete with new retail chains such as Walmart and Target who could offer a far greater range of products at much lower costs. This led to the downfall of the traditional mail order business and the eventual shut down of businesses and bankruptcy of iconic brands such as Sears.[11]

In the 1980s and the 1990s, suburban malls comprising multiple branded outlets became a popular concept across the United States initially and eventually in many parts of the world. In addition to the retail buying experience, customers were attracted to these locations due to dining and entertainment options offered under a single roof. Specialised retail chains in sports, fashion, food, luxury products and electronics got an impetus during this phase with a rapid expansion of their footprints and revenues from multiple locations.

The late 1990s and the first decade of the 21st century created an enthusiastic response to the internet, which dramatically changed our lives. Retail was also impacted by the internet boom, which saw the entry of new players like Amazon and eBay who disrupted the then existing brick-and-mortar retail businesses. Several established players struggled to adapt to the advent of digital technologies in their businesses. Companies like Sears and Toys 'R' Us continued to follow their outdated policies and practices and lacked the agility and the foresightedness to embed technology in their operations, which resulted in mounting losses in their business. Meanwhile, the digital-era retailers could leverage technology for inventory planning, customer personalisation and optimisation of the supply chain. Gap Inc. was slow to make the moves around technology, thus resulting in competitors like Zara, H&M and others overtaking them with their savvy tech strategies to enhance market shares. Macy's, too, has been impacted due to lagging behind in investment in digital technology, resulting in losses and several stores having to be shut. Much later, they managed to rejuvenate the business by offering digital interventions and omnichannel experience to their customers. However, in the meantime, Amazon and Walmart have moved ahead with their omnichannel experiences for their customers.[12] Lately, retailers have been using the storefronts for creating in-store personalisation, thus disrupting direct-to-consumer approaches, using superior immersive product experiences prior to purchase with VR, AR and interactive displays. We have also been witnessing examples of no-contact checkouts and hyper-personalisation through brands such as Amazon Go.

The Rise and Fall of the Mail Order Business

The mail order business was, for a long time, an independent business and, for a while, a subset of retail business—a format that enabled customers to access products from far and wide. The mail order business took off in the late 19th and early 20th century, specifically in the US market, with companies such as Sears, Roebuck & Co. and Montgomery Ward offering a wide range of products to their customers.[13] By producing attractive catalogues with thousands of products, they could reach customers far and wide—those who did not have access to such options otherwise. Rural customers in the American markets found this particularly advantageous coupled with the offer of return and refund if they didn't like the products on arrival and, in later years, payment in instalments too. After a while, the mail order business model became international, and in the era after the Second World War, the patronage of the expanded base of customers helped the businesses to increase their revenues substantially. At its peak, in the early 1980s, the mail order business reached an estimated annual revenue of US$30 billion with a significant share of the business with companies such as Sears, JCPenney, Montgomery Ward and Spiegel.[14]

In time, mail order business customers embraced e-commerce. Instead of physical catalogues, digital content provided information about the products in much more user-friendly formats, enabling access to a vast range of products at competitive prices, enhanced flexibility, convenience, independence and support where required to make purchase decisions. New businesses like Amazon have come into the e-commerce space with reduced overheads, building upon the advantages of mail order businesses and in-person retail formats in life-altering ways. Mail order retail laid the foundation for today's e-commerce: the key tenets for the retail business, the convenience factor and access to a wide choice of products have been drawn from the mail order business and embedded into e-commerce.

Since 2010, retail has transitioned from the traditional marketplace recreated on the internet where buyers and sellers interact directly or through intermediaries to influence marketing and social commerce. User-generated content is being effectively utilised to reach out to audiences who are sliced and diced and precisely targeted based on the enormous data being generated through every touch point of the customer. Use of mobile phones as a medium of connection to the retail experience has resulted in mobile-first designs making the buying process simple and easy to handle.

AI Applications in the Retail Industry

Retail is one of the domains where AI and other emerging tools are already being deployed for gathering insights regarding buying patterns and coming up with solutions that enhance customer delight. Hyper-personalisation, prediction of customer needs and preferences with greater accuracy and perfection of the buying experience across online and offline modes would be the focus of AI and digital technologies in the coming years. In this context, let us examine the domains in retail where AI solutions would have a significant impact and how retail businesses should be equipped to implement AI solutions.

AI-led Seamless Shopping Experience

The shopping experience is one of the applications where AI is being used to make security and the buying process seamless.

While face recognition and biometric payments create enhanced security that identifies suspicious behaviour and enables quick access without the need to use passwords, the checkout technologies being implemented by companies like Amazon Go remove the hassles of payments and time spent in long queues for checkouts. To maximise sales and create customer delight, with the help of geolocation and data analytics, AI recommendation engines could suggest real-time discounts to the stores to be made available to the individual customer or a group of customers who are in the vicinity of the store, thus making the entire shopping experience much more engaging and purposeful.

Personalised Recommendations

Current recommendation systems are built around patterns and trends of datasets of similar customers and their shopping preferences, buying behaviour and browsing history. Future recommendation systems would be hyper-personalised, that is, the recommendations would be highly personalised and tuned to individual preferences and buying patterns, and context-specific based on situations or real-time needs. For instance, as you are walking up the street at dinner time, it would suggest restaurants offering your dietary preferences, or on a hot summer day, the recommendation engine could suggest ice cream options of your choice available at special prices. Visual- and style-embedded recommendation engines could also have the ability to remember and contextualise the needs of the individual and suggest the right options instead of the shopper having to recall/know the product or style. In stores where there are store assistants stationed, they could be empowered on a real-time basis with customer data indicating their preferences of products, style and price points based on their previous browsing history or purchases, thus enabling them to personalise the sales process and minimise the time for sales conversion. For instance, in a store selling expensive ortho footwear, if the store assistant has access to a customer's previous purchase or browsing history, the recommendation engine would indicate options that the store assistant could provide to the customer, thus making the shopping experience personalised and satisfying.

Conversational AI

Amazon Echo, Apple HomePod and Google Home are examples of tools that enable voice shopping. Voice assistants would get more sophisticated as they would be able to understand and interpret complex shopping queries, going beyond simple keyword matches. Chatbots and virtual assistants would become intuitive and make suitable recommendations. Domino's Pizza Bot orders food and tracks delivery.[15] Walmart's Easy Reorder simplifies shopping with AI-powered recommendations,[16] and Target's Redcard offers personalised deals.[17] Over a period of time, they could provide voice-enabled comparisons of products or suggest additions to the carts. In future, when integrated with AR and VR, conversational AI would provide an enhanced customer experience.

AR and Virtual Try-Ons

AR is being used currently in virtual showrooms. For instance, Warby Parker has created an AR application that enables customers to try on eyeglass frames virtually, thus helping customers feel comfortable with the options being considered before reaching the decision for purchase.[18] Houzz and Williams-Sonoma use an AR application to help customers visualise furniture and home décor in their own space to determine the right choice of products.[19] L'Oreal uses AR to enable customers to virtually try on cosmetics and make-up.[20] Tiffany & Co's engagement ring experience[21] and De Beer's Diamond Experience[22] are aimed at interactive storytelling, leading to enhanced customer experience. Louis Vuitton hosts AR fashion shows, which offer immersive fashion experiences.[23] Automobile manufacturers such as Audi, BMW and Tesla help customers to visualise cars in 3D formats and explore car features and designs.[24] Social commerce platforms such as Shopify AR create AR experiences for e-commerce and provide an integrated AR shopping experience.[25] Fashion brands partner with influencers for AR-powered product showcases. For instance, influencers use Sephora's Virtual Artist or Ulta Beauty's Virtual Try-On to showcase make-up looks.[26] Heritage Indian brands are creating immersive experiences for their customers through AI and AR. The legacy brands include Britannia, Tata Tea and ITC.[27]

AI can use a shopper's picture or measurements to create digital avatars for virtual try-ons. It is anticipated that AR-powered virtual try-on capabilities will become more widely used in the coming days. Smart mirrors can transform the retail business with innovative AI and AR applications. While they are currently being deployed to enable customers to try on fashion and convenience-related products and provide them with real-time haptic feedback to help them speed up their decision-making process, in due course of time, AI algorithms would personalise recommendations based on the analysis of customer preferences and purchase patterns. Some examples of businesses that are using smart mirror technology include H&M, which has installed smart mirrors with Microsoft Azure-powered voice assistants at its New York Times Square store, and Adidas and Tommy Hilfiger, which encourage customers to try various options virtually and thus reduce the return rates.[28]

The trends in using AR to enhance the shopping experience will grow significantly in the coming years.[29] The combination of AR and AI technologies would bring XR into the mainstream, enabling further personalised experiences and interactive applications. For instance, we would be experiencing generative AR glasses that are able to identify objects and enrich them with AR information generated on demand, offering real-time and personalised experiences. Immersive customer experiences would become more enriching. With the integrated applications combining AR, spatial computing, Web3 and non-fungible tokens, customer engagement would be enhanced, linking products with immersive experiences.

Smart Inventory Management

Inventory management and fast-moving items have been closely monitored by manufacturers for a while now. Moving away from stock-and-sell approaches to smart inventory management involving predictive analytics has been effective with those businesses where data is systematically organised so that it could be sliced and diced as required to come up with optimal stocking as well as manufacturing plans. Predictive analytics can be used to know which items would be required in which stores based on seasonality, specific occasions and target audiences. Many organisations struggle with data access, formats of organising the data, ownership of data and the time taken to reorganise or clean up the data to build/maintain models. There is also the added challenge in integrating data from multiple devices/modes/channels and making them amenable for analysis. In future, robotics and blockchain technology will play a significant role in handling and tracking stock and minimise human errors. IoT-enabled smart shelves and intelligent inventory replenishments will ensure that what customers need is always in stock.

AI-led Loyalty Programmes

To make shopping a more pleasurable experience, AI could help with personalising loyalty programmes. Unlike the generic loyalty programme, personalised loyalty programmes are linked with individual shopping patterns, and rewards or discounts could be customised and aligned with customer interests and what they value most. To increase retention of customers and encourage repeat purchases, AI could gamify the loyalty programmes by encouraging referrals or social media participation and provide associated graded rewards. Hilton Honors uses AI to provide personalised offers, room upgrades and tailored experiences to its loyalty programme members.[30] Customers of American Airlines who are part of its loyalty programme have been offered personalised promotions and dynamic offers over the years. The airline is looking at ways to use AI itself—but it's just hoping to save time, not let AI bots dictate the price customers pay.[31] Domino's Pizza offers discounts and rewards to its loyalty programme members using its AI-powered virtual assistant.[32] Starbucks Rewards is able to use its AI tool to make personalised offers based on customer analytics.[33] As the business's abilities to manage and organise the data matures, personalisation at scale would be feasible for each segment. Predictive analytics would use the data to fine-tune its loyalty programmes with the understanding of anticipated customer behaviour and preferences. AI would help in cost savings and increased sales with targeted and personalised loyalty programmes for its customers. [34]

Fraud Detection and Customer Protection

Online transactions have led to huge losses for several e-commerce companies. As per Juniper Research 2022, merchants worldwide faced losses exceeding US$48 billion payment fraud due to online payment transactions.[35] AI could help address this problem by identifying suspicious behaviour with the use of biometrics and preventing fraud. Authentication can be made more foolproof and seamless by using facial recognition or fingerprint scanning without having to use passwords. Predictive analytics could be deployed to identify potential threats. AI-powered drones and robots could be deployed to monitor stores and warehouses. Blockchain technology ensures secure data storage and transmission. A few examples of how AI is powering fraud detection and security in the context of the retail business include Amazon's use of AI-powered access control, Walmart's AI-powered surveillance systems and Target's implementation of an AI-driven fraud detection system.[36] In future, regulatory compliances will increase, and retailers will have to rely upon AI-led security systems with greater focus on safety considerations in the customer experience. The opportunities to integrate AR, VR and other technologies with AI would also lead to integration issues and security-related risks. Chief technical officers of retail businesses should be mindful of such risks and mitigate the risks by smart deployment of AI to thwart fraudsters.

Future of AI in the Retail Industry

The advancement in AI tools along with other digital technologies would make integration of data and insights more robust. The tightly coupled information would make it feasible to create hyper-personalised experiences, autonomous stores and smart supply chains that would make the cost of such servicing affordable and the retail process seamless in the dynamic world. Sustainability and waste reduction agendas would be embedded into the retail process as much as human and machine collaboration will become far more effective in the future.

Talent Requirements of Retail Industry for the AI Era

To succeed in the exciting yet complex AI-driven environment, the retail industry would need a varied talent force. The capabilities that the retail industry should possess include understanding changing customer behaviour and preferences, implementing AI-powered customer service, leveraging data analytics for decision-making, enhancing inventory management and supply chain efficiencies, creating immersive shopping experiences, strengthening cybersecurity measures and moving away from generic marketing strategies to a personalised marketing strategy. Personnel currently in retail businesses would require to be trained and equipped with various skills to contribute or would have to be replaced with new talent that has the relevant skills. At the same time, due to AI and automation, several roles that are currently handled by humans need to be examined to decide which of them could be redefined with new skills and which roles will become redundant. Let us examine these roles next in Tables 5.3 and 5.4.

Table 5.3 Evolving Roles in the Retail Industry

Functional Area	Roles Likely to Disappear / Evolve	Drivers of Change	New / Emerging Roles	Description / Key Skills Needed
Store operations & customer experience	Cashiers; manual billing staff	Self-checkout, UPI/QR/BNPL, cashier-less stores	Frictionless store experience specialist	• Manages self-checkout, smart carts, store apps & queue-less experience • Skilled in digital customer experience, issue resolution & device troubleshooting
	Floor sales associates (product push)	AI product recommendations, hyper-personalisation	Personalised retail experience adviser (AI-augmented)	• Uses customer data & AI prompts to tailor product suggestions • Strong customer empathy, data-assisted selling & digital POS skills
E-commerce & omnichannel	Store-only merchandisers	Unified commerce, endless aisle, app-first shopping	Omnichannel merchandise planner	• Integrates store + online assortment, demand signals & fulfilment • Analytics, channel planning & supply visibility skills

Functional Area	Roles Likely to Disappear / Evolve	Drivers of Change	New / Emerging Roles	Description / Key Skills Needed
	Call-centre support agents	Chatbots, WhatsApp commerce, AI assistants	Omnichannel customer care specialist	• Handles assisted commerce across chat, social & voice • Skills in CRM, conversational commerce & sentiment management
Supply chain, fulfilment & logistics	Manual store inventory clerks	Radio frequency identification (RFID), vision tracking, automated replenishment	Real-time inventory visibility analyst	• Uses IoT/RFID analytics to maintain shelf availability • Requires data monitoring, exception handling & replenishment logic
	Warehouse pickers (manual)	Dark stores, robotics, micro-fulfilment	Robotics & micro-fulfilment coordinator	• Oversees warehouse robots, pick-to-light systems • Skills in automation workflow & safety protocols
	Manual last-mile routing roles	Route AI, gig delivery, drones	Last-mile optimisation specialist	• Uses AI route planning, gig workforce management & cost-to-serve analytics to optimise delivery
Merchandising & category management	Manual category managers (gut-based)	Predictive analytics & AI category planning	AI-driven category & space planner	• Uses data, AI & computer vision to optimise assortment, planograms & shelf productivity • Skilled in analytics & retail maths

	Visual merchandisers (store-only)	Phygital retail, AR try-on	Digital experience & phygital merchandiser	• Designs AR try-on, in-store screens, digital planograms • Skills in UX, visual storytelling & digital assets
Marketing, loyalty & CRM	Mass-campaign marketers	Precision marketing, AI audience segmentation	Retail growth & loyalty personalisation manager	• Runs AI-led loyalty; recency, frequency and monetary value segmentation; hyper-personalised offers • CRM, customer data platform & campaign analytics required
	Manual market research analysts	Social listening, AI insight engines	Consumer insights analyst (GenAI-driven)	• Uses AI to extract insights from social, app, CRM & market signals for brand/category decisions
Payments, fintech & revenue models	Cash-handling staff; billing supervisors	UPI, BNPL, wallet/credit integration	Retail payments & fintech manager	• Manages BNPL partnerships, fraud, chargebacks & loyalty-payments integration
	Rigid pricing teams	Dynamic pricing, competitor AI crawlers	Dynamic pricing & promo optimisation lead	• Designs flexible pricing & promo scenarios using AI competition & demand signals
Sustainability & ESG in retail	Generic sustainability officers (reporting)	Circular retail, packaging rules, carbon focus	Circular retail & ESG programme lead	• Builds recycling, refill, take-back programmes, ethical sourcing & ESG reporting • Partnership & compliance skills required

Functional Area	Roles Likely to Disappear / Evolve	Drivers of Change	New / Emerging Roles	Description / Key Skills Needed
	Waste & shrinkage controller	Computer vision & IoT loss prevention	Retail loss prevention data analyst	• Uses connection validation/ IoT to detect shrinkage, fraud & stock loss patterns • Analytics, risk & compliance skills needed
Technology, data & product	Store-level IT support (basic troubleshooting)	Retail tech stack, POS + app + order management system + CRM integration	Retail tech & systems integrator	• Integrates, POS, CRM, order management system and warehouse management system apps • Cybersecurity, API, vendor & data governance skills
	Manual data entry/store reporting roles	Automation, AI copilots, digital workflows	Retail data product analyst	• Designs AI workflows for store ops, builds dashboards & derives data-led intervention • SQL, business intelligence & domain knowledge needed
HR, talent & workforce development	Paper-based HR generalists	Gig workforce, skill-based staffing, digital HR	Retail workforce architect	• Designs skill-based role pathways, gig-mix staffing, AI skill development & talent mobility across omni-retail

	Classroom-led trainers	Microlearning, AR/VR skill training	Immersive retail learning and development designer	• Creates AR/VR training for store scenarios, product knowledge & digital selling • Experience design & learning science
In-store services & value-added retail	Standard beauty advisers; stylist roles	Experiential retail, personalised advisory, consultations	Tech-enabled experience specialist (beauty/wellness/fashion)	• Uses AI skin/fit diagnosis tools, virtual try-ons & personalised consultations • Consultative selling and digital fluency
Security, risk & compliance	Physical security guards	Computer vision, digital fraud, cyber-risk	Cyber-physical retail security analyst	• Integrates CCTV analytics, POS fraud, cybersecurity & store safety to reduce risk

Source: Curated with inputs from ChatGPT

Table 5.4 Understanding the New Roles in the Retail Industry

Net-New Role	Why This Role Is Emerging (Key Drivers)	Where It Will Exist (Retail Formats)	Key Skills Needed
Phygital experience designer	Blending physical and digital retail for immersive shopping experiences	Fashion, beauty, electronics, flagship stores	• AR/VR • UX • Journey design • Visual storytelling
Self-checkout & autonomous store experience manager	Rise of cashier-less stores & frictionless checkout	Supermarkets, convenience, airports	• Device ops • Customer experience • Issue-resolution • Analytics
AI-powered retail personal stylist / adviser	AI-generated fashion/beauty recommendations and digital persona styling	Fashion, beauty, luxury	• AI styling tools • Body/skin analysis • Personalised curation
Metaverse & virtual store manager	Virtual storefronts for brand engagement and commerce	Fashion, luxury, electronics	• Virtual worlds • Avatar retailing • Community management
Retail media network strategist	Retailers becoming ad platforms monetising first-party data	Supermarkets, e-commerce, big box retail	• Adtech • Data monetisation • Media planning
Conversational commerce curator	Commerce shifting to WhatsApp, voice and chat commerce	All formats, especially India & South East Asia	• Conversational AI • Sales scripts • CRM • Bot tuning

Retail subscription & membership architect	Shift to recurring revenue & subscription models	Grocery, beauty, pet care, fashion	• Subscription design • Loyalty economics • Retention
Community commerce manager	Creator-led and community-based retail influence	Direct-to-consumer, lifestyle, beauty, food brands	• Influencer management • Social commerce • Community building
Ethical sourcing & traceability analyst	Transparency on product origin, sustainability, labour ethics	Fashion, grocery, electronics	• Supply chain traceability • ESG audits • Labour condition applications basics
Returns experience & reverse commerce designer	Growth of returns, need for sustainability & resale loops	Fashion, footwear, electronics	• Reverse logistics • Customer experience • Recommerce • Repair ops
Digital shelf intelligence analyst	Computer vision & AI to track competitor stock keeping units, pricing, and share of shelf online	Fast moving consumer goods (FMCG), consumer goods, e-commerce	• Computer vision tools • Pricing intel • Competitive analytics
Retail content & livestream shopping producer	Rise of live-video shopping & entertainment commerce	Beauty, fashion, electronics	• Live content production • Scripting • Host management
Retail e-sports & gaming partnerships lead	Retail–gaming collabs for Gen-Z engagement	Electronics, fashion, QSR, convenience	• Brand collabs • Gaming ecosystem • Activation design
Last-metre delivery experience designer	Experience differentiation between door & doorstep moment	E-commerce, QSR, grocery	• Customer experience design • Logistics • Packaging • Hyperlocal insights

Net-New Role	Why This Role Is Emerging (Key Drivers)	Where It Will Exist (Retail Formats)	Key Skills Needed
In-store robotics & automation supervisor	Robots for shelf scanning, cleaning, customer assist	Supermarkets, hypermarkets, warehouse stores	• Robot ops • Tech troubleshooting • Safety
Retail data privacy & consent steward	Consumer data privacy, AI ethics & consent management	Chains, omni-retail, e-commerce	• DPDP/GDPR • Consent user experience • Data ethics
Sustainability-led store architect & zero-waste designer	Sustainable store design & refill/reuse formats	Grocery, beauty, lifestyle	• Green design • Circular retail • Materials knowledge
AI shopping companion designer	Designing AI-based shopper companions for app & in-store	Fashion, electronics, grocery apps	• AI prompt flows • Persona algorithms • UX writing
Recommerce & rental marketplace manager	Second-life retail and 'product as a service' models	Fashion, electronics, furniture	• Refurbishment • Pricing • Marketplace ops
Neighbourhood micro-fulfilment hub manager	15-minute & hyperlocal delivery hubs	Grocery, QSR, convenience	• Ops management • Last-mile analytics • Workforce gig management

Source: Curated with inputs from ChatGPT

Banking, Insurance & Financial Services Industry (BFSI)

The financial services industry has been one of the earliest adopters of advances in AI and has been willing to experiment and take initiatives that have resulted in path-breaking changes in the industry. A study of the financial services industry indicates that the successes of the businesses in the industry have been intricately woven around finding pathways despite regulations and economic downturns, changes in customer profiles and requirements and technology advancements. Hence, there is the need for disruptions and adaptation.

Evolution of the Financial Services Industry

In earlier times, the barter system was a fairly common mode of transaction that various civilisations followed. It involved exchange of goods and services as part of early economic exchanges.[37] This is evidenced in civilisations such as Mesopotamia, ancient Rome, Greece, China, pre-colonial Sub-Saharan Africa and pre-Columbian nations. In India, too, cowrie shells, grain, cattle and salt were used as part of the barter system during the Indus Valley civilisation (3300–1300 BCE). Ancient Indian traders and merchants conducted money-lending and goldsmith businesses.[38]

Although public banking was invented in the 12th century by Venetian merchants, it was during the Renaissance period that the initial formats of the banks in the form of loans and deposits started to get formalised.[39] Around 1500, the Americas, Africa and Asia were colonised, and global trade increased substantially. This necessitated the creation of formal financial intermediaries with money lending becoming a common practice. Hawala methods, originating in South Asia, started to become popular.[40] Industrialisation in Europe led to the setting up of large factories and production facilities to export goods across the globe. This resulted in the setting up of central banks and companies offering life insurance and property insurance to manage risks. The New York Stock Exchange was founded in 1792,[41] which, in turn, nurtured the development of securities trading, and investment banking as a specialised offering started taking root.

The United States of America and Europe witnessed rapid industrialisation with private and national banking systems gaining momentum after the 1900s and during the Second World War. This period also witnessed the Great Depression, which led to the stock market crash and several measures to streamline financial operations in various countries. In the United States, the Securities and Exchange Commission was created in 1934 to safeguard the interests of investors and regulate the stock market.[42]

In India, while money-lending practices continued, the British set up the banking system in Calcutta, Madras and Bombay to primarily support trade and raise investment for national projects like the railways. These banks were eventually merged into the Imperial Bank of India, which later became the State Bank of India.[43]

The post–Second World War phase provided opportunities for nations to rebuild and grow rapidly. Several erstwhile colonies like India and Indonesia became independent, and this also created avenues through their growth and impetus for the financial services industry to expand. Global financial institutions such as the International Monetary Fund and the World Bank were set up, and they could play a significant role in the development of countries and, specifically, in the financial sector. Credit cards were introduced, which changed the manner in which consumers started to spend. Mutual funds were introduced, allowing diversification of portfolios for investors. As the number of transactions of financial services institutions grew, computers were introduced to process data and reports.

With the advent of microprocessors and desktop computing in the 1980s, technology started to play a key role in the transformation of businesses. Online banking was introduced in the 1990s, which would eventually act as a game changer for the financial services industry and its customers.[44] Along with this, deregulation efforts, particularly in the United States, helped businesses to introduce several innovative financial products in the market.

The financial crisis of 2008 led to regulatory changes and more stringent risk management practices. With digital technology and telecommunications leapfrogging, enabling the industry and customers to have dramatically different experiences, the financial services industry has been at the forefront for adopting mobile technology, blockchain, cryptocurrencies, cloud computing, AI and much more. As a result, the industry has been witnessing breakthrough innovations in the offerings, not just in the United States but around the world as well, based on the local needs through an integrated service line—fintech. Several path-breaking propositions have emerged through fintech start-ups across the world, disrupting the existing processes and established players in the market.

The slow response or lack of adequate investment in digital efforts has negatively impacted the financial services business. The rate of change and the dynamics of change are stupendous in this sector, and only nimble-footed and technology-savvy entities can survive and succeed. A digital-first strategy is being implemented by several companies now. There is a need for constant review of the digital approach, regulatory changes and compliance requirements on the basis of new tools and technologies available. Wirecard was an upcoming European fintech company that had attracted large investments. Despite its lead with the digital payment solutions, its missteps in reporting and accounting scandals led to the downfall of the business, which ultimately resulted in bankruptcy.[45] Paytm is another example from the Indian fintech business. It was a darling of the Indian financial services market and had attracted investments from Alibaba and Softbank. However, its inability to comply with regulatory requirements and financial lapses led to sharp drops in its market value, and after regaining the confidence of the regulatory bodies, investors and customers, it is only in August 2025 that the payment aggregator licence has been approved.[46] In the meantime, Softbank, which had invested around US$1.5 billion in One97 Communications, the owner of Paytm, exited at a loss of around US$150 million in 2024.[47]

Future of AI in the BFSI Industry

In the early days, the financial services industry comprised primarily banks whose focus was to receive deposits and lend money to customers. It has come a long way in terms of sophisticated product offerings and the technology-centric approach to growth and innovation. It is expected that this trend will continue, with advancements in AI having the potential to continually disrupt the financial industry. Inclusive finance and expansion of global trade will receive further momentum due to technological investments in the financial services industry. Recognising this, several organisations have started making investments in AI and other related areas to remain competitive in the marketplace. Traditional banks are threatened with the entry of fintech start-ups, which are innovating, removing the intermediaries from the system and deploying AI-powered smart systems that are overcoming the age-old practices and assumptions for servicing customers.

Organisations have already deployed AI-powered tools for enhancing process efficiency through RPA and improved customer service through virtual assistants and chatbots. For instance, American Express has deployed AI-powered virtual assistant Amex Bot, which handles over 5 million customer enquiries each month and has reduced call centre operational costs by 15 per cent.[48] State Bank of India's chatbot system handles as much as 25 per cent of the queries that Google processes each day.[49] According to ICICI Bank, the use of its chatbot 'iPal', launched in February 2017, has led to quicker responses with 90 per cent accuracy and reduced operational costs.[50] Initially, several private banks had taken the lead in the deployment of chatbots for servicing customer queries.[51] Lately, chatbots are being widely deployed in public-sector banks as well, and, in the coming years, they are likely to replace humans in many roles that involve handling customer interactions.

Algorithms are already fuelling trading, and the pace and the complex insights they bring to trading are simply unmatched by humans. In due course, these models will get even more sophisticated as they would also be able to bring into trading market intelligence and predictive analytics based on such information, which would help AI tools execute transactions with minimal human oversight. Goldman Sachs has created an AI-led trading platform to support trading with algorithms and improve investment strategies, which has resulted in $100 million savings annually according to their reports.[52]

Personalisation and hyper-personalisation would be the benchmark capability of every financial institution. With the ability that AI has to analyse vast amounts of data, it should be possible to offer customised products in banking, insurance and other allied services. Based on social media status, spends and ratings, it would be possible to assess the creditworthiness of individuals. This could form the basis for lending, which could be used in the short term as an additional parameter for determining creditworthiness and, in the long term, possibly even replace the credit scoring models. HDFC Bank has explicitly positioned Data, AI and machine learning at the centre of banking's evolution towards Banking 3.0, framing it as the core of the bank's future.[53] The Bajaj Finserv app's AI-powered service chat has cut service requests by 70 per cent.[54] Lendingkart, the Indian fintech company providing working capital loans to small and medium-sized companies through its online platform, has been using AI-powered credit risk assessment such as financial documents, transaction history and social data, thus reducing its reliance on traditional scoring methods. As a result, as per company reports, there has been a 95 per cent automation rate in loan processing, leading to expediting loan disbursements and 40 per cent reduction in loan defaults.[55]

Ant Group, an affiliate of the Chinese company Alibaba, has built an alternative to the traditional credit scoring model. It uses Zhima Credit (known as Sesame Credit) to assess the creditworthiness of over 500 million users with the help of data related to mobile phone usage, social behaviour and transaction history. Its AI-powered micro-lending platform is able to process 98 per cent of loan applications with no human intervention within three minutes.[56] These examples indicate the possibilities for hyper-personalisation with speed and precision resulting in customer delight.

Intelligent robot advisers would be able to analyse clients' financial scenarios, preferences and market trends to offer real-time advice to customers. Instead of depending upon analysts to recommend investment strategies, robot advisers would be able to offer such advice, saving the conversion or response time and the costs involved in hiring the services of expensive human resources. Groww, the Indian fintech firm providing investment options of stocks, exchange-traded funds and mutual funds to its customers through its online platform, has been using an AI-led robo-advisory system to offer personalised investment options based on the risk profiles and financial goals of each customer. Groww has attracted 25 million users in 2023,[57] and annualised returns for its customers have improved by 8–10 per cent as compared to non AI-managed portfolios.

Similar to wealth management, investment management would also get a shot in the arm with AI tools as more dynamic information related to market status, investor goals and risk tolerances as well as sentiment analysis based on market trends and social media are factored into the algorithms. UBS has reported that there has been a 20 per cent increase in client engagement as an AI-led predictive system is enabling it to provide custom wealth management services to its clients based on their individual goals, risk appetite and market trends.[58]

Use of AI will get deeply entrenched in cybersecurity, fraud prevention and risk management. AI tools would be able to alert about potential breaches or frauds or discrepancies arising out of regulatory compliances on a real-time basis and help with correction of lapses or actions thereof. This would help organisations to avoid paying huge penalties on account of lack of adherences. American Express has deployed AI models on its platform that processes around 6 billion transactions per annum. These models analyse patterns and carry out predictive analytics that throws up potential frauds, which have helped reduce 50 per cent fraudulent transactions as per their reports.[59] Mastercard, too, has developed its AI-led fraud detection system, which has helped reduce fraud incidents to the tune of 50 per cent for merchants using its technology.[60] JPMorgan Chase has developed an AI-led risk management platform called COiN (Contract Intelligence) that helps to efficiently review complex legal documents, contracts and trade documents. What would have taken 360,000 hours of manual work to review 12,000 documents previously is now done in a few seconds.[61]

Although Metaverse has entered the mainstream, it is expected to pick up momentum in the coming years.[62] Visa has filed patents for metaverse-related technologies. Mastercard has introduced virtual payment cards for metaverse transactions. JPMorgan Chase has launched Onyx, a blockchain-based Metaverse platform. There are still challenges around the regulatory frameworks and security apart from the critical volume required for scaling for AI-powered systems to take advantage of Metaverse.

Sustainability and environment consciousness would be the driving forces with the customers, and customers would be keen on such product offerings that are centred on them. AI tools would analyse ESG data to evaluate investment opportunities.

The trinity of Jan Dhan, Aadhar and UPI—the innovative initiatives of the Indian government—has transformed the lives of those who had recourse only to expensive local moneylenders until recently. Now they are able to access the banking system and a streamlined credit system in India. As of August 2024, 45 crore beneficiaries have been covered under the Pradhan Mantri

Jan Dhan Yojana,[63] and as of October 2024, 50 crore UPI users are registered.[64] UPI has enabled financial inclusion with 60 per cent of UPI users belonging to rural areas and 45 per cent to semi-urban areas.[65] These initiatives have been path-breaking, and with the data and the access provided, it is possible to create further inclusive programmes with the help of AI models customising for various segments. There are several examples of fintech start-ups from India that are making inclusive finance a reality with their AI-powered systems. Mobikwik has over 40 per cent customers in rural India out of its base of 100 million customers, offering them affordable micro-insurance, micro-credit and digital savings products. Using AI-powered systems, Mobikwik is able to assess creditworthiness of customers in real time, leveraging alternative data such as utility bills, mobile phone payments and e-commerce transactions.[66] Another fintech company, Rupifi, has been servicing over 100,000 micro-, small and medium enterprises (MSMEs) all over India through its AI-powered system with 35 per cent of them not having prior credit history.[67]

Future AI Applications in the Financial Services Sector

It is estimated that the financial services industry would double its spending on AI by 2027 with the sales of AI systems expected to increase 29 per cent annually.[68] The future of AI in the financial services industry can totally redefine the industry in terms of the key stakeholders, their roles and their engagements. Let us examine some of these dimensions next.

AI-Driven Decentralised Finance (DeFi) Systems

The implementation of DeFi, which operates on blockchain technology, could have far-reaching implications for the financial services industry, including removal of intermediaries like banks and brokers, enabling direct peer-to-peer financial transactions. As a result, AI algorithms could facilitate real-time automated portfolio management, smart contracts, and automatic detection of potential frauds and manipulation.[69]

AI for Predictive Financial Health Monitoring

Financial institutions would be able to offer proactive solutions for customers who are likely to face financial difficulties by alerting them in advance. AI-driven systems would be able to report risk trends by monitoring the customer's financial status, behaviour and mental status continually and propose suitable options to invest/divest.[70]

AI-Supported Integrated Financial Views

AI could help create an integrated view of financial scenarios across different industries or ecosystems, thus making the finance management process seamless for customers. This could lead to design of financial products cutting across different sectors, integration of data from multiple sources, namely, retail, health, credit scores and so on and connection of all investments across insurance, banks, stocks and so on to get an integrated view.[71]

AI-Powered Quantum Computing in Finance

Quantum computing is yet to unleash its full potential and is expected to emerge as an important force multiplier on AI soon. This would lead to higher levels of precision and accuracy in risk modelling, portfolio optimisation and market trends due to which decision-making with respect to investments, trading and interest rates would become far superior.[72]

AI-Driven Financial Sovereignty and Digital Identity

Consumers would be able to control their digital identities and financial sovereignty with the help of AI in future. Blockchain would enable individuals to protect their personal data, and financial institutions could use AI to authenticate and verify the identities. The scope of digital wallets would expand and go beyond payments and offer verification and asset tracking in a secure and decentralised manner.

The Emerging Talent Requirements for the AI Era

With continuous innovation and advancements in AI and related technologies, their applications in the financial services industry provide a vast scope for further innovation in products, customer servicing and operations. End-to-end automation of processes and personalisation with better understanding of customer behaviour and emotions would be feasible. Regulation and compliances will also undergo significant changes, and ethical functioning of businesses would be a challenge that AI has to address. In this context, there would be a radical change in the talent required for the industry. Some of the existing roles will become redundant and some of them will exist, but new or additional skill sets would be required. Additionally, new talent with these skill sets would also be required. An estimated 2.5 lakh permanent jobs would be created by 2030, driven by growth in Tier II/III cities in the Indian BFSI sector as per *Adecco India Report* 2025.[73] Let us examine the changes in the talent landscape of the financial services industry in Tables 5.5 and 5.6.

Table 5.5 Evolving Roles in the BFSI Industry

Functional Area	Roles Likely to Disappear / Evolve	Drivers of Change	New / Emerging Roles	Description / Key Skills Needed
Retail & branch banking	Branch tellers; manual cashiers	UPI/QR, digital onboarding, branch-lite models	Digital relationship banker (AI-augmented)	• Manages customer portfolios via video banking & AI copilots • Skills in digital Know Your Customer (KYC), conversational banking & cross-sell through analytics
	Traditional customer service executives	Chatbots, WhatsApp banking, virtual assistants	Omnichannel customer experience manager	• Orchestrates service across chat, voice, app & branch • Skilled in journey mapping, Net Promoter Score and escalation via AI insights
Lending & credit	Manual loan officers; field verifiers	AI underwriting, eKYC/video KYC, account aggregators	Digital credit & risk analyst (AI-scored)	• Uses AI-driven credit models, alternative data & account aggregator consent flows • Must know model interpretation & bias checks
	Physical collections agents	Digital collections, behavioural nudges	Digital collections & recovery strategist	• Runs AI-driven repayment nudges, segmentation, and digital collection journeys • Behavioural science + data ops
Payments & cards	Card-focused product managers	Wallets, UPI, tokenisation, central bank digital currency	Real-time payments product manager	• Designs instant payment journeys, cross-border UPI, ISO 20022 flows and value-added services on real-time payments rails

Functional Area	Roles Likely to Disappear / Evolve	Drivers of Change	New / Emerging Roles	Description / Key Skills Needed
	POS device sales staff	SoftPOS, QR, tap-on-phone	Merchant experience & acceptance lead	• Builds value for micro-, small and medium enterprise merchants with SaaS + payment bundles • Requires go-to-market, merchant analytics & fintech UX skills
Wealth management & investments	Traditional relationship managers for high-net-worth (relationship-only)	Robo-advisory, fractional investing, AI portfolios	Hybrid wealth adviser (human+AI)	• Combines personalised advisory with AI portfolio modelling • Skills in behavioural finance, systematic investment plan/systematic transfer plan strategy and digital advisory tools
	Paper-based research analysts	GenAI research, real-time market intelligence	AI-enabled investment research curator	• Aggregates & validates AI-generated research • Ensures compliance, explainability & risk disclosures
Insurance (life, health, general)	Field agents reliant on manual onboarding	Digital issuance, embedded/affinity insurance, API-led	Embedded insurance partnerships manager	• Builds insurance APIs into e-commerce, travel, mobility & fintech platforms • Partnership & product bundling skills needed
	Manual claims processors	AI image/video claims, telematics, IoT	Claims automation & fraud intelligence lead	• Uses AI/machine learning for claims triage, anomaly detection & fraud rings • Domain, data science and forensics skills
Risk, compliance & fraud	Document-heavy compliance officers	Regulatory tech-nology (RegTech), continuous compliance, AI monitoring	RegTech & compliance automation specialist	• Deploys tools for automated KYC/anti-money laundering • Conducts model risk testing • Ensures regulatory reporting accuracy

	Manual anti–money laundering analysts	AI + network graph-based anti–money laundering	Financial crime & threat intelligence analyst	• Uses network analytics, open-source intelligence & typology modelling to detect complex laundering & cyber financial crime
Technology, data & cybersecurity	Traditional IT support roles	Cloud-native BFSI, AI copilots, automation	AI banking product engineer	• Builds AI-powered workflows, copilots for staff & customers • Needs LLM usage, prompt engineering & domain knowledge
	Data entry/ reporting staff	Automated reporting, Reserve Bank of India/ Securities & Exchange Board of India/Extensible Business Reporting Language API filings	Banking data product owner	• Owns data models, lineage, access & quality • Bridges tech, compliance & business using data mesh principles
	Traditional cybersecurity analysts	Identity-first, zero-trust, API fraud	Cyber-fraud & identity security architect	• Designs zero-trust, identity-proofing, API and device-risk analytics • Deep security and fraud prevention skills
Corporate & institutional banking	Relationship manager roles focused on relationship-only	Platform banking, API-ecosystem models	Corporate banking solutions adviser	• Helps corporate clients digitise finance ops with API cash management, supply chain finance & treasury automation tools
	Manual trade finance officers	Blockchain, electronic bill of lading, trade digitalisation	Digital trade & supply chain finance specialist	• Manages e-documentation, tokenised assets, cross-border trade rails • Knowledge in International Chamber of Commerce rules & digital trade platforms

Functional Area	Roles Likely to Disappear / Evolve	Drivers of Change	New / Emerging Roles	Description / Key Skills Needed
Product, strategy & innovation	Product managers with slow-release cycles	Open banking, A/B experimentation, fintech competition	Bank-fintech ecosystem strategist	• Designs co-create models with fintechs • Manages APIs, revenue-share constructs • Strong partnership & regulatory navigation
	Traditional analysts (deck/report-led)	Scenario AI & data-led strategy	AI-enabled business strategy analyst	• Uses data, simulation & GenAI to model scenarios • Ensures governance & strategic prioritisation clarity
HR, learning & workforce	HR generalists (policy/admin)	Skills-based orgs, talent analytics	BFSI workforce & skills architect	• Designs future skill maps, capability academies, AI upskilling & role transition journeys across BFSI
	Classroom-only trainers	AI learning, microlearning, simulations	Immersive BFSI learning and development experience designer	• Builds compliance + sales training using simulations, AR/VR & adaptive learning • Learning science + design tech
Operations & shared services	Large operations back-offices (manual processing)	Automation, AI copilots, workflow orchestration	Banking automation & copilot orchestrator	• Designs human+AI work allocation systems • Reduces manual load • Improves turnaround & compliance
	On-shore only ops teams	'Follow the Sun' and nearshore and gig experts	Distributed operations network manager	• Manages multi-site ops with productivity, quality & risk • Cross-cultural operations leadership skills required

Source: Curated with inputs from ChatGPT

Table 5.6 Understanding the New Roles in the BFSI Industry

New Role	Why This Role Is Emerging (Key Drivers)	Primary BFSI Segments	Key Skills Needed
AI model risk & ethics officer (financial services)	AI in credit, underwriting, surveillance requires fairness, explainability & ethical guard rails	Banks, non-banking financial companies (NBFCs), insurers, fintech	• AI governance, model risk • Reserve Bank of India/ISO ethics guidelines
Digital public infrastructure product architect	India Stack, Open Network for Digital Commerce, Open Credit Enablement Network, UPI account aggregator ecosystem	Banks, fintech, neo-banks	• Digital public infrastructure protocols • API design • Ecosystem partnerships
Embedded finance partnership designer	BFSI products embedded into e-commerce, mobility, health, agri & small and medium enterprise workflow	Banks, insurers, NBFCs	• Platform strategy • API economy • Co-creation models
Financial generative pre-trained transformer/ SLM trainer for financial services	Need for domain-trained SLMs for BFSI	Banks, fintech AI labs, RegTech	• Data annotation • Prompt engineering • BFSI domain
Tokenised assets & digital securities specialist	Rise of tokenised bonds, funds, real-world assets, central bank digital currencies (CBDCs)	Investment banks, asset management, exchanges	• Blockchain, tokenisation • Custody, compliance

New Role	Why This Role Is Emerging (Key Drivers)	Primary BFSI Segments	Key Skills Needed
CBDC product & ecosystem manager	Rollout of digital rupee & CBDCs for cross-border corridors	Banks, fintech, central bank programmes	• CBDC rails • Wallet UX • Offline payments • Security
Financial behavioural science strategist	Behavioural nudging in collections, saving, investing, fraud prevention	Banks, insurers, wealth, NBFCs	• Behavioural economics • Data experiments • Nudging
AI-powered hyper-personalisation designer	1:1 personalised finance experiences at scale	Retail banking, wealth, insurance	• Data science • Personalisation engines • Customer psychology
Green finance & ESG lending analyst	Climate-linked loans, ESG scoring of borrowers & investments	Banks, development finance, funds	• ESG frameworks • Climate finance • Impact metrics
Financial wellness & money coaching adviser	Rising middle-class stress, need for financial well-being	Banks, neo-banks, HR partnership programmes	• Human coaching and digital tools • Behavioural finance
Cyber-fraud threat intelligence analyst	Sophisticated fraud rings, deepfake scams, mule networks	Banks, cards, payments, fintech	• Open-source intelligence • Network analytics • Crypto-fraud detection
Risk tech & RegTech solution integrator	Automated compliance and regulatory reporting tech adoption	Banks, insurers, NBFCs	• RegTech tools • Automated KYC/anti-money laundering • API/regulatory mapping
Credit-in-the-cloud product owner	Credit products built as micro-services and cloud workflows	Banks, fintech, lending platforms	• Cloud credit stacks • Account aggregator data • Bureau and alt-data modelling

Super-app financial services curator	Cross-selling BFSI inside lifestyle super-apps	Fintech, payments, Telcos	• Product bundling • Ecosystem business development • Urban+vernacular strategy
Digital trust & consent steward (BFSI)	DPDP Act, data portability & consent-based finance	Banks, insurers, wealth management firms	• Consent UX • Privacy engineering • Data policy
Gig-economy & creator wealth solutions designer	New income models needing new credit, insurance & tax solutions	Banking, insurtech, wealthtech	• Product innovation • Segment insights • Creator economy
Climate & catastrophe risk data scientist	Climate risk as a core banking and insurance risk driver	Insurance, reinsurance, banks	• Climate models, • Geospatial, actuarial and machine learning
Insurance parametric product specialist	Parametric products triggered by events (rainfall, flight delay, crop)	General insurance, insurtechs	• Parametric design • Satellite/IoT data • Actuarial innovation
Small and medium enterprise embedded credit stack developer	Lending inside small and medium enterprise, enterprise resource planning systems, POS, agri, supply chain workflows	Banks, NBFCs, agri/ microfinance institution/ lending tech	• API lending • Cashflow underwriting • Workflow UX
Wealth-as-a-service (WaaS) platform manager	White-label wealth infra for non-banks & brand platforms	Wealthtech, asset management companies, fintech infra providers	• Partner management • Modular productisation • Compliance mapping
Crypto/DeFi risk & compliance analyst*	Web3 and crypto-linked transactions (where permitted)	Crypto exchanges, banks (per regulation)	• DeFi • On/off-ramp risk • Travel rule compliance

* Adoption of crypto roles depends on country-specific regulatory stance in Asia.

Source: Curated with inputs from ChatGPT

Leadership Imperatives for the Service Industry in the AI Era

Given the impact of change that is beginning to happen in the services industry due to internal or external forces as a result of continuously evolving technology trends, leadership would have to adapt and steer the businesses in very different ways as compared to the earlier times as can be seen from Table 5.7. While the core of leadership would have to continue to be centred on people, inspiring them to attain higher levels of performance to keep pushing the boundaries of growth and profitability, it has become critical for leaders to have an in-depth understanding of technology and AI trends. In this ability lies the current and the future potential of the business. Success is no longer measured by how many customers are served but by how smartly customers are served in real time with personalisation.

The success metrics in the traditional bank would have been branch expansion to improve customer service, whereas in the AI-led banking system, customer touch points and servicing would be through deployment of intelligent chatbots. The founder of Walmart, Sam Walton, focused on cost control through economies of scale.[74] Presently, the focus of Doug McMillion and Satish Meena, the CEO and AI strategy head of Walmart, respectively, is around the 'Intelligent Retail Lab' aimed at data-driven store optimisation.[75] Isadore Sharp, the founder of Seasons Hotels, centred his business on treating guests and employees alike with dignity and respect,[76] whereas now Seasons Hotels has adopted virtual concierge bots and machine learning models to predict guest preferences for providing customised experiences.[77] In summary, traditional leaders in the service industry built human-driven cultures with process orientation, whereas in the AI-led era, successful leaders are combining data insights with the human touch to foster algorithm-driven empathy.

Table: 5.7 Service Industry Leadership in the Traditional vs AI-Led Era

Dimension	Traditional Service Industry Leadership	AI-Era Service Industry Leadership
Decision making	Hierarchical and experience-driven; relies on intuition and past performance	• Data-driven, agile and model-assisted • Uses AI analytics for predictive insights and adaptive decision-making
Leadership style	Transactional or transformational; focused on people management and customer service quality	• Techno-empathetic and ecosystem-oriented • Blends emotional intelligence with algorithmic intelligence
Organisational structure	Vertical hierarchies with clearly defined roles and standard operating procedures	• Networked and decentralised • Relies on cross-functional, AI-augmented teams and autonomous decision nodes
CRM	Manual and relationship-based; personalised service delivered by staff	• Hyper-personalised and algorithmic • AI agents predict and fulfil customer needs proactively
Performance metrics	Efficiency, customer satisfaction and compliance	• Innovation velocity, data accuracy, ethical AI use and customer lifetime value driven by personalisation
Innovation approach	Incremental and process-based improvements (lean, Six Sigma)	• Continuous and generative • AI enables rapid prototyping, automation and new service models
Talent & skills focus	Soft skills, domain expertise and operational know-how	• Digital fluency, AI literacy, prompt engineering and human–machine collaboration capabilities

Dimension	Traditional Service Industry Leadership	AI-Era Service Industry Leadership
Leadership development	Mentorship, experiential learning and hierarchical promotions	• Continuous reskilling via digital platforms • Flatter growth paths with AI-enabled performance analytics
Culture & values	Stability, trust and service consistency	• Agility, experimentation, ethical governance and transparency in AI usage
Risk management	Focus on operational and financial risks	• Focus on algorithmic bias, data privacy, cybersecurity and reputational risks linked to AI outputs
Employee engagement	Employee motivation through interpersonal leadership	• Human–AI co-working engagement • Leaders motivate teams to trust AI while retaining creative autonomy
Customer experience leadership	Frontline managers lead through hospitality and empathy	• AI experience designers and 'customer experience scientists' lead through predictive personalisation and digital empathy
Success definition	Stable growth, loyal customers and consistent brand image	• Scalable innovation, adaptive resilience and sustainable differentiation through AI insights

Source: Curated with inputs form ChatGPT

6

AI Transforming Manufacturing and Life Sciences

Manufacturing Industry

Manufacturing as we understand it today—of products for diverse segments such as industry, consumer, health and materials for construction, to name a few—has evolved substantially over several generations. Thanks to automation, not only has manufacturing scaled meteorically over time, scaling of production and global access have been feasible on account of innovation, demand and science and technological advancements aligning with one another. Beginning with design of products to their production, their supply chain to distribution and logistics, all of these functions have been disrupted several times with the advancements in science and technology. While automation has made the manufacturing industry more productive and efficient, the advent of AI has been yet another important milestone in the evolution of the manufacturing sector to achieve benefits from hitherto unexplored contours. In this chapter, we shall examine some of the key milestones in the evolution of the manufacturing sector leading up to the AI era and how leaders have had the vision and foresight to drive innovation causing these disruptions or have built successful businesses arising out of the opportunities they seized upon from time to time.

Prior to the industrialisation phase right until the late 18th century, goods were produced in homes in what was known as a cottage industry. Manufacturing was predominantly labour-intensive and decentralised but catered to the needs of immediate localities where the cottage industry existed. Most of the products were handcrafted and dependent upon locally available natural raw materials such as agricultural produce. The skills of the artisans played an important role, and some of them used some basic tools to produce the items, which were usually in small quantities. At times, they were custom-made and sold. Mostly, the artisans or artisans, guild passed on their hereditary knowledge to others in the family, and at times, different processes or manufacturing of parts of the product were distributed across different members of the family. Mostly, the quantities produced were in small batches due to the high labour component, and hence it was not a scalable proposition. Therefore, the products were expensive and accessible only to a few. As the products were expensive and it involved a long wait time for them to be readied, products once bought were preserved for long periods of time.[1]

First Industrial Revolution (1760–1840)

The invention of the steam engine dramatically changed the manufacturing process as it transitioned from dependence on water mills and manual labour. Steam power made it feasible to envisage centralised large-scale production with the advantages of lesser time and lower costs. Goods could be made available across multiple locations, and thus, mechanisation, initially through looms and later on through other manufacturing processes, brought about quantum jumps in efficiency.

Second Industrial Revolution (1870–1914)

The feasibility of the mechanical production of electric power provided an impetus to the Second Industrial Revolution. Production of electric power on a large scale for distribution was first conceived in the late 19th century. The first central power station was established in New York. The contributions of Thomas Alva Edison and Nikola Tesla made it possible to power machines reliably with electricity. This breakthrough enabled manufacturers to reduce dependence on water or steam, making it feasible to plan for mass production and, hence, higher volumes of output with higher levels of efficiency and lower costs. The automobile industry picked up momentum through the pioneering efforts of Henry Ford, who introduced assembly lines for manufacturing with workers acquiring specialised skills in different tasks. This was the turning point for lowering the cost of production and laying the foundation for consumer goods industries.[2]

The Second Industrial Revolution was also witness to advancements in telecommunications thanks to the contributions of Alexander Graham Bell and Guglielmo Marconi through telegraphy, telephone and wireless telegraphy, which enabled enhanced international communication and, hence, boosted productivity and personal relationships.[3] These breakthroughs laid the foundation for the later-day developments related to internet, mobile networks, satellite communication and fibre optics.

Third Industrial Revolution

During the period between 1969 and 2010, automation enabled by computers and digital technologies started playing a major role, leading to higher levels of accuracy and control over manufacturing processes. With the advent of microprocessors, there was a phenomenal change in the computing world. Desktop computers and personal computing for a wide range of users became feasible as a result. Human errors could be reduced, and increased productivity became feasible because of automation.[4] The World Wide Web was invented in 1991,[5] and mobile phones and GPS became widely accessible. This phase also saw the beginnings of e-commerce, AI and IoT. With the help of computer-aided design and computer-aided manufacturing, it became easier for the industry to create a variety of designs and production facilities.

Fourth Industrial Revolution

The period 2010 to the present day (2025) is popularly known as Industry 4.0. In this phase, we are experiencing smart factories integrating digital and physical systems, with machines, products and systems communicating with one another for optimised production. The maturity of technologies such as AI, IoT, 3D printers, blockchain, robotics, AR and VR have had a profound impact on the automation and productivity of manufacturing processes. Being able to carry out predictive analytics to prevent malfunctioning or production stoppage (the sensors providing real-time data on machine and product performance to take actions expeditiously), rapid prototyping with the help of 3D printing, fostering security and controls through blockchain technology, augmenting the workforce through robotics and visualisation of customer experiences through AR and VR technologies have catapulted manufacturing capabilities to higher levels of efficiencies and innovation. The speed and the quantum of benefits to the industry from these technologies have been ably facilitated by 5G networks and cloud computing capabilities developed by the telecommunications and digital industry in parallel.[6]

Emerging Fifth Industrial Revolution

The Fifth Industrial Revolution, which commenced in the 2020s, is presently concurrent with the Fourth Industrial Revolution. This phase is slated to bring about transformation through what is being touted as sustainable and human-centric manufacturing. The focus is on conserving depleting resources (namely, raw materials, energy and water) and promoting circular economy principles to reduce waste. Cobots (human and robots working together) are likely to be prevalent in the workplace. Quantum computing, autonomous systems, XR and Internet of Bodies are expected to leapfrog and become drivers of the manufacturing processes. It is anticipated that with these developments, there would be enhanced quality of life, higher levels of conscious action towards environmental sustainability and empowered decision-making at multiple levels.[7]

The DNA for Change

The ability of organisations to withstand the jolt from constantly evolving technological changes, foresee these trends, embrace the appropriate technologies that suit the industry and reskill/encourage the existing teams to adapt their processes and businesses would be the key to survival and excellence. Many organisations have had their share of struggles during such transitions and could not survive for long. Let us examine some examples of companies that have managed to withstand the strong currents of change and some others that have been swept aside.

Several cottage industries, guilds and home-based production centres could not adapt to the power of the steam engine and folded. Boulton & Watt (United Kingdom) were pioneers of the steam engine that powered factories and mills. They enabled several companies to shift from manual processes to mechanised production.[8] Lowell Textile Mills in Massachusetts adopted steam-powered looms and pioneered large-scale textile manufacturing processes in the United States, which enabled them to expand their business and enhance their productivity.[9] During the Second Industrial Revolution, with the spread of electricity, General Electric became a leader in the consumer electronics industry with its pioneering efforts in electrification in manufacturing and household products. However, a combination of strategic misses, professional mismanagement and inability to adopt the right technologies at the right time have been the death knell for the iconic organisation as it was in its heyday, which has since been split into three entities.[10] Only time will tell whether any of these entities will rise from the ashes like a phoenix and shine once again!

There are several other examples of companies whose technology strategy backfired or did not fire at the right time due to which they have gone out of the reckoning. Kodak and Polaroid were two companies well known for camera and films that had almost a monopoly in the market. However, they failed to foresee the digital impact, and once digital photography was born, these companies became irrelevant in the marketplace.[11]

Once a leader in telegraphy, Western Union did not effectively transition into the new age of telecommunications, losing ground to companies that embraced telephone technology. As the digital age progressed, Intel dominated the microprocessor market for several years, providing essential components for computers and digital devices. Their products fuelled the rise of personal computers and the tech industry. Intel's bold byline, 'Intel Inside', virtually meant most computers shipped were built around Intel's microprocessors. However, Intel failed in the race for a share in the AI era, allowing Nvidia to take a substantial lead over it. Nvidia overtook Intel's market value for the first time in 2020, and by 2025, Nvidia's market cap had reached an astronomical US$4 trillion, more than double the combined values of AMD, Arm, Broadcom and Intel. Today, the position of Intel has been taken over by Nvidia as one of the three large tech equity benchmarks, and there are talks about its future including possibilities of being bought by one of the large tech companies.[12]

Nokia created the world's first international cellular network and, for almost a decade until the early 2000s, was the global leader in mobile phones. However, its late entry into the smartphone market meant that iPhone and Android technology had taken a significant lead over Nokia, who then had no option but to exit from this business.[13] Blackberry Motion was another manufacturer of smartphones that was successful until the late 1990s with its device, which had an arched keyboard. When touchscreen displays became commonplace in the mobile industry, Blackberry continued to protect its products and technology, little realising that its products had outlived the industry. Finally, in 2017, Blackberry officially announced the end of its smartphone business.[14] Motorola's cell phones were considered for the hardware quality. However, with customers becoming familiar with the software features other products offered and Motorola's continued thrust on hardware with innovation in software not forthcoming, Motorola was left behind in the shift to 3G.[15]

To remain competitive in the marketplace, businesses must be cognizant of the sweeping changes in technology and gear up at the right time to back the right technologies that would define the future of the business. In the context of AI, several areas of manufacturing and allied services are getting impacted, and it would be useful to examine them to decipher how leading manufacturing companies are building strategies to enhance their operational efficiencies while delivering superior value to their customers and remaining competitive in the marketplace.

AI Technology Solutions in Manufacturing

AI has made deep inroads in several leading organisations in the manufacturing domain over the last few years. Based on the impact realised by these organisations, other organisations have been made to recognise that they need to invest in AI or they will perish. Let us examine a few examples.

BMW has implemented AI-powered computer vision systems that have resulted in reduction in false detection instances and overall enhancement of quality. An extra layer of quality assurance is enabled as an AI solution compares vehicle data with live images of designated models to identify discrepancies, and AI-driven robots weld half a million metal studs onto vehicle frames daily and ensure precision.[16]

Siemens has been using predictive analytics driven by Smart Insights (SI), a platform for IIoT that provides data-driven insights for smart manufacturing. Siemens uses this platform to monitor the health of equipment at their manufacturing facilities so that downtime reduction and lower maintenance costs could be feasible.[17] At their Amberg production facility in Germany, Siemens has managed to achieve a 50 per cent decrease in unplanned downtime[18] and 30 per cent decrease in maintenance time at its American factory in Charlotte.[19] AI-driven systems have also helped Siemens to reduce quality defects. L&T has deployed AI in predictive maintenance, leading to enhanced operational efficiency with around 10 per cent higher profitability through improved worker efficiency.[20] Maruti Suzuki has managed to increase efficiency through its AI-led efforts to optimise its production lines, particularly for vehicle assembly and parts manufacturing, improving precision and reducing waste.[21] AI-led preventive maintenance products have been developed by several other companies such as ASEA Brown Boveri, Honeywell, Parametric Technology Corporation, General Electric, Siemens and others that help them make their offerings more robust within their manufacturing facilities and also help their customers in critical manufacturing business domains to predict and prevent asset failures.

Foxconn has implemented AI-driven visual inspection methods comprising computer vision, machine learning and deep learning in several processes related to production with the help of its partnerships with Nvidia and Google. For example, the Automated Optical Inspection system is used to inspect printed circuit boards for defects, which has helped in the reduction of inspection time by 50 per cent and enhanced the accuracy by 90 per cent. Its Small Quality Inspection system has helped in reducing defect rates in smartphone displays by 30 per cent. Foxconn also uses AI-powered X-ray inspection to analyse X-ray images of electronic components, which helps in the detection of hidden defects and reduces false positives by 40 per cent.[22]

AI-driven supply chain optimisation is being implemented by several manufacturers as supply chains are the lifeline of the factories. The combination of machine learning, deep learning, NLP and IoT has enabled organisations to build optimised supply chains and carry out effective demand forecasting. General Electric has been using an AI-powered system to accurately predict and streamline logistics costs that could enable a 10 per cent reduction in logistics costs. This would represent global cost savings to the wind industry of up to US$2.6 billion per annum by 2030 based on the industry growth projections.[23] Tata Steel was recognised by the World Economic Forum in 2019 as one of forty-four Lighthouses in the adoption of Fourth Industrial Revolution technologies.[24] According to a McKinsey Report, the team at Tata working on the superheating model pulled together operational data generated from sensors or recorded manually and, after the initial pilot, managed to refine the model and identified more than twenty-five performance indicators such as temperature, speed and others.[25] The analytics model enabled the team to realise 80 per cent of the targeted improvements, resulting in US$70 to US$80 million of value and 2 to 3.5 percentage points of incremental earnings before interest, taxes, depreciation and ammortisation.[26] JSW Steel is the other company that has implemented AI-powered solutions successfully to monitor and control the steel-making process, optimising parameters like temperature and chemical composition for better product quality. The AI-powered platform manages close to 3,000 critical assets across ten plants and uses data from more than 13,500 sensors in real time. This has resulted in the company being able to reduce energy consumption by 10 per cent and prevent unplanned downtime as per the company annual reports.[27] Hindalco, too, reduced raw material costs by 10 per cent by optimising procurement strategies with AI-led systems.[28]

The production facility of Bosch at Bamberg, Germany, is working towards its goal of zero defect production with the help of AI platforms with its highly automated and connected manufacturing system that is able to make terabytes of data readable in a matter of seconds.[29] Proctor & Gamble has managed to improve its inventory management and achieve reduction of costs by implementing its AI-driven system for demand forecasting and supply chain optimisation by working on the totality of the supply chain, including working collaboratively with retailers.[30] Nike has been able to reduce inventory over-stocking due to the AI-powered sales forecasting system, which is part of its digital-first supply chain strategy.[31]

AI-powered robotics are being deployed for manufacturing processes by several organisations. Notable among them are automobile companies such as Tesla, BMW, Siemens and Daimler, who are using robots of their own or developed by specialist companies such as FANUC Robotics, KUKA Robotics, Universal Robotics and others for vehicle assembly, welding, inspection, material handling, painting and overall manufacturing optimization.[32] Mahindra & Mahindra integrates AI with robotics in its assembly lines to improve precision and speed and reduce human error, which has resulted in 15–20 per cent increase in production efficiency.[33] Bajaj Auto has deployed cobots from Universal Robots, which helped achieve zero annual maintenance costs alongside reduced power consumption.[34] Use of robots in factories has not only improved efficiency and accuracy but also enhanced the flexibility required to adapt to changing production needs.

AI algorithms are being used for product development for creating multiple design options. This generative design approach is being followed by Airbus to create lightweight aircraft brackets. New Balance and Nike are using this approach to provide customised shoe insoles and shoe options to give a personalised look, feel, fit and performance.[35] Application of this approach to design is increasingly being favoured by manufacturers in domains such as aerospace, consumer products, industrial equipment and automative products.

Digital twin is yet another interesting approach towards optimisation and prediction. For this, real-world physical assets and systems are replicated virtually as a digital twin, and simulation is carried out. By blending real-time data, AI and IoT sensors, manufacturers are able to enhance reliability, optimise production costs, reduce maintenance costs and support effective decision-making. Siemens' digital twin of a gas turbine predicts maintenance needs. GE Aviation's digital twin optimises engine performance. The National Aeronautics and Space Administration uses the digital twin of spacecrafts for mission planning. Tesla uses the digital twin of EVs for performance optimization.[36]

Energy management and sustainability goals have become critical to businesses. AI-driven systems help in optimisation of energy consumption and reduction of waste. Siemens, Schneider Electric and Honeywell are some of the leading examples of organisations using AI-driven energy management systems that help with analytics regarding prediction of likely usage of energy and thus assist in the planning process to reduce wastage and environmental impact.[37]

Apart from these areas that are unique to manufacturing processes, the universal AI-driven systems customised to the functioning of production systems are also widely being deployed. This includes AR systems for training of production and maintenance staff, virtual assistants to handle queries from customers related to problems faced and resolution thereof, and cybersecurity to safeguard manufacturing processes from cyber-attacks.

Future of Manufacturing in the AI Era

AI has already taken significant strides in the manufacturing arena. With further capabilities being developed as AI platforms mature, advancements in other technologies together with integration with other technologies will create the necessary momentum for further transformation in the manufacturing sector. Let us examine some of these dimensions of potential impact due to advancements in AI and allied technologies.

Autonomous Robots

Robots are already replacing humans in performing repetitive tasks in factories, thereby resulting in higher levels of accuracy, desired quality levels and avoidance of human errors. As the next step, robots will become autonomous in the production arena, equipped with the required skills and intelligence to adapt to new tasks to cater to custom orders and personalised productions without the need for extensive programming interventions. For complex tasks to be performed, a swarm of robots would be required to work in a coordinated fashion. Robotics-as-a-service (RaaS) is another strand of development that is likely to be tapped into for tasks that are commonly carried out and plugged into their respective production systems. The presence of collaborative robots (cobots) in the production environment will increase, and they would be expected to work alongside humans, learning from them and adapting to changes, thus improving overall performance.

Flexibility in Production Centres

With enhanced automation of production processes and deployment of robots for the requisite skills, for certain products, it may be possible to take back production to those locations where they were being originally manufactured and reduce the dependence on a global supply chain. AI-driven systems could make local production economically viable and environment-friendly as there would be reduced carbon footprints.

Customised Manufacturing

On the one hand, AI-driven systems would provide tools to customers to define their individual requirements. On the other hand, the combination of advanced robotics and smart factories would enable factories to adapt production facilities to cater to individual needs. The combination of 3D printing and GenAI design along with smart robotics would make it feasible for manufacturers to move towards mass customisation.

Sustainability-Centric Production

The realisation of having to conserve resources and energy is increasingly driving consumers and producers to adopt production methods to reduce consumption and costs. With the network of suppliers, producers and customers adopting AI technologies that would enable them to use analytics for improved resource management leading to reduced wastage and scrap and overall better prediction, forecasting and planning, it is anticipated that AI will act as the catalyst towards sustainability goals.

Workers' Safety

Wearables with predictive analytics would enable manufacturing organisations to be forewarned about potential accidents or injuries to workers and take real-time and proactive action to prevent accidents. Timely action may include alteration in the plant and machinery and fine-tuning the performance of certain equipment to ensure a safe working environment for employees.

Skill Development for an AI-Driven Environment

Workers would be required to be trained continually. With the goal of customisation and resource conservation being paramount, AI systems would enable workers to be trained for new skills, new tasks and techniques of production and mentor them in real time. They would also need to learn to work alongside smart robots to perform certain tasks together and use data-driven insights to fine-tune the production processes for better outcomes.

Edge AI in Manufacturing

Deployment of AI at the edge of the network where data is generated for enhancing real-time decision-making would be path-breaking. This could result in instantaneous processing and analytics with minimal communication delays. This would also mean less dependence on cloud computing and empowering decision-making on the edge. With enhanced edge AI solutions, the possibilities for real-time inventory management, further optimisation of supply chain, real-time preventive maintenance actions and real-time optimisation of energy consumption would become feasible. However, a lot of work remains to be done to overcome several challenges, namely, dealing with the diversity and complexities of edge devices, security issues and integration requirements.

Role of Quantum Computing in Manufacturing

Quantum computing could be helpful to address complex logistics, speed and precision-driven predictive analytics and granular defect detection in highly sensitive and critical scenarios. To move in this direction, we need to overcome the challenges of quantum control and scalability, security concerns and error correction methods and acquire the skilled resources required for developing products and technology. Leading technology majors such as Microsoft, IBM and Google are working in this area, which may result in some breakthrough technologies in the near future.

Transitioning to Industry 5.0

As AI enables manufacturing businesses to progress towards Industry 5.0, innovation and human creativity would have to be in the driving seat to take advantage of the automation and analytics capabilities and the connectedness of everything. Thus, it would be the test of human ingenuity to identify how humans are able to get the most out of the machines designed, created and trained by them, sharing their own intelligence with them. In turn, the machines would be able to generate intelligence of a new kind and possibly of a higher order, the depth of insights and the vastness of which are humanly impossible to achieve alone. However, decision-making and the ability to make sense of all the possible options and insights made available will remain with the humans. Hence, there is a need for a healthy collaboration between the humans and the machines.

Talent Requirements for the AI Era in the Manufacturing Industry

Several large players in the manufacturing industry have embraced AI and other digital technologies and have started realising significant outcomes for their businesses, resulting in many of them committing to an AI-first strategic approach. It is also the industry where we find AI getting embedded in and integrated with various other technologies. Hence, there is a rapid change in the manner in which business processes are getting transformed. As a result, as the manufacturing industry readies itself for the future waves of AI, its leaders have recognised the need to reskill their workforce continually and also identify the roles that are becoming redundant or getting redefined. Let us examine the changes in the roles as a result of the transition in the manufacturing industry in Tables 6.1 and 6.2.

Table 6.1 Evolving Roles in the Manufacturing Industry (India & Asia-Pacific Context)

Functional Area	Roles Likely to Disappear / Evolve	Drivers of Change	New / Emerging Roles	Description / Key Skills Needed
R&D, design & engineering	Manual drafters; 2D-only design engineers	Digital twins, simulation-led engineering, generative design	Generative design & simulation engineer	• Uses AI and physics-based models to optimise components/products • Skills in computer-aided manufacturing + AI tools and digital twin modelling
	Prototype engineers (physical-first)	Virtual prototyping & additive manufacturing	Additive manufacturing & rapid prototyping specialist	• Operates 3D-printing ecosystems, topology optimisation, materials science & short-run prototyping
Production & shop floor operations	Assembly line operators (manual repetitive tasks)	Industrial robotics, cobots, automation	Human–robot collaboration technician	• Works with cobots, configures safe human–machine workflows • Requires robotics basics, safety & calibration
	Manual machine setters/operators	Computer numerical control auto-calibration, remote monitoring	Smart factory technician (IIoT-enabled)	• Monitors machine health dashboards • Configures IIoT devices • Performs data-led interventions & root-cause checks
Quality & inspection	Manual quality control inspectors (visual/manual checks)	Vision systems, non-destructive testing automation, predictive quality	AI-powered quality analytics lead	• Uses computer vision, statistical models & anomaly detection for real-time quality assurance • Statistical process control and data skills

Functional Area	Roles Likely to Disappear / Evolve	Drivers of Change	New / Emerging Roles	Description / Key Skills Needed
	Paper-based quality documentation roles	Digital quality management systems, blockchain traceability	Digital quality & traceability analyst	• Manages digital quality records, blockchain trails & compliance dashboards across suppliers and plants
Maintenance & asset management	Reactive maintenance technicians	Predictive maintenance, digital twins, sensorisation	predictive maintenance & reliability engineer	• Uses vibration/thermal data, machine learning models & comprehensive enterprise facility management platform to forecast failures • Requires condition-monitoring & analytics skills
	Separate mechanical/electrical maintenance roles	Convergence of mechatronics & automation	Mechatronics & automation engineer	• Integrates mechanical, electrical, PLC, robotics & automation tech for end-to-end equipment reliability
Supply chain & logistics	Manual planners & schedulers (spreadsheet-led)	Real-time supply chain visibility, AI planning	Connected supply chain planner (control-tower model)	• Uses digital control towers with scenario planning • Skills in sales and operations planning, network optimisation & AI planning tools
	Storekeepers & manual inventory tracking	RFID, IoT, automated warehouses	Smart warehouse & intralogistics coordinator	• Operates autonomous mobile robots, automated storage systems & sensor-based inventory • Skills in warehouse management system, robotics & safety

ESG, energy & sustainability	Generic environmental, health & safety) / corporate social responsibility) officers	Carbon mandates, renewable integration, circular production	Decarbonisation & circular manufacturing lead	• Designs Scope 1–3 reduction plans, circular material loops, green certifications & supplier ESG programmes
	Manual waste handling staff	Zero-waste factories, resource recovery	Industrial waste-to-value engineer	• Converts process waste into energy or raw materials • Skills in industrial waste chemistry, ESG & partner ecosystems
Workforce, safety & skill development	Safety officers (compliance-only)	Connected workers, wearables, AR/VR safety training	Connected worker experience & safety technologist	• Deploys wearables, AR/VR safety simulations & digital standard operating procedures • Skills in health, safety and environment + digital adoption
	Classroom-only trainers	AR/VR, microlearning, skill passports	Immersive learning & skills mobility designer	• Builds VR/AR modules, competency-based credentials & internal talent mobility pathways
IT/operational technology (OT), cyber & data	Traditional IT support roles	IT–OT convergence, cybersecurity for factories	OT cybersecurity & industrial resilience architect	• Secures Supervisory Control and Data Acquisition system (SCADA), PLC, IIoT networks • Incident response & cyber-physical security expertise

Functional Area	Roles Likely to Disappear / Evolve	Drivers of Change	New / Emerging Roles	Description / Key Skills Needed
	Manual data entry/reporting roles	Smart manufacturing execution system, AI copilots & automation	Manufacturing data product analyst	• Builds digital workflows for shop floor data, business intelligence dashboards & AI use cases • SQL, analytics & domain expertise
Procurement & vendor management	Manual vendor selection & audits	Smart contracts, supplier risk analytics	Supplier risk & digital procurement analyst	• Uses AI for vendor scoring, ESG compliance & smart contracting • Strong analytics + negotiation knowledge
After-sales, service & product life cycle	Field service technicians (reactive)	IoT-enabled remote service, servitisation	Product service & remote diagnostics engineer	• Uses IoT data for remote troubleshooting & predictive service • Skills in customer-centric service analytics
Smart manufacturing & Industry 4.0 transformation	Lean officers (process only, no tech)	Industry 4.0, smart plant networks, AI-first operations	Industry 4.0 transformation manager	• Leads road map for automation, AI, IIoT, digital twin & workforce upskilling • Strong change management + tech fluency
Innovation & new business models	Traditional product managers (hardware-only mindset)	'Product + Service + Data' business models	Product-as-a-service business architect	• Designs subscription/usage-based models for industrial products, integrating service, data & digital ecosystems

Source: Curated with inputs from ChatGPT

Table 6.2 Understanding the New Roles in the Manufacturing Industry (India and Asia-Pacific, 2025–2030)

Net New Role	Why This Role Is Emerging (Key Drivers)	Manufacturing Segments Where This Appears	Key Skills Needed
Digital twin systems architect	Digital twins for plants, lines, machines & supply chains; simulation-led decisions	Automotive, electronics, pharma, heavy engineering, FMCG	• Simulation tools • IIoT • Data modelling • Physics-based AI
AI-first production orchestration manager	AI-driven dynamic scheduling & production flow optimisation	Discrete & process manufacturing	• AI/machine learning for ops, manufacturing execution system + enterprise resource planning + IIoT integration, scenario planning
Robotics & cobotics fleet supervisor	Fleet of collaborative robots & autonomous systems on shop floor	Automotive, electronics, FMCG, food processing	• Robot ops, safety, programming, uptime & vendor management
Industrial metaverse experience designer	Virtual factories for training, design, maintenance & remote collaboration	High-tech, aerospace, automotive, tier-1 suppliers	• XR design • 3D content • Human–machine interaction
Green hydrogen & clean energy systems lead	Transition to net-zero energy, hydrogen-based industrial fuels	Steel, cement, chemicals, heavy industries	• Hydrogen tech • Energy systems • Carbon accounting
Carbon & circular materials scientist	Low-carbon materials and circular product design	Packaging, textiles, automotive, electronics	• Material science • Life cycle assessment • Recycling tech • Circular design

Net New Role	Why This Role Is Emerging (Key Drivers)	Manufacturing Segments Where This Appears	Key Skills Needed
Smart materials & nano-manufacturing engineer	Smart/self-healing materials, nano-precision manufacturing	Semiconductors, electronics, medical devices	• Nanotech • Cleanroom • Micro-fabrication
Industrial data marketplace product owner	Monetisation of machine & process data for ecosystem partners	Industrial original equipment manufacturers, tier-1 suppliers	• Data economics • API ecosystems • Platform strategy
Cyber-physical threat intelligence analyst	Security for converged OT+IT; attacks on PLCs/ SCADA & IIoT	All asset-intensive sectors	• OT cybersecurity • Threat intel • Red teaming
Ethical AI & autonomous systems auditor	Governance of AI-led production, robotic decisions, safety & compliance	Smart factories & multinational plants	• AI governance • Safety standards • Compliance frameworks
Human-digital workplace experience designer	Designing worker-centric digital shop floor interactions	All modern factories, especially with ageing workforce	• UX for frontline tech • Change management • Ergonomics • Inclusion
Micro-factory & localised production network manager	Distributed, small-footprint, hyperlocal manufacturing networks	Apparel, food, electronics, 3D printing–enabled sectors	• Network design • Micro-plant ops • Community supply chains
Servitisation & outcome-based manufacturing lead	Shift to 'product + service + performance guarantees'	Industrial original equipment manufacturers; machinery; heating, ventilation and air conditioning; elevators	• Contracting • Key performance indicators • Data-driven service-level agreements

Retrofit & brownfield digitalisation specialist	Need to digitise legacy plants instead of greenfield	Engineering, procurement & construction firms, MSME clusters	• OT/IIoT retrofitting • Vendor management • ROI modelling
AI-powered product teardown & re-design engineer	Circularity + cost pressure → redesign for reuse/refurbish	Electronics, automotive, consumer goods	• Value engineering • Teardown analysis • AI design tools
Quantum manufacturing R&D analyst (early-stage)	Future of quantum modelling for materials & optimisation	Advanced materials, pharma, high-tech	• Quantum basics • Simulation • Applied research
Sustainability-linked finance & compliance coordinator	Financing tied to ESG metrics & sustainable performance	Large manufacturers & green-fund recipients	• ESG reporting • Finance • Incentives & audit alignment
Industrial biomanufacturing process developer	Growth of bio-based manufacturing & synthetic biology	Textiles, packaging, chemical substitutes	• Bioprocess design • Fermentation • Scale-up
Workforce digital ethics & well-being officer	Automation, AI, augmentation → new well-being/ethics needs	Multi-factory enterprises	• Employee well-being • Tech-ethics • Policy • Inclusion
Industrial talent cloud & skills exchange manager	Talent sharing across factories, gig technicians & skill marketplaces	MSMEs, clusters, multi-plant enterprises	• Skill taxonomies • Gig workforce ops • Credentialing

Source: Curated with inputs from ChatGPT

Leadership Imperatives for the Manufacturing Industry in the AI Era

Leaders are aware that the changes in the way businesses would function and new jobs would be performed would impact the industry as a whole. As a result of changing business processes and the new roles being created, their workers have to be trained to embrace the change from being blue-collar workers to adapting to an environment where they would be guided by AI for diagnostics and maintenance on the shop floor. Thus, their focus would shift from supervising humans to enabling humans to accept cobots in the work environment and facilitating collaboration between humans and machines. Disruptions caused by Covid-19 and the reality of wars in various parts of the world—Russia versus Ukraine, Israel versus Palestine and the turbulences in the Middle East—have been wake-up calls to the leaders of the manufacturing businesses to streamline their supply chains with better visibility across the value chain and robustness to avoid material shortages. This has resulted in the urgency of leaders to adopt AI-enabled predictive global supply chain systems that meet with ethical and compliance standards.

Autonomous manufacturing lines are replacing manual or machine-supported assembly lines. Hence, it is critical for leaders to have a thorough understanding of cyber-physical systems. While decision-making could be centred on experiences, they would be driven by data and intelligence coming through multiple sources. Hence, an in-depth understanding of how to nurture the development of decision frameworks by integrating sensors, robotics, digital twins, safety, cybersecurity, diagnostics and predictive maintenance would be essential. All businesses would have access to a whole host of technology and AI tools. However, the decisions that leaders make about investments, their risk appetite on the future trajectories of how technology is likely to define their growth pathways and their choice of manufacturing technologies, products and locations, to name a few, would determine their current competitiveness and their survival in the future. The questions of ethics, governance and data ownership are tough questions that do not have easy answers, and leaders of the manufacturing industry, like all other industry leaders, need to work in unison with hi-tech industry leaders, innovators and governments to find the pathways that would work for all. Table 6.3 provides a detailed description of leadership focus and priorities for the AI era.

TABLE 6.3 LEADERSHIP IMPERATIVES FOR THE MANUFACTURING INDUSTRY: TRADITIONAL VS AI ERA

Dimension	Traditional Manufacturing Leadership	AI-Era Manufacturing Leadership
Core leadership focus	Efficiency, standardisation and scale. Leaders aimed to maximise output, minimise waste and maintain consistency.	Intelligence, agility and sustainability. Leaders optimise systems dynamically through data, automation and predictive analytics.
Leadership philosophy	Stability through control—focus on precision, discipline and mechanised reliability	Agility through orchestration—focus on data-driven decisions, adaptability and human–machine collaboration
Leadership style	Hierarchical and command-driven. Leadership authority came from technical expertise and tenure.	Distributed and collaborative. Leadership authority comes from data fluency, cross-domain coordination and systems thinking.
Decision-making model	Experience-based, sequential and reactive. Leaders relied on production logs, inspections and monthly reports.	Predictive, real-time and continuous. Leaders use AI dashboards, digital twins and analytics for instant insight and proactive decisions.
Operational leadership	Focused on throughput, machine uptime and defect reduction via manual supervision	Focused on predictive maintenance, process optimisation and AI-led quality by design

Dimension	Traditional Manufacturing Leadership	AI-Era Manufacturing Leadership
Data and intelligence use	Data captured for audits and historical reference. Little integration between plant, procurement and distribution.	Data is the factory's nervous system—integrated through IoT, edge computing and AI models, enabling autonomous control loops.
Innovation approach	Incremental process improvement (Kaizen, Lean Six Sigma). Innovation was gradual and human-driven.	Continuous innovation via AI and simulation—digital twins enable rapid prototyping, scenario testing and autonomous optimisation
Technology adoption	Automation limited to physical machinery (computer numerical control), PLC, robotics	Convergence of AI, robotics, IoT and quantum computing for cognitive manufacturing—machines learn and self-correct
Organizational structure	Vertical, functionally siloed departments (production, maintenance, quality, procurement)	Networked, cross-functional 'smart cells' with shared data layers connecting design, production and logistics
Workforce and people leadership	Labour-intensive, repetitive and manually supervised roles. Leadership focused on compliance and safety.	Hybrid human–machine workforce. Leadership focuses on upskilling, safety in cobot environments and ethical AI deployment.
Supply chain leadership	Linear, reactive logistics; limited visibility across suppliers and distributors	Predictive and resilient supply chains—AI forecasts demand, mitigates disruptions and ensures traceability
Quality & risk management	Manual inspection, reactive quality checks and corrective actions post-production	AI-led predictive quality and risk assessment; sensors detect anomalies in real time, reducing defects and downtime

Dimension	Traditional Manufacturing Leadership	AI-Era Manufacturing Leadership
Customer orientation	Production to forecast—one-size-fits-all products for mass markets	Production to personalisation—AI enables customised, small-batch manufacturing responding to real-time demand
Sustainability & ESG leadership	Compliance-oriented; energy conservation treated as cost-saving	Proactive; AI tracks emissions, resource use and waste reduction, integrating sustainability into business performance
Governance and ethics	Leadership accountability centred on output and safety metrics	Governance includes algorithmic accountability, data transparency and ethical use of automation
Leadership competencies	Engineering knowledge, process control and people supervision	Data literacy, digital fluency, ecosystem thinking and sustainability vision
Metrics of success	Cost, yield, downtime and efficiency	Innovation speed, carbon footprint, resilience and AI-driven ROI

Source: Curated with inputs from ChatGPT

In this context, the life sciences industry is yet another industry that is grappling with a similar set of questions and challenges in the context of AI. Several functions such as design, production and supply chain have similar characteristics and performances, although there are other dimensions that are unique to the life sciences industry driven by its own ecosystem. It, therefore, felt prudent to examine some of the dimensions of this industry that would play dominant roles in defining the future of AI's own trajectories while they are in the throes of immersion into AI.

Life Sciences Industry

The life sciences industry comprises businesses and institutions that research, develop and commercialise products related to biology, medicine, biotechnology, pharmaceuticals and healthcare. Institutions and firms engaged with life sciences play a significant role in advancing scientific knowledge, developing new technologies and treatments, improving global health and driving economic growth and innovation. Solutions for enhancing quality of life—medical treatments, pharmaceutical discoveries, invention and design of devices or improved yields in agriculture—are intrinsically linked with the pace of development in science and technology. From the ancient days of using primitive tools and localised knowledge, civilisations have progressed over centuries on the strength of new breakthroughs supported by advancements in computing, communication and cross-pollination of ideas.

Evolution of the Life Sciences Industry

The beginnings of the need for therapeutic and medical solutions have been driven by the need to survive and combat the adversities in the environment, whether it was to protect against the vagaries of the weather or animals or other warring humans. Solutions aimed at human preservation or therapeutic treatment were essentially localised and developed through trial-and-error methods—tested primarily on an opportunistic basis. Some of these principles and methods have been codified by the masters of these practices or their followers in due course of time. History and mythology are replete with examples of the interventions of masters or gods whose efforts were idolised and celebrated.

In Greek mythology, Apollo and his son Asclepius are considered the gods of healing. The symbol of Asclepius, the rod of Asclepius, is a staff with a single serpent coiled around it and remains the universal symbol of medicine today.[38] In Hindu mythology, Dhanvantari is considered the god of Ayurveda and physician of the gods. His birthday and the divine origins of healing and health are celebrated two days before Diwali as Dhanteras.[39] As per Chinese mythology, Shennong, the divine farmer, is considered the god of agriculture and herbal medicine and is credited with writing the *Shennong Bencao Jing* (Divine farmer's classic of

Materia Medica), the oldest text on Chinese herbal medicine.[40] Egyptian mythology considered Imhotep and Sekhmet the gods of medicine and healing.[41] Brigid and Eir were considered goddesses of healing in the Celtic and Norse mythologies respectively.[42] Sukunahikona-no-Mikoto in the Japanese Shinto tradition, Patecatl in the Aztec tradition and Osain in the African-Yoruba tradition were considered the gods of healing.[43] The common theme found across cultures is the use of natural elements such as water, sun and herbs as the divine tools to cure medical problems, and priests and healers served as channels between divine medicine and human suffering.

Emergence of Modern-Day Scientific Medicine

The formal scientific approach to medicine, agriculture and related fields commenced in Europe during the 16th to 19th centuries coinciding with the Industrial Revolution. The modern-day empirical scientific medicine could be attributed to Andreas Vesalius, whose book *De Humani Corporis Fabrica* was published in 1543 challenged older anatomical traditions.[44] After the French Revolution, hospitals and medical treatments were reorganised in France. The Rothamsted Experimental Station in England (United Kingdom) was founded in 1843 and is often cited as one of the first continuous scientific agricultural research stations.[45] In Germany and France around the mid-19th century, the application of chemistry to agriculture became systematic (for example, the work of Justus von Liebig in Germany).[46]

The early foundations of the life sciences domain were centred on advancements in biology, medicine and chemistry through the key discoveries of cell theory in 1838, Louis Pasteur's germ theory of disease and Mendelian genetics in the 1860s, leading to primitive drug development in the late 1890s.[47] The formalisation of the pharmaceutical industry commenced in the 1900s.[48] The discovery of penicillin and the introduction of insulin for diabetes in the 1920s gave an impetus for mass production in the 1950s.[49] Simultaneously, medical devices for X-ray and electrocardiography also started to become key aids for medical treatments.[50] Many drug merchants across the United States such as Squibb, Merck, Parke Davis, Smith Kline and others, who were originally engaged in wholesale procurement and sale of malarial drugs, started expanding their product portfolio and their presence in the markets.[51]

The field of molecular biology became prominent with Watson and Crick's discovery of the DNA double helix in the 1950s.[52] The study of biochemistry and genetics as scientific disciplines led to numerous drug discoveries, supported actively by the investment in academic and industrial research by the United States of America through the National Institute of Health.[53] In parallel, the regulatory body Food and Drug Administration's power increased with important legislative and organisational changes.[54] The late 1970s witnessed a surge in the founding of biotech companies and the emergence of genetically engineered drugs.[55] The ambitious human genome project was launched in 1990,[56] and contract research and outsourcing models started gaining momentum in the 1980–1990 period.[57] The first ten years following the year 2000 have experienced advances in bioinformatics, systems biology and personalised medication with the completion of the human genome project.[58]

Digital Adoption by Life Sciences Companies

Studies on digital adoption in healthcare companies have shown that the uptake of companies has been enthusiastic with blockchain and IoT but slow in manufacturing and supply chain, resulting in limited outcomes.[59] Zymergen was an American biotech company founded in 2013 that applied genomics and machine learning to design organisms that produce chemicals. Although the company positioned itself as a tech-driven company and focused on its discovery platform, it neglected its biomanufacturing and commercialisation efforts. As a result, the company finally wound down for a much smaller value than expected and was acquired by Ginkgo Bioworks.[60]

An industry survey in India, a bespoke study conducted by Cognizant, found that while 71 per cent of life sciences organisations had planned manufacturing as the primary focus for digital innovation, only 10 per cent had moved beyond planning to implementation.[61] A study of the Indian pharma industry found that seven out of ten digital projects fail to deliver results despite heavy investments. The reasons for projects not yielding the planned outcomes include poor adoption, legacy spreadsheets still in use and redundancy of digital tools.[62] At times, over-investment in technology platforms without sufficient focus on process change, workforce skills and data readiness have also been the reasons for failure to realise the benefits from tech investments as envisaged. The key takeaways from these examples include following through tech investments with robust execution plans. With tech access being available to all companies, only those firms who move with speed and adapt their processes to changes in technology, market needs and regulatory requirements would be able to stay ahead of their competition. Recognising this, many organisations have started inducting AI in their business models to create compelling value propositions for their customers.

The Immersion of AI in the Life Sciences Business

From 2010 onwards, AI and machine learning have started to get integrated into drug discovery and healthcare systems. A number of devices, telehealth and wearables have been introduced and adopted by customers.[63] Companies such as Pfizer and Moderna could develop Covid-19 vaccines with the help of mRNA platforms.[64] AI is supporting scientists in sifting through large datasets to identify new drug targets and predict molecule-target interactions. Traditional drug discovery takes ten to twelve years or more and involves huge investments. AI helps in accelerating the process and reducing costs. Further, with the explosion of data through imaging, real-world data, biomarker data and genomics, the use of AI has become extremely helpful in studying and analysing the complex data. GenAI is being used to design molecules and predict properties. In clinical trials, AI helps to select appropriate patient cohorts, predict drop-outs and optimise the overall trial timelines and operations. It is also helping in mining real-world data to identify patterns and side effects for different population segments.

PandaOmics, the AI platform of Insilico Medicine, helps pharmaceutical companies to accelerate target identification, biomarker modelling and compound generation by leveraging large datasets derived from patients and sample sets.[65] NantWorks, BostonGene, ExpanseWorks and CarisMPI are among the leading companies that are using AI engines for multiomics data integration and target identification.[66] There are also Indian start-ups that are building businesses on the strength of AI applied to the omics/systems-biology domain. Proteomica, a spin-off from the Indian Institute of Technology Bombay, is an example of a venture that is blending AI with omics. Proteomica specialises in developing digital health solutions for personalised, evidence-based wellness utilising proteomics and multiomics.[67] Sravathi AI is another Indian start-up that is working on the continuum from target discovery through to drug design in the systems biology/omics value chain.[68] Vgenomics is using AI along with genomic data to accelerate diagnosis and target discovery aimed at rare diseases.[69]

Life sciences companies are using AI in manufacturing in biologics production with sensory data, prediction of equipment failures, process cycle time reduction and optimisation of processes, and in supply chain optimisation with demand forecasting and inventory optimisation. Pfizer has reported that the AI-powered manufacturing processes aimed at detecting anomalies in production, reduction of process cycle time and yield improvement have resulted in an increase in throughput by 20 per cent and reduction in cycle time by 25 per cent. Pfizer could also deliver the oral medication for Covid-19 faster because of the deployment of AI-enabled optimisation in manufacturing and supply chain.[70] Novartis has deployed digital twins of its manufacturing lines by using AI/machine learning with the partnerships built with Amazon

Web Services, thus making production more robust, reducing downtimes.[71] Apart from pharma companies, specialist software companies such as Blue Yonder support drug manufacturers in their supply chain optimisation and play a significant role in risk reduction, lowering of cost and improvement of responsiveness with their solutions.[72]

AI is being used in the design and development of devices and analysis of images. Siemens Healthineers has integrated AI into its imaging systems and diagnostic workflows, which enables the generation of consistent imaging across sites and standardisation in diagnostics.[73] With the democratisation of mobile access, medical device manufacturers such as AliveCor have been able to democratise access to diagnostics, reduce hospital costs and detect medical conditions earlier with their AI-enabled portable devices.[74] Pathology is an important part of diagnostics. Use of AI has been improving the speed, throughput and accuracy in pathology that help with treatment pathways. Ibex AI provides diagnostic solutions that help pathologists analyse tissue slides for cancer efficiently.[75] The extensive use of AI in diagnostics would help developing countries like India with cost-effective wearables and devices and treatment for hitherto unaddressed diseases.

The potential for further AI integration is significant in the entire value chain of drug discovery, manufacturing processes and supply chain and in the device design and diagnostics support systems. However, the stakeholders engaged in designing and implementing AI-driven solutions recognise that the quality and access to data is complex and that data may not be standardised. The methods used by AI models for arriving at decisions have to be made transparent as they concern the health and safety of consumers. Regulatory approvals would be required for new AI models, and they also need to be validated through appropriate channels. Ethical concerns, bias creep and patient data privacy are concerns that are yet to be addressed by all the stakeholders concerned while building AI models. While there is a huge potential for deployment of AI in life sciences in India, which could lead to customisation for different population sets at low costs with genomic diversity, data volumes and patient populations being large, there are still challenges of data infrastructure, interoperability and regulations that need to be addressed.

AI and the Future of the Life Sciences Industry

The AI in the life sciences market is estimated at US$3.61 billion in 2025, projected to grow to around US$11.11 billion by 2030 (≈ 25.2 per cent compound annual growth rate).[76] In the coming years, there would be widespread adoption of AI and GenAI in drug discovery. The next decade will mark a shift from AI-assisted to AI-driven life sciences innovation, fundamentally redefining how science is conducted and how therapies reach patients. There would be convergence of AI with other emerging technologies such as IoT, blockchain robotics and edge/IoT in diagnostics. There would be close collaboration among AI companies and pharma biotech companies.

AI-designed drugs are likely to become more common, and AI-supported drug discovery processes would support expeditious development of drugs with lowering of costs. Instead of the dependence on the traditional lab-based experimentation, drug discovery would increasingly move towards AI-based target identification and molecular design. This would also help in developing drugs for addressing rare or neglected diseases. Robotics and AI and 'lab-in-the-loop' systems would be implemented to automate lab workflows,[77] and virtual screening of a vast range of compounds would also improve the time and cost of drug development. Scientists would not only use AI as a tool but also develop a close collaboration with AI. AI would help scientists by taking on tasks such as sifting through research literature and resolving some of the research bottlenecks and free up the scientists to do more 'thinking' and 'original' work. Embedded AI governance frameworks would ensure traceability, auditability and fairness across product and clinical outcomes.

AI models driven by systems biology will help in mapping disease pathways and simulate interventions that were previously invisible. Therefore, personalised and precision medicine would become mainstream, facilitating customised treatment plans. Risk prediction models for chronic diseases would become more accurate. Population-specific therapeutics would become more feasible. Clinical trials would become smarter, decentralised and more cost-effective with AI playing a significant role in optimising trial design, identifying patient cohorts across diverse populations and predictive analytics ensuring minimal drop-outs. Digital twins would simulate patient samples, and AI-enabled trials could facilitate continuous trials with real-time data insights. The combination of digital twins, AI and IoT will make pharma plants fully autonomous, and with better demand prediction, batch production would be adjusted in real time and supported by real-time quality checks. Biomanufacturing units, like smart factories, are using AI sensors for continuous monitoring and self-correction.

While the potential of AI adoption and the efforts initiated by several corporates are encouraging, ethics and data privacy issues continue to be daunting. These matters should be high on the agenda to be addressed by the combined efforts of the government, industry and key technology players.

India's pharma R&D employment will shift 20–25 per cent towards data-driven and automation-linked roles.[78] Bioinformatics, genomics and digital trial operations are expected to create 50,000–70,000 new high-skill jobs by 2030.[79] A new workforce model will emerge at the intersection of biology, data science, AI, ethics and engineering. India has an exciting opportunity to build the new-age bio-AI talent that would drive biotech innovation. To make this a reality, new formats of partnerships are necessary between pharma, AI start-ups, cloud providers and research institutions. Let us examine the changes in the roles as a result of the transition in the life sciences industry in Tables 6.4 and 6.5.

Table 6.4 Emerging Roles in the Life Sciences Industry

Functional Area	Roles Likely to Disappear / Evolve	Drivers of Change	New / Emerging Roles	Description / Key Skills Needed
Research & discovery	Manual lab technicians; animal testing coordinators	AI-driven simulation, in-silico trials, automation	AI-integrated drug discovery scientist	Combines biology, chemistry & machine learning for molecular design, predictive modelling and digital twin simulations
	Traditional biostatisticians (manual statistical analysis system–based work)	Cloud analytics, GenAI summarisation	Computational biologist (GenAI-augmented)	Uses AI for omics interpretation, integrating transcriptomics, proteomics & clinical data
Clinical development	On-site clinical research associate	Rise of decentralised clinical trials, remote monitoring	Digital / decentralised trial manager	Manages wearables, telemedicine platforms and regulatory-grade digital patient data
	Data entry specialists for clinical data	Automated e-source capture	Clinical data curator	Validates, harmonises & de-biases multi-source data (electronic health record, IoT, genomics)
Manufacturing & quality	Manual inspection quality check roles	Sensor-based continuous monitoring	Continuous quality intelligence lead	Builds predictive quality control models using IoT sensors and anomaly detection
	Shop floor batch operators	Smart factories, robotics	Bioprocess automation engineer	Designs robotic workflows, integrates SCADA/AI systems for Good Manufacturing Practices plants

	Documentation officers (paper-based Good Manufacturing Practices)	Blockchain, digital audit trails	Regulatory blockchain compliance officer	Ensures traceability and auditability of data across sites
Regulatory affairs	Dossier preparation clerks	AI-powered submission generation	RegTech analyst	Uses NLP tools to create & validate global submission of documents in real time
	Compliance coordinators	Shift to continuous regulatory monitoring	AI policy & ethics manager (pharma)	Interfaces with regulators and ensures explainability, data sovereignty compliance
Sales, marketing & med-affairs	Medical reps focused on hospital visits	E-detailing, tele-promotion, digital key opinion leader engagement	Omnichannel medical engagement manager	Manages digital medical communications through AI-driven CRM & content automation
	Manual market research analysts	Predictive analytics, NLP	Healthcare insights analyst (GenAI-driven)	Generates brand insights from social, patient and prescribing data
	Static product trainers	Microlearning, immersive AR/VR	AR/VR learning experience designer	Builds digital learning environments for healthcare professionals' education
Data science & informatics	Biodata entry roles	Automation, pipelines	Biodata architect	Designs life sciences data lakes for multiomics & clinical integration
	Disconnected data scientists (no domain depth)	Need for domain-specific AI models	Life sciences machine learning engineer (SLMs–trained)	Builds domain-tuned SLMs for pharma/biotech workflows

Functional Area	Roles Likely to Disappear / Evolve	Drivers of Change	New / Emerging Roles	Description / Key Skills Needed
Supply chain & logistics	Inventory clerks	Blockchain, IoT, predictive logistics	Cold-chain data analyst	Optimises vaccine & biologics transport with real-time sensor analytics
	Manual procurement roles	Smart contracts, vendor analytics	Pharma supply chain intelligence manager	Integrates AI procurement tools with compliance & ESG dashboards
Corporate & strategy	Legacy business analysts	AI scenario modelling	Bioeconomy strategist	Plans national/state bioeconomy projects integrating AI, biotech & sustainability
	HR generalists (paper-based compliance)	Talent analytics, AI-driven skilling	Life sciences workforce architect	Designs future skill maps and manages AI upskilling and talent transitions
Public health / policy interface	Traditional corporate social responsibility project officers	Outcome-based models, AI impact measurement	Digital health ecosystem designer	Connects ASHA (accredited social health activists)/primary health data with national disease intelligence systems
	Epidemiology data coders	Real-time surveillance platforms	AI epidemiologist	Uses AI for outbreak prediction, pattern detection & vaccine planning

Source: Curated with inputs from ChatGPT

Table 6.5 Understanding the New Roles in the Life Sciences Industry

New Role	Why This Role Is Emerging (Key Drivers)	Where in Life Sciences (Segments) It Applies	Key Skills Needed / Description
AI drug discovery platform architect	GenAI + machine learning + digital biology platforms accelerating target identification & lead optimisation	Pharma, biotech, contract research organisations	• Builds/owns AI-driven discovery stack • Needs biology + machine learning + cloud architecture knowledge
Digital trial & decentralised study manager	Rise of remote/hybrid trials, wearables, real-world data capture	Clinical development, contract research organisations, pharma	• Manages virtual/hybrid trial platforms • Skills in telemedicine, remote monitoring, data integrity
Bioprocess automation & digital manufacturing engineer	Smart/continuous manufacturing, biologics scale-up, IIoT	Biologics manufacturing, pharma manufacturing, contract manufacturing	• Designs digital workflows, automates bioprocess • Needs bioprocess + automation + data analytics
Ethical AI & autonomous systems auditor (life sciences)	Use of AI in drug/test design, autonomous labs; need for governance, explainability	R&D, discovery labs, biotech	• Assesses AI systems and ensures compliance & ethics • Needs AI governance, regulatory understanding, bio-domain knowledge
Industrial biomanufacturing process developer	Synthetic biology, biomanufacturing of chemicals/ therapies	Biotech, life sciences manufacturing	• Develops bio-based manufacturing methods • Skills in fermentation, bioprocess, scale-up, sustainability

New Role	Why This Role Is Emerging (Key Drivers)	Where in Life Sciences (Segments) It Applies	Key Skills Needed / Description
Real-world evidence & omics integration lead	Huge growth in omics + electronic health records + real-world data for regulatory/commercial use	Pharma, regulatory affairs, market access	• Integrates genomics/proteomics + patient data • Needs data science + clinical/biologic domain + regulatory knowledge
Digital trust & consent steward (life sciences)	Data privacy, patient consent, cross-border data flows (DPDP/GDPR and so on)	Digital health, clinical development, biotech	• Manages consent frameworks, vendor risk, data governance • Needs privacy law, data architecture, stakeholder management
Industrial data marketplace product owner (life sciences)	Machine/clinical/omics data monetisation, ecosystem platforms	Pharma, Biotech, MedTech	• Builds data monetisation platforms, API ecosystems • Requires product management, data economics, domain context
Human-digital collaboration experience designer (lab/clinic)	Labs/clinics becoming smart, need UX for digital-biology + human workflows	Discovery labs, clinical sites, MedTech	• Designs experience for scientists/clinicians using AI/automation • Needs UX, change management, domain fluency
Carbon & circular biomanufacturing lead	Sustainability, circular biology, bioeconomy demands	Manufacturing, biotech, pharma	• Designs low-carbon manufacturing, material loops, circular processes • Skills in sustainability, bioengineering, process design

Source: Curated with inputs from ChatGPT

Leadership Imperatives for the Life Sciences Industry in the AI Era

While many entities in the life sciences industry have started training the workforce and planning for the emerging roles in the AI era, more than ever before, leaders have to actively lead, encourage and facilitate partnerships between academia, bioinformatics specialist firms and AI solution providers as the data from various partners would need to be brought together for building AI models. Data streams would include other sources as well, for example, omics, wearables and multiple types and categories of healthcare providers who would be bound by their own agreements with their customers. Leaders have to brace themselves to not only champion AI-led drug discovery processes and scientific integrity but also develop clarity for complex questions related to data ownership and accountability.

Furthermore, leaders would need to develop innovative strategies to build cross-industry bridges like the case of ABB and Thermo Fisher blending process engineering capabilities with biopharma analytics.[80] Institutionalising AI-led adaptive trial designs, patient monitoring and ethical governance would require the attention of leaders. Investment in automation, drug release timing and regulatory compliances would be an ongoing balancing act for leaders. All of this would pose another significant challenge to be addressed by the leaders: that of ownership of innovation, outcomes and intellectual property. Table 6.6 provides the detailed outline of how leadership in the AI era would evolve in the life sciences industry.

Table 6.6 Leadership Imperatives for the Life Sciences Industry: Traditional vs AI Era

Dimension	Traditional Life Sciences Leadership	AI-Era Life Sciences Leadership
Core leadership focus	Discovery and safety through scientific rigour and compliance; long R&D cycles with limited integration across teams	• Speed, precision and ethical innovation powered by AI • Real-time collaboration across discovery, clinical, manufacturing and patient ecosystems
Leadership philosophy	Science-led, cautious, hierarchical; success measured by accuracy, approvals and incremental innovation	• Data-led, agile and collaborative • Success measured by discovery velocity, ethical AI use and patient outcomes
Leadership style	Expert-centric and authority-driven; decisions made by senior scientists and clinicians	• Networked and cross-disciplinary • Leaders integrate data scientists, clinicians, ethicists and technologists
Decision-making model	Sequential, hypothesis-driven, reliant on manual experimentation and retrospective analysis	• Non-linear, simulation-driven, using predictive modelling, GenAI and in-silico validation
R&D and discovery leadership	Based on lab experiments, trial-and-error molecule design and lengthy human trials	• AI-enabled drug discovery and clinical simulation • Leaders oversee hybrid teams of biologists and AI modellers
Clinical trials & evidence generation	Dependent on physical recruitment, site monitoring and manual data logging	• Adaptive, decentralised trials using AI for patient selection, outcome prediction and synthetic control groups
Data & technology use	Fragmented lab and patient data; limited computational power; siloed bioinformatics	• Integrated AI pipelines combining omics, electronic health records, imaging and real-world data for continuous insight generation
Regulatory leadership	Compliance after experimentation; reactive responses to audits and changing regulations	• Proactive compliance with continuous monitoring, explainable AI and algorithmic traceability built into the workflow
Ethical orientation	Ethical oversight confined to human and animal testing norms	• Expanded ethical mandate covering algorithmic bias, genomic privacy, consent and equitable access to AI-enabled therapies

Innovation leadership	Dependent on serendipitous discoveries and incremental lab breakthroughs	• Systematic, data-driven innovation via generative design, knowledge graphs and AI-assisted hypothesis generation
Manufacturing leadership	Batch-based, manual quality assurance and reactive error correction	• AI-driven continuous manufacturing • Predictive quality control and 'right-first-time' production guided by data analytics
Organisational structure	Vertical and function-based: R&D, clinical, regulatory and marketing operated independently	• Horizontal and integrated: cloud-connected platforms link research, production, compliance and patient engagement
Leadership competencies	Scientific expertise, regulatory understanding, risk aversion and perseverance	• Data literacy, ethical foresight, interdisciplinary agility and digital transformation vision
Talent & workforce leadership	Focused on laboratory scientists, clinicians and regulatory specialists	• Blended teams of biologists, data scientists, AI engineers, ethicists and patient experience designers
Patient engagement	Transactional—patients as trial participants or end users	• Relational—patients as data partners • AI enables continuous feedback and personalised care pathways
Collaboration ecosystem	Partnerships limited to academia, contract research organisations and government funding bodies	• Open innovation networks involving cloud providers, AI start-ups, universities and health systems
Risk & governance	Managed via documentation and periodic audits; low tolerance for failure	• Managed through real-time AI dashboards; leaders embrace agile experimentation while upholding ethical and regulatory guard rails
Sustainability & access	Global access and affordability often secondary to profitability	• AI supports equitable healthcare delivery, local manufacturing and personalized medicine • Leaders link ESG to social innovation
Metrics of success	Number of drugs approved, patents filed, regulatory compliance	• Time-to-discovery, patient outcomes, data transparency and ecosystem impact

Source: Curated with inputs from ChatGPT

7

The Surge of Automation with AI at the Edge

IT IS HUMAN NATURE to seek more material gains with minimal labour. Get more with less. The concept of automation must have been born somewhere in that pursuit to explore different options to seek greater returns, hundreds of years ago. This quest, when channelised well with novel ideas, available technologies and ingenuity, has led to wonderful innovations. These innovations have changed the ways in which humankind lives, operates and thrives on this planet.

The journey of industrial manufacturing spans across a few centuries, and the journey of automation goes hand in hand with it. Automation has played a critical role in shaping the manufacturing sector and, in turn, the world as it is today. In the First Industrial Revolution, mechanical machines helped improve the speed of manufacturing. It also reduced the human-introduced variability in the goods produced, even though these machines operated on steam or other rudimentary energy sources and were inefficient with frequent breakdowns. In the Second Industrial Revolution, the availability of electricity and its ease of distribution made it possible to make the machines more efficient and reliable. The advent of assembly-line manufacturing dramatically improved industrial manufacturing productivity, irrespective of what the factory was producing. Further, electronic technology and its derivatives like computers and industrial control systems brought about a massive change in the scale and speed of manufacturing. As of 2025, the industry is experiencing the impact of the internet and its extended application in the IIoT. IIoT is a hyperscale interconnection of sensors, equipment, devices, machines and humans that interact and integrate the physical and digital worlds. This unification is giving rise to a new world—a meta-world. A meta-world is a virtual ecosystem that combines digital technologies like VR, AR, AI and systems that conduct commerce (for example, cryptocurrency) with the real world. It creates a shared space where people can connect, interact and conduct their business. It is also known as the 'metaverse'. Metaverses are expected to transform the way humans live, allowing them to interact with the virtual world along with machines and computers, without residing in the same physical space. We are already using early concepts and innovations of such metaverses for learning, working, shopping, socialising and entertainment. Automation in manufacturing is bound to leverage this concept to further enhance manufacturing capabilities and stretch the realm of possibilities.

The rise of AI and its application in the manufacturing sector holds an exciting promise to transform the industrial world, going beyond mere enhancements on the shop floor. AI, combined with conventional automation systems, can deliver the promise of 'autonomous manufacturing'—a dream that eliminates the need for humans at manufacturing locations, enhancing safety, reliability, efficiency and productivity. Autonomous manufacturing has the potential to eliminate human fatalities in difficult and hazardous manufacturing locations and sidestep expensive mistakes caused by manual operations. Similar to the concept of a driverless car, an entire manufacturing facility can be self-operated, self-controlled and self-sustained with minimal human intervention. There is a popular concept of a futuristic factory with only a dog and a man at the manufacturing facility.[1] The man's responsibility in this concept is to feed the dog, and the dog's job is to ensure that the man does not interfere in the manufacturing process of the factory. Far-fetched as it may sound, this concept may not be far from reality.

We started this conversation with the human quest to attain more with less. This may be a path leading us to the pinnacle of an uber-automated world. However, the aim behind this is not to promote human idleness but to make humans more creative, productive and happy. Automation combined with AI can positively impact the quality of our lives in ways that we may still not be able to clearly foresee or fathom. Those who are passionate about automation—stay tuned. The best in automation is yet to come!

Key Trends Shaping the Future of Industrial Automation

1. AI and machine learning integration
   i. Predictive maintenance: AI will anticipate equipment failures before they occur, reducing downtime.
   ii. Autonomous decision-making: Machine learning models will optimise supply chains, energy use and process quality without human intervention.
2. IIoT
   i. Machines, sensors and systems will be interconnected in real time.
   ii. Data-rich environments will enable granular control and diagnostics at every step of the production process.
3. Edge and cloud computing
   i. Edge computing will allow faster, local decision-making on factory floors.
   ii. Cloud platforms will unify data from global operations for enterprise-wide optimisation.
4. Collaborative robots (cobots)
   i. Cobots will work *alongside* humans in safer, smarter ways.
   ii. They will be used especially in assembly lines, quality inspection and packaging.
5. Digital twins
   i. Virtual replicas of factories, machines or processes will enable *simulation*, *testing* and o*ptimisation* before physical implementation.

6. Cybersecurity-driven automation
   i. As automation increases, so do cyber threats.
   ii. Future systems will have built-in AI-powered *threat detection* and *response.*
7. Sustainable manufacturing
   i. Automation will help reduce waste, energy usage and emissions.
   ii. Carbon footprint tracking will be embedded into systems via automation tools.
8. Human–machine collaboration
   i. Future automation will *augment* rather than replace human roles—especially in decision-making, supervision and exception handling.
9. Low-code/no-code automation tools
   i. Operators and engineers will design workflows and automation logic without deep coding knowledge.
10. 5G and next-gen connectivity
    i. Ultra-fast and reliable networks will allow *real-time data exchange* across distributed industrial sites.

We will discuss a few of these key trends in this chapter.

The 3 Ps: Process Automation, Plant Machinery, People Enablement

Any conversation on manufacturing automation quickly tends to get very technical and complex. To make it a bit simpler and to logically divide the areas of automation, it is helpful to divide the entire scope of automation into three simple categories. Let us call them the 3 Ps of automation: *p*rocess automation, *p*lant machinery and equipment, and *p*eople enablement. These are the three pillars of any manufacturing facility, big or small.

Process automation controls the physical process of manufacturing, starting from the raw materials through every step of value addition to the finished products. Sophisticated automation improves the process, safety, efficiency, throughput and quality of the products. Automation for plant machinery and equipment helps control the complex procedures that use this equipment for various critical manufacturing operations. Automation helps in increasing the plant's effectiveness, reducing upsets and breakdowns and increasing the life of expensive machines and equipment.

The people who are responsible for various departments of the manufacturing facilities can also be aided by automation. Automation makes the workers effective, helping them know what is happening and why and what actions may need to be taken in case of any abnormal situations. Companies who are global leaders in their respective manufacturing industries take this comprehensive approach to deploy automation for their process of manufacturing, plant equipment and people workflow. Unlike a decade ago, before they embark upon a large roll-out, they now have a way to check out the impact and benefits in a virtual world using digital twins.

Digital Twins: Helping Take Automation to the Next Level

The world over, manufacturers are under intense pressure to meet global demand under increasingly challenging circumstances. In a resource-constrained environment where talent gaps and supply chain shortages are the norm, digital twins are emerging as a frontrunner technology for scaling capacity rapidly, increasing resilience and driving more efficient operations. In fast-paced, continuous operations, manufacturing digital twins—real-time virtual representations of the entire manufacturing facility—provide manufacturers with the ability to support faster, smarter and more cost-effective decision-making. They can deepen manufacturers' understanding of complex physical systems and production operations, optimise production scheduling or simulate 'what-if' scenarios to understand the impact of new product introductions and so on.

Digital twins are a computer-simulated representation of a physical system. They are also real-time virtual renderings of the physical world. Digital twins can be developed for individual products, assets in the factory, the entire manufacturing facility and end-to-end systems across the complete enterprise. While each of these twins answers different, specific questions, they all enhance the understanding of complex physical systems and improve their operations, automation philosophy and overall decision-making.

Process Twin

This is a fully digital representation of individual products, which captures the as-built condition in detail, assisting with root-cause problem solving of quality defects, warranty analytics and product improvements.

Asset or Equipment Twin

A real-time representation of factory assets, informed through PLCs, sensors and IoT devices, these twins enable predictive maintenance and help optimise manufacturing yield, energy consumption and throughput.

Manufacturing Facility Twin

A complete manufacturing plant or factory is digitally represented using data feeds from assets, manufacturing execution systems, enterprise resource planning and human–machine interfaces, enabling dynamic, automated production scheduling and what-if scenario analyses.

Enterprise Twin

This is the most extensive digital twin, covering large portions of the supply chain from suppliers to production and distribution centres. These twins can help unlock advanced planning benefits as they work across a larger part of the system and not just a specific aspect.

When most people consider digital twins, they think of the visualisation and simulation tools used to develop innovative new products. Offshore oil platforms, racing sailboats, luxury automobile engines, hotels and train stations are just some of the things that have been designed and refined using advanced digital simulations. These use cases represent a fraction of what digital twins can accomplish. It is helpful to think of digital twins less as a tool for designers, engineers and manufacturers and more as a laboratory in which nearly any organisation can optimise its most precious resource—information—to continually push the boundaries of what it can accomplish. By using data to mirror real-world situations, digital twins can be deployed to create, fine-tune or entirely re-imagine nearly any complex process or system, including supply chains, public transit systems and manufacturing assembly lines.[2]

Connected Automation: IIoT

Automation accompanied by digital transformation is at the very core of business today, yet many manufacturing companies still struggle to execute on this imperative. The Covid-19 pandemic has made this imperative even more pressing: companies that don't act with urgency to get through the crisis and recovery mode risk falling behind at a time when they can least afford to. Among the slow adopters are those companies struggling to implement the IIoT, considered as pivotal to the future of manufacturing. The IIoT approach helps connect the three Ps mentioned earlier—process, plant equipment and people—in a unified automation system. Effective digital transformations are business-backed and business-led. Digital transformation is about envisioning how technologies like IIoT can redefine value creation by accelerating and scaling existing operations, rethinking how customers are served and reinventing business models. It's a complete re-imagination of the way work is done. Above all, it is about a new way of competing in the manufacturing sector.

IIoT, combined with other manufacturing automation technologies, is already delivering significant value to many manufacturers, big and small. One reality business leaders cannot ignore is the role they must play in driving digital transformation, achieving end-to-end impact from IIoT. Adopting advanced digital technologies takes enterprise-wide commitment from the top leadership. To ensure widespread adoption and momentum, companies must view digital transformations as a business-led transformation. Business leaders must start with a clear vision and then consider the technologies that they will need to advance that vision. While some efforts may fail, leaders must learn from them and try again by encouraging cooperation and collaboration among business units and forging a strong sense of unity. The entire enterprise must pursue digital transformation as one, with a strong sense of collaboration and urgency—urgency because digital transformation is a matter of competitive advantage. No company can be completely ready for such a transformation as it is a journey and not a destination. Transformation is a work in progress, and agile methods that support and enhance it can ease this transformation. Adoption delays only result in a painful catch-up game, which is often futile.

Finally, leaders must consider the capabilities that will accelerate and reinforce transformation, such as a scalable IIoT architecture or a technology partnership in an ecosystem that will reinforce and amplify the benefits. They must demonstrate the positive impact an IIoT-based digital transformation can bring to all the stakeholders and help build sustainable employment in the future, which is a true win-win-win for employees, partners and the entire business.

Industrial Cybersecurity: An Imperative for Digitalised and Connected Automation

As the world becomes more digital and connected, the threat of cyber-attacks grows with it. This is an obvious vulnerability.

Therefore, it is important to understand it and make provisions. The work to prioritise assets and risks, evaluate controls and develop remediation plans can be a tedious, labour-intensive affair. Specialists must review thousands of risks and controls and then make ratings based on individual judgement. Some organisations mistakenly approach this work as a compliance exercise rather than a crucial and mandatory business process. Without prioritisation, however, the organisation will struggle to deploy resources effectively to reduce cybersecurity risk. Financial considerations may turn board members off from the need to invest in these safety measures if they aren't aware of the implications it can have.

All data and systems are not created equal. In any organisation, some of the data, systems and applications are more important than others. Some are more exposed to cyber-risks, and others are more likely to be hacked into. Critical assets and sensitivity levels also vary widely across sectors. For manufacturing systems, for example, the most sensitive asset is typically production control and information systems. Some other data such as corporate social responsibility programmes and their funding may even be publicly available. Risks to critical data include breach, theft and ransomware attacks. In the last few years, several manufacturing organisations have had to shell out a ransom to hackers that had seized control of their manufacturing systems. In similar incidents, a few oil and gas operating companies were brought to their knees by cyber-attacks that incapacitated their production and financial systems.[3]

Each industry has specific needs and unique priorities. An oil and gas operating company needs to protect its hazardous operations and safely run its complex chemical processes. Any attack on its operations and transactions systems can compromise its entire business. An aerospace-systems manufacturer needs to protect intellectual property as well as system designs and process methodologies. A financial services company requires few controls for its marketing materials but is vulnerable to fraudulent transactions; its consumer and M&A database, furthermore, will need the best protection money can buy. Attackers can be individuals or organisations, such as criminal syndicates or governments with significant resources at their command. The attacks can be simple or sophisticated, the objectives varying from immediate financial reward to competitive or even geopolitical advantage.

Automation systems today, and in the future, need to pay special attention to these details and require specialised industrial cybersecurity protection to avoid attacks. Automation providers must continuously upgrade and enhance their systems and software to help their industrial manufacturing customers to manage vulnerabilities.

Once these vulnerabilities are identified and addressed with a properly strategised and supported industrial cybersecurity cover, the full potential and benefits of connected automation and its associated IIoT ecosystem can be realised.

AI: Taking Automation to Autonomous

Rapid developments in the field of AI have paved the way for multiple possibilities. One such possibility is to blend AI with automation technologies and to create a new world of 'intelligent automation'. The buzz around GenAI is loud and ubiquitous. Much is being said about this branch of AI. However, in the world of mission-critical manufacturing facilities, applied automation must be 'deterministic'. Everything that needs to happen must be firm and non-probabilistic. Hence, the AI technology must be much more developed and trustworthy. The outcomes from an AI algorithm that are fed to the automation system must be dependable and error-free, else the consequences can be disproportionate and, at times, disastrous. To ensure this, many enterprises are perfecting the more difficult branch of AI—machine learning. Machine learning is a subset of AI that allows computer-based systems to learn and improve without being explicitly 'programmed'. It uses algorithms to analyse large amounts of data, learn from the insights and then make informed decisions. As machine learning models can learn from data without relying on rules-based programming (otherwise known as unsupervised learning), with sufficient 'training' and vast amounts of data, it can become deterministic. Machine learning came into existence as a scientific discipline in the late 1990s as steady advances in digitisation and cheap computing power enabled data scientists to stop building finished models and instead train computers to do so.

Change is coming so fast that human-in-the-loop involvement in all decision-making is rapidly becoming impractical. Looking three to five years ahead, we expect to see far higher levels of AI as well as the development of distributed autonomous systems (DAS). These self-motivating, self-contained agents, formed as corporations, will be able to carry out set objectives autonomously without any direct human supervision. Some DASs will certainly become self-learning and self-enhancing. One school of thought views DASs as a threatening proposition.[4] But by the time these systems fully evolve, machine learning would have become invisible in the same way technological inventions of the 20th century disappeared into the background. The older technologies get refined and rooted in the newer evolving technologies. As they mature, they are taken for granted. Upon maturity, they are expected to be harnessed and put to appropriate use. When automation moves towards autonomy, the role of humans will be to direct and guide such machine learning–based algorithms in the background to seek even more highly complex, multidimensional goals and objectives that are otherwise extremely difficult to achieve manually.

No matter what fresh insights such DASs bring out, only human managers can decide the essential and relevant questions, such as which future business problems a company or a manufacturing facility is really trying to solve. Just as humans need regular reviews and assessments, so do these 'intelligent systems'. Their work will also need to be regularly evaluated, refined and perhaps even 'fired' or shifted to pursue entirely different 'roles' by AI-aware executives with real-life experience, wisdom gathered over time and industrial domain expertise. The solution will be neither machines alone nor humans alone but the two working together effectively.

Before we get to the fully developed DAS, there is one more stage—intelligent process automation (IPA). In simple terms, IPA 'takes the robot out of the human'. IPA leverages a set of new technologies that combines fundamental process redesign with robotic process automation and machine learning. It is a suite of business-process improvements and next-generation tools that assist the knowledge worker by removing repetitive, replicable and routine tasks. It can radically improve manufacturing by simplifying interactions and speeding up processes. IPA mimics activities carried out by humans and, over time, learns to do them even better. Traditional levers of rule-based automation are augmented with decision-making capabilities thanks to advances in deep learning and cognitive technology. IPA promises radically enhanced efficiency, increased worker performance, reduction of operational risks and improved response times and customer journey experiences.[5]

Digitally Native Manufacturing: An Innovative Concept in Manufacturing Automation

Digitally native plants are new-generation operating plants that are self-evaluating, self-learning and self-optimizing. These autonomous plants will run at the highest overall equipment effectiveness and lowest operational risks and have operational flexibility to be profitable in a dynamic market environment. They will be built on a scalable digital platform that enables direct 'edge to cloud to edge' communication architecture where feasible, potentially flattening the conventional Purdue Model. The Purdue Model is a framework for industrial control systems security that helps protect OT from malware and other attacks. It is based on the idea that separating IT from industrial control systems and industrial infrastructure can help keep these environments secure.[6] Disruption of Purdue Model–based architecture will lead to a fundamental shift in the way the life cycle of a plant and its automation will be managed.

Manufacturing automation providers of digital technology, control systems, sensors, valves, IT hardware and software and advanced applications will have to think differently to deliver a digitally native plant. The operators will need to upskill their workforce and redesign the organisation and work processes to fully leverage the potential. The autonomous plants will challenge existing industry guidelines and best practices around safety and reliability and will need plant operators to influence governing bodies to ensure alignment with the new technology and organisational capabilities. This is a fundamental re-imagining of various models and process manufacturing.

Throughout the life cycle of a plant, digitally native plants can achieve the following objectives:

1. Manufacturing plant: design phase
   i. Minimise total cost of ownership over the life of the plant by tightly integrating digital technologies (for example, advanced simulation, digital twin) from design to operations to optimisation
2. Building the manufacturing plant
   i. Reduce commissioning, start-up time and time to full-capacity operation by instituting digital-ready instrumentation and control requirements from design, automating procedures and software-defined control to future-proof OT systems
3. Stabilisation and successful operations
   i. Run flexible operations to adjust to market demands at lowest costs and higher efficiency with real-time automated and AI-optimised control
   ii. Significantly reduce plant personnel requirements with autonomous and streamlined plant workflows from operations, maintenance and compliance, using advanced tools with human-in-the-loop automation
   iii. Minimise risk to digital and capital assets through real-time visibility to cyber threats and opportunities
   iv. Overdrive ESG goals with real-time sensing and analytics of process and emissions and closed-loop corrective actions for driving sustainability goals

4. Organisation and operating model
   i. Maximise the effectiveness of the workforce with 'connected everywhere' industrial workers armed with sensors, VR/AR and digital handheld devices that provide guided instructions and on-demand training over high-speed cellular or wireless networks that are always connected
   ii. Upskill and reskill the workforce through AI-driven knowledge platforms, anywhere anytime 'experiential training' and frictionless access to remote experts

Digitally native plants are built with a strong edge-to-cloud strategy. Cloud provides the advantages of faster software deployment, lower maintenance cost through shared infrastructures and automated updates, unlimited and flexible computing and storage scalability and lower carbon footprint through shared resources and efficiencies of scale. The smart edge-to-cloud architecture delivers optimised performance, scale, latency and security based on the application requirements. Unlike the past, adding sensors (sensorisation) and connecting the machine to the edge network can now be done through a plug-and-play model. This is a new-age concept that encompasses all the latest technologies blended together for a greenfield manufacturing facility. It has great potential to bring a paradigm shift in the way the industry designs, builds, operates and improves manufacturing plants in the future.

Industrial Automation: A Vital Ingredient for 'a Developed India' Dream

As we all know, manufacturing plays a vital role in the development of a nation. India wants to be a developed nation by 2047, a hundred years after Independence. It will soon become the third largest growing economy.[7] Manufacturing must become a cornerstone of India's economic growth. As of now, the Indian manufacturing industry generates roughly 17 per cent of India's gross domestic product (GDP), with it targeted to reach approximately 25 per cent by the end of 2025.[8] The Indian manufacturing sector is steadily moving towards more automated and process-driven manufacturing, which is projected to improve efficiency and enhance productivity. To boost productivity, efficiency and global competitiveness, state-of-the-art automation is a must in conventional manufacturing industries such as automotives, engineering, energy and chemicals, pharmaceuticals and consumer durables. But it also needs to be incorporated as an integral part of new industries such as e-commerce, giga-factories, electronics and semiconductors and green fuels such as sustainable aviation fuel, compressed biogas, green hydrogen and so on. What got us here will not take us to the desired destination. Indian businesses will need to compete in global markets. Digital transformation with modern automation is a key aspect in gaining an edge in this highly competitive marketplace.

India must develop the capacity to export goods worth US$1 trillion by 2030. To get on this road to becoming a major global manufacturing hub, embracing industrial automation is imperative. India must continue to develop its physical and digital infrastructure to raise the share of the manufacturing sector in the country's economy and work hard to establish itself as an important link in global supply chains.

A globally competitive manufacturing sector is India's greatest potential to drive economic growth and job creation in this decade. Several factors contribute to this potential. A few of these favourable factors are availability of power/energy, long-term employment prospects and basic skills that can be honed further combined with a growing domestic market. This gives India a significant opportunity to engage in international markets. However, to convert that opportunity into reality, a few things must happen such as expanding exports from India (global scale and quality manufacturing), aggressively localising imports ('Make in India'), encouraging internal demand (fiscal and monetary policies) and contract manufacturing (taking advantage of the 'China+' movement). With digital transformation being a crucial component in achieving an advantage in this fiercely competitive industry, technology has sparked creativity. The manufacturing sector in India is gradually shifting to more automated and process-driven manufacturing, which is expected to increase the efficiency and boost production of the manufacturing industry. Indian businesses are gradually adopting Industry 4.0 through the Government of India's initiatives like the National Manufacturing Policy. This will enable the government to achieve its target to increase the share of manufacturing in the GDP of the nation from 14–16 per cent in financial year 2024–25 to 17–18 per cent by financial year 2026–27 and move towards the aspirational goal of 25 per cent eventually.[9] The financial incentives provided by the Indian government under the Production Linked Incentives (PLI) scheme for manufacturing businesses is also expected to help the manufacturing sector in modernising its production facilities to be at par with global manufacturing standards.

Furthermore, the Indian government has announced incentives of up to ₹18,000 crore (approximately US$2.2 billion) to boost local manufacturing in sectors such as auto components, automobiles, chemicals, electronics and medical devices, to mention a few.[10]

This is not just about boosting the manufacturing sector but also about creating much-needed jobs for the youth of the nation. One good example of such a success story is the manufacturing of smartphones in India. The smart mobile phone manufacturing industry anticipates creating up to 250,000 direct and indirect jobs at a steady rate, driven by government incentives and increased global demand.[11] Major players are expanding their workforce to meet growing production needs. This model needs to be repeated in several other manufacturing sectors.

Automation has a significant role to play here to enable job growth as manufacturing facilities grow. To begin with, it can help bridge the gap between a new inexperienced worker and a seasoned worker with more than twenty years of experience. Automation can equip a raw worker to perform closer to the level of expertise expected and help train a new batch of recruits. New-age automation can enable manufacturing businesses to skill people differently, using systems aided by AI/machine learning for higher throughput and productivity while helping to achieve world-class quality at affordable costs. Additionally, smart automation can substantially improve employees' workplace safety.

The benefits are many, and the good news is that it will create jobs for the new-generation workers and, in parallel, drive India's ambition to be a developed nation.

MSME Inclusion: A Critical Must

A simple internet search can reveal to us that the MSME sector in India is a key contributor to the country's economy, providing jobs, driving exports and contributing to economic development. Here are some data points:[12]

1. Job creation: The MSME sector employs over 110 million people.
2. Helping the nation's exports: MSMEs account for about 50 per cent of India's exports.
3. Significant contribution to the GDP: The MSME sector contributes about 30 per cent to India's GDP.
4. Contribution to the manufacturing sector: MSMEs make up 45 per cent of India's manufacturing sector.
5. Overall development: MSMEs help develop rural and backward areas.
6. Accretive growth: The MSME sector has grown significantly, aided by government initiatives and entrepreneurial spirit in India. The MSME sector is growing at a higher rate than GDP growth (approximately 7 per cent).

The new automation technologies are inclusive of MSMEs. Otherwise, a large portion of the manufacturing sector and a significant part of the GDP will be deprived of it. Therefore, while top manufacturing companies adapt to these technologies, automation providers must consider MSME needs and requirements.

Automation can significantly improve production processes in the MSME manufacturing sector. It can help manufacturers reduce labour costs, increase productivity and lower the risk of human error by automating repetitive tasks and processes. Automation can also give manufacturers more flexibility in production, allowing them to respond quickly to changing market and consumer demands.

A good automation deployment in the Indian MSME industry will help with:

1. Business and revenue growth
2. Enhanced workplace safety
3. Cost optimisation and improved profitability
4. Higher productivity driven by better decision-making
5. Product quality and consistency improvements to mention a few.

Barriers for MSMEs to adopt a good level of modern automation have been cost-to-benefit considerations, lack of access to the relevant technology and automation products, and poor understanding of the applications of such modern technology in production facilities. Once these barriers are overcome, the adoption rate of modern automation will grow rapidly. Today, the large automation providers focus on the needs of large corporates. It is understandable as the large corporates are the automation vendors' largest revenue drivers. Adoption of new technologies can bring a pivotal shift in such a disproportionate focus and can prove to be a win-win for both the automation providers and the MSME sector.

As an example, growth in cloud-based pay-as-you-use models can make the latest automation and control technologies available to a large number of manufacturing MSMEs at a relatively lower cost. This is because the combined cost of hardware, software and the operational expenses can now be distributed over a large number of MSMEs and, hence, can be made affordable to them while satisfying the business expectations of automation providers. Imagine a cluster of MSMEs that need a SCADA system for their operations. Individual MSMEs may not be able to afford a sophisticated SCADA system. However, if the SCADA system is hosted on a common cloud that can be accessed by a group of MSMEs, the cost per MSME comes down. Similarly, when such digitisation is deployed at a manufacturing facility, it needs a cybersecurity cover to protect itself from malware and cyber-attacks. Individual MSMEs may not be able to afford independent cybersecurity solutions. However, if hosted in a cloud-based architecture, the same cloud-hosted SCADA can be cyber-secured at a fraction of the cost. This concept can be extended to several automation technologies that can be made affordable and scalable for a cluster of MSMEs. Much work needs to be done to facilitate such systems, and MSMEs should be educated to adapt to them.

With such an approach, the MSME sector can be modernised, made world-class in its manufacturing capabilities and further integrated into the global supply chains to make India a significant manufacturing hub. Therefore, it is mandatory to include MSMEs in this journey to embrace modern automation.

In Conclusion

The journey of automation has come a long way. It is aggressively embracing new and diverse technologies to become even better. Progress in the field of AI is adding several new dimensions to automation and is marching towards autonomous systems. The manufacturing sector is poised to benefit significantly with the help of such automation systems.

As India prepares itself to be in the top three economies on the planet, the manufacturing sector is going to play a vital role in its nation-building ambition. MSMEs, being a large part of this sector, will need to be included in this mission. A globally competitive and differentiated manufacturing competence will need advanced automation adoption by MSMEs and large corporates. The good news is that this offers ample scope for renewed imagination, innovation and creativity for the nation. It needs to be embraced with arms wide open.

With inputs from Ashish Gaikwad, Managing Director, Praj Industries Limited, and former Managing Director, Honeywell Automation India Limited.

8

AI Changing Our Lives

THE WAY WE WORK will undoubtedly change substantially as the technologies of AI mature and usage in organisations matures beyond the early hype. What is not so clear and possibly more ominous is the impact that AI will have on the way we live, learn and interact with other humans and with AI itself. There are three schools of thought emerging—one that this is just a passing fad that will have little or no impact in the long term on the way we live, and the second an extreme viewpoint that says we will all be relegated to moronic followers of AI wizards who will run our lives. A third and possibly wiser view that emerges from previous experiences argues that our lives will be made substantially more comfortable and we are entering an era of self-assured comfort and happiness.

To analyse these possibilities in detail, this chapter takes us on a tour of all the activities that fill our lives from cradle to grave and explores possible evolutionary and revolutionary impacts. But to tease the imagination, let us point you to two experiences that we have had in the past few months. The first was a movie made in 2022 titled *The Artifice Girl* about a revolutionary AI-embedded robotic girl who is created to catch online predators. The intelligence of the character gets sharper and deeper as the movie progresses and finally confounds not only the creators but the robot itself. The movie ends with a truly poignant scene of the robot teaching herself dancing to relieve the boredom of dealing with human beings—quite a paradox![1]

The second experience was a packed auditorium in Manhattan, New York, in September 2024 when celebrity historian and author Yuval Noah Harari spoke on his latest book *Nexus*. He made a stunning assertion that dictatorial forms of government would benefit greatly from the inherent centralisation of power that AI supports. To illustrate his point, he asked the audience to imagine the all-knowing KGB in the high-espionage days of Russia. AI would have given them the power to not only track the movements of every citizen in the country but also to use their entire words and deeds footprint to predict who would be a future threat to the regime. Threats could be eliminated even before they themselves thought of committing acts against the regime. Do the Israel Defence Forces already use such tools in their systematic targeting and eliminating of individuals in the Hamas and Hezbollah? If they don't today, they will tomorrow![2]

We will start our tour of future AI touch points with a child's early contact with the world through education, progress through skills that make young people job-ready and look at the evolving world of healthcare and entertainment. We will then look at mobility and how this whole field is changing with AI. Finally, we look at the way relationships will evolve and change in an increasingly AI-charged world.

Education Models for the Future

Education has evolved substantially since the days when all kids in India were sent to a playschool at the age of three and graduated to nursery, kindergarten and finally to a regimented school curriculum designed for rote academic learning rather than any personalised learning discovery process. Content and pedagogy designed for the average student tended to exclude the bored intelligent lot and the weak learners. Indian readers may recall that it is only after the movie *Taare Zameen Par* hit Indian screens that challenges like dyslexia became known to the average Indian parent.[3] In this context, there is an enormous added value that AI can provide in the planning and delivery of personalised education.

In the classroom, AI can provide valuable assistance in grading. Ganesh remembers that in his tenure at Harvard Business School, the professor disappeared after every class to individually grade students on class participation. When learning moved to a synchronous online mechanism called HBX with seventy students arrayed on a screen in front of the professor, it made it possible for an intelligent AI eye to observe each student and potentially give assessment recommendations to the professor. This assistance provided by AI to grade finalisation automatically frees up more time for course preparation and instruction.

Classroom organisation, too, can be transformed through algorithms that can ensure that similar profiles are matched and learning opportunities are created from peers with different yet interesting experiences. While most of us may have grown up with a 'best friend' who stuck with us through school and sometimes college, progressive schools like the United Nations International School in New York experiment with changing classmates at regular intervals and also matching kids of different nationalities to give the children a truly global experience.[4] In packed classrooms like the ones we have in municipal schools in India, such assortments may be difficult to achieve, but AI algorithms can help in identifying pairing possibilities based on class performance and a 'big brother is watching you' approach to enhance classroom behaviour!

Classroom content generation and test paper generation is a very easy application of technology and may not require AI, but generating additional content or easier explanations with otherwise abled children in the classroom may make the learning experience more homogenous. AI can also assist in predictive and prescriptive analytics based on classroom behaviour and test result patterns. The real value of an AI-assisted approach through ten to twelve years of a student's progress through school education would be to have an assistive friend who monitors, provides nudges when necessary and makes the entire learning process more personalised, adaptive, pleasurable and productive!

It could be argued, and indeed we, the authors, believe, that extensive AI usage might quell the desire in children to seek out the truth on any subject on their own and reduce the pleasure of search and discovery that is so much a part of the learning process. However, the history of technology has shown that every advancement and aid to the capabilities of the human brain results in new explorations and the use of the brain in newer avenues of pursuit. The learning process has to be more expansive. The test papers have to probe intelligence rather than memory, and new pathways to learning will need to emerge to tease the imagination of the young learner.

Impact on Skills Development

There has been tremendous progress conceptualised and delivered in the last few years in the area of skills. A case in point is corporate learning, where organisations have procured hundreds of e-learning course modules for their employees only to find that both usage and course completion rates have been abysmal. The reasons for this poor response are many but can mainly be attributed to a feeling of 'why on earth should I learn this stuff?' in employees and the inability of purely e-learning approaches to personalise the learning to individual needs.

Enter AI, and the entire approach and pedagogy can be transformed. A wonderful India-developed platform, Skills Alpha, works through a five-phase model that is transforming learning effectiveness in organisations by:[5]

1. Capturing previous appraisal and performance data about the employee
2. Engaging through a bot to discuss the career aspirations of the person and explore various options and the unlearning, reinforcement learning and new learning needs to be qualified for the chosen role
3. Analysing the track record of learning that the person has demonstrated through available data and choosing the right pedagogy for maximum learning effectiveness. This could be as simple as choosing video courses rather than text or increasing levels of complexity in course design for the individual.

4. Measuring learning effectiveness through the courses completed by the person and also integrating the outcomes of courses taken outside the learning platform with quantitative and qualitative data capture
5. Assigning a mentor who has traversed the track a few months or years earlier to guide the person over learning doubts and difficulties and later help the person to navigate situations that may have an adverse career impact

The future of AI in enabling better skills development is only limited by our imagination. With so much data available as the social construct of each individual on the internet, it is within the realm of reason to assume that every step of skills development can be re-engineered for learning effectiveness.

Beyond the skilling process itself, there are many contemporary skills that get individuals jobs and careers that can be transformed by AI. Cases in point are many and can be broadly categorised in three buckets.

1. Industry-related skills, where awareness needs to be built on the nuances of the industry that people are getting trained for. In the previous chapter, we have detailed the opportunities for AI in many industry sectors, and job seekers in these sectors would do well to be trained by AI-on-AI opportunities. Whether it is superior shop floor techniques for the manufacturing industry or intelligence predictive analytics for people entering healthcare, every industry has nuances that need to be quickly learnt and mastered to build career success.
2. Technical skills can also be taught with large doses of AI input. A welder can master his craft better if he is watched and guided by AI on better techniques suited to his hand flexibility, and a supervisor managing an automated plant can be guided on potential failure points to look out for through years of past performance and failures and likely future occurrences.
3. Soft skills are where AI can probably play a very

> substantial role in building better supervisors and managers. Every situation is different in a working environment, but there have been situations where decisions taken on impulse without adequate data have resulted in suboptimal outcomes. Predictive and prescriptive analytics can be brought into play to enhance the percentage of good decisions made by managers and leaders. AI can play a significant role in enhancing the style flexibility of supervisors too. AI can analyse the behaviour patterns of each member of a team and guide the supervisor on responses as well as the mode of taking corrective action with any delinquent subordinate. Over thirty years ago, one of the authors had an opportunity to go through an interactive learning course where an aspiring leader could sit at a console with seven or eight people at a conference table on the video screen in front of him or her. In a situation where one member seemed to be dozing off in the meeting, the leader would be presented with three or four options: to ignore, to request attention or to admonish in a loud voice. Watching the response would guide towards a better action in each situation. Today, with AI researching every past action and outcome for each individual, the guidance could be very granular, customised to each team member. The possibilities are truly infinite, and much can be predicted and used to guide actions in future.

The most endangered skills will be those that have enabled nearly a million Indians to build global careers in the world of IT and BPO services for third-party as well as global capability centres that dot the Indian landscape. These are programming or coding, testing and offshore maintenance services. Coding has for long been the sought-after skill for youth across the country, and it is necessary to understand whether this will become entirely irrelevant in the years to come or whether there are still areas that young career aspirants can and should pursue.

AI is certainly capable of generating code for any development environment and can also correct or complete code written by programmers for previous applications. Detecting and fixing bugs, testing for completeness and optimisation are all within the purview of AI code generators. Development cycles in large systems development projects can definitely be accelerated by applying 'dual intelligence', an approach that has been advocated by new data company GTT Data Solutions as the optimal approach to combine human and AI to tasks and programs of the future.[6]

What then are the areas where human intelligence will continue to score over AI, at least in the foreseeable future? When one of us asked our personal AI what it saw as its current limitations, it quickly confessed to falling short in human judgement and empathy, context and intent understanding, creativity and navigation of ambiguity and complex decisions. The passionate trainers of LLMs would scoff at these and throw a couple of graphics processing units at the AI to overcome these limitations faster. The Chinese creators of DeepSeek would enhance its distillation and inference capability to discern emotions and modify behaviour based on what it perceives. However, there is no doubt that the data-information-knowledge-wisdom quartet that many of us have traversed will take AI a lot of learning to master. This may raise the issue of what a young inexperienced software engineer should learn to start his career in these complex times, which may have to be answered differently with every cycle of AI evolution.

Healthcare for a Changing World

With ageing populations in every country, the provision of health to all segments of the population is proving to be the biggest challenge for country leaders and healthcare providers. The nature of diseases has also been changing. Ageing problems related to diabetes, cardiac ailments, nervous and muscular weakening, memory loss and the onset of Alzheimer's disease and much-dreaded cancer are becoming more and more common and widespread as life expectancy increases and more people look forward to longer retirement periods and want to work and enjoy life through the autumn of their existence.

All this has placed substantial demands on primary and secondary healthcare systems in every country. The pressure on advanced economies like the United States of America, Western Europe, Japan and the ASEAN (Association of Southeast Asian Nations) countries is being matched by the expectations from governments in developing nations like China, India and much of the Global South to invest more and demonstrate care for their citizens through improving focus on their well-being.

We can broadly categorise the potential role of AI in four buckets: accuracy of data capture and timely dissemination, effective preventive care and early diagnosis, predictive and prescriptive healthcare for each citizen, and improvement of healthcare ecosystems in communities and countries. If addressed holistically with a real desire to transform, the results can be thoughtful and, in many cases, dramatic!

Timely and accurate data capture has many challenges. Data quality has always been suspect with many cases going unreported and undiagnosed. In advanced countries, data privacy considerations have also inhibited sharing of critical data, creating an inability to consolidate and come to any aggregate conclusions. AI has the potential to change this, gathering information from formal sources and informal exchanges, but the fine line between sharing and privacy has to be watched all the time. Availability of clean medical records for each citizen, to be made available to the doctor or surgeon the patient chooses to confide in, is one of the most fundamental imperatives, and AI has a role to play in identifying potential data sources as well as possible flaws in the gathered data.

In preventive care and diagnosis, AI has already started playing a very major role, with AI-driven risk assessments in communities based on living and eating habits and AI taking the lead in developing a baseline and triggering actions for disease prevention during normal times as well as during significant events like floods, cyclones and even epidemics. A number of measuring and early warning devices are prevalent today. Many hospitals in India use a number of devices to continuously track health in ageing populations and for post-hospitalisation patients who need regular monitoring. This also takes away the pressure from physical health check facilities and monthly visits to a general practitioner in already overcrowded medical systems. AI assistance in pathology, medical imaging analysis and telemedicine for remote consultations has already significantly improved the efficiency and effectiveness and nationwide uniformity of medical consultations. The use of mixed-reality solutions like VR consultations with 'experts', which may soon happen in the metaverse, can have significant psychological and real impacts on citizens.

AI-Powered Chatbots for Patient Support

In the area of predictive and prescriptive medicine, significant advances are being made through AI-driven risk assessments, health monitoring and the availability of rich machine learning data to support the diagnosis and treatment prescription for any patient. AI is assisting doctors and surgeons before, during and after the interaction with patients. AI is also encouraging many young career aspirants to choose healthcare because of the amount of support they can get from technology. It is also providing hospital administrators, nurses, paramedical staff and doctors a learning environment that gives them cutting-edge skills and understanding of diseases and treatment.

Improvement of the health ecosystems in communities and countries could well be the long-term boon that AI bestows on society. Medical research speed and quality enabled by large-scale processing of data through disease-specific LLMs and accelerated clinical trials will lead to faster drug discovery and AI-facilitated collaborations between large and small medical research facilities and research establishments and pharmaceutical boutiques and giants. Ganesh had a discussion with the global chief of one of the world's largest technology firms at a CEO dinner in South India.

The American CEO was celebrating the installation of what was then the most significant AI computing environment in an Indian medical and research facility, and when Ganesh mentioned his daughter was a research head at one of the largest such facilities in North America, he was told that the facility there had seen the first installation of the same AI environment. Messaging with his daughter during the dinner, Ganesh told the CEO that she had not seen much value from the installation, and he received a quick counter: 'That's the exact point of AI. It taps into the brains of top-notch brains like your daughter and helps lesser trained researchers and practitioners in other parts of the world to learn and adopt the same principles.' Sales pitch or reality? Only AI can tell!

In the United States of America, the use of IBM Watson Health systems, Microsoft Health Bots, Google's DeepMind Health and Amazon's Comprehend Medical solutions are omnipresent, and institutions like Mayo Clinic, Stanford Health and the Memorial Sloan Kettering Cancer Center have been exemplars in using AI solutions. From an environment where a major proportion of healthcare information has been unstructured to the use of AI in a majority of healthcare organisations and widespread use of AI for diagnostics and treatment, there is no doubt that enhanced use of AI will improve transparency, reduce healthcare costs, greatly reduce errors and improve the quality of patient care.

Impact on Entertainment

The best way to introduce this section on the role of technology, specifically AI technologies in entertainment, would be to start with an example from the 1990s that underscores the increasing importance of entertainment in our lives. In an interesting collaboration, two of the authors, Uma in her role as CEO of Zee Education, the learning arm of Zee Telefilms, and Ganesh, then CEO of APTECH, a household brand for computer education, decided to launch a television-based computer education programme called *The A to Z of Computers*. In what was going to be a significant departure from the video and television-based education programmes that had been launched by some highly renowned government institutions, they decided that education would work best if it was mixed with entertainment. A young couple, Shyam and Angel, were introduced as the anchors of the programme. The then prime minister Narasimha Rao endorsed the programme, and history was created by the number of learners who benefited from this unique mix of education and entertainment.

Today, this example is no longer the exception. It has become the rule that boring books and learning content no longer suffice for an increasingly impatient generation of youth who seek quick gratification and interesting experiences in education, enlightenment or just entertainment. For instance, virtual and augmented reality could be used to change the aquarium experience for young children. All of us have been taken by parents to aquariums where there are fish swimming in various tanks, and we are expected to read the engraved descriptions to understand the characteristics of each fish. Very little learning truly happens, but by using these new technologies, children can be encouraged to pick one out of a dozen fish outlines on paper and also to draw and paint on it to develop the fish they like. This fish is scanned, and the children will see their fish appear and swim in the audio-visual environment that is created. Then can follow an amazing hour or more when the children's fish encounter water companions and discover their characteristics by experiencing their actions and even avoiding predators like sharks. The learning and retention experience through this highly interactive process would be many times better than wandering around an aquarium, though the fish are simulated and not live.

In this context of expectations, we dive into the role of AI in entertainment. These range from the somewhat mundane acceleration of content production to quick dissemination to the more complex areas of hyper-personalisation, the use of AR and VR, and the enormous opportunities that lie in the area of gaming. For the entertainment enthusiast or the commercial opportunity seeker, this is arguably the most productive area for growth in the use of AI.

The composition of new scripts, music and audio and video special effects is the obvious area of AI deployment where the development of a new story idea with language that is appropriate for the target segment can be quite easily done by technology and delivered across multiple media. Companies like Kantar Media and Nielsen are able to capture audience response to every variation in screenplay and sound effects to enable producers of OTT seasons to learn from the experiences of previous seasons and garner additional viewership as the popularity of shows goes up with targeted variations.[7] However, the borderline between AR and fake representation on audio and video of popular stars of the silver screen will need careful tracking to avoid doubts about the reality of what people are watching, which will steer attention away from the narrative or the story itself.

In the area of content dissemination and distribution, the use of AI in choosing the appropriate channel for distribution of any content has been implemented with good impact on viewership for the last few years. Entities like Facebook and Google have practised AI-enabled targeted advertising for many years and also used the power of their acquisitions to garner intelligence from one app and use it to showcase purchasing options across the network. Entertainment will soon be served up on predicted demand to each individual in a family or community based on perceived preferences. Will this completely eradicate the concept of family entertainment, and will the group visit to the cinema for a popcorn and movie evening become an anachronism? Maybe not immediately but eventually without a doubt! One cannot rule out either the power of persuasion that AI can catalyse. Influencer marketing has been a phenomenon restricted to millennials and Gen Zs for some time, but influencers will be able to plant ideas in the minds of many citizens, which will be reinforced by marketeers seeking to exploit a forming opinion to sell more of their brand.

Harari provides a real-world and somewhat disturbing description of the role social media and specific apps can play in forming public opinion and fomenting a whole movement in society. The case in point is the targeting of the Rohingya community in Myanmar, which was initially caused by one religious activist who posted divisive and hate-filled comments against the community on a well-known social media app. There were, as there always is, voices of reason that tried to assuage the feelings of the Myanmar majority, which is when, Harari suggests, the social media app realised that fanning the flames of hatred had more potential for attracting eyeballs and maximising time spent on the app than the peace-generating attempts. It follows that the negative comments could be given more prominence while the positive ones were not highlighted, resulting in more voices against the Rohingyas and more commercial value for the app.[8]

While this example may not be related to entertainment, it shows the power of AI to influence at scale. Movie makers could well be using influencers and social media apps in the future to manipulate the ratings given to their productions, leading more and more unsuspecting viewers to endorse their work to avoid being part of a minority. Will that result in genuine entertainment being forsaken at the altar of manipulated public opinion? Only time will tell!

Impact on Mobility

Mobility is becoming the biggest differentiator between the developed and developing countries, and the investments being made in road, rail and air infrastructure and newer and more sophisticated means of transportation are very substantial in countries like India and other aspiring leaders from the Global South as they seek to make their impact through goods and services made and delivered better, faster and cheaper than incumbents in the Western world.

In India, the government, through the Ministry of Electronics and Information Technology's software technology parks, established in 1991 the Centre of Excellence (CoE) for Autonomous, Connected, Electric and Shared Mobility (ACES), appropriately called the MOTION CoE. With Ganesh serving as chief mentor since inception, MOTION has seen more action than most other CoEs, with large enterprises, mentors, collaborators and start-up entrepreneurs lining up to take advantage of the knowledge and capital flows facilitated by the CoE.[9] In discussions over the last couple of years, AI has been the centrepiece of conversation, given its impact on safety enhancement, efficiency and accessibility apart from sheer convenience. A case in point is the ride we took from Newport, New Jersey, to visit the Bochasanwasi Akshar Purushottam Swaminarayan Sanstha temple near Princeton. Our friend, who picked us up in his Tesla, just entered the address in his car and confirmed the driving route and was then chatting with us for the next hour without an eye on the road. The car navigated perfectly through the highway system and busy traffic in some of the towns we drove through, and we emerged fresh and unconcerned with all the traffic encountered on the ride.

Self-driven cars have been around for some time with the combination of electric mobility and AI completely transforming both driving efficiency and comfort, and the real impact will be on shared mobility with smart driverless buses operating on city streets and trucks on lonely interstate expressways. Drone taxis, drone delivery of packages and AI-coordinated convoy driving or truck platoons will soon become the order of the day, and our trains, too, can become fully supported to avoid accidents of any kind. In the EV area itself, what we have seen in the ACES CoE, and indeed what is happening worldwide, is optimisation of battery usage and placement of charging infrastructure for maximum convenience and efficiency. The mobility ecosystem also gets transformed with AI-enabled management of ride share availability, traffic flows and signals management, enhancement of current route planning and optimisation and scheduling of public transits on roads, rail and water.

Use of AI in mobility will also greatly enhance the ability of senior citizens and the physically challenged to become more independent with a host of new gizmos like smart wheelchairs and canes and voice-enabled guidance mechanisms enhancing their confidence. Over the next ten years, a major share of new cars will be electric, and over half of all transport mechanisms can be autonomous. Apart from Tesla, the automatic ride-hailing capabilities being implemented in the United States[10] and the advent of new players in China[11] and Korea[12] seeking to challenge the domination of the West and Japan in automobile brands will drive convenience higher and price points lower.

In the future, we can expect to see trends towards fossil fuel elimination and sustainability drive major AI innovations in mobility and integration of transportation systems, both private and public, with mainstream smart city infrastructure. Automatic guidance available from command-and-control centres of smart cities to individual autonomous automobiles will optimise travel efficiency, and the rides like the one we had to the temple in New Jersey will become the rule, not the exception. Traffic congestion may become a thing of the past, and safety can reach new and predictable levels. One can expect that public acceptance and trust will be easier to get in this area than in banking and healthcare through cybersecurity, and management of complex traffic scenarios will continue to be a daunting factor in the move towards an increasingly drive-free world.

Impact on Entrepreneurship

Entrepreneurship in all its forms is what is expected to change the fortunes of many young people in a world that is increasingly starving for jobs. In India, the government has launched a campaign to motivate young people to be job givers rather than job seekers through its flagship initiatives 'Startup India Standup India' and Start up Village Entrepreneurship Programme. Indeed, many thousands of people have chosen entrepreneurship and its excitement instead of settling for a mundane job. A case in point is The IndUS Entrepreneurs (TiE) in the western city of Pune, where a group of over eighty seasoned entrepreneurs have taken on the mandate of supporting hundreds of entrepreneur aspirants with a series of programmes that encourage them, provide them learning opportunities and nurture them to success. TiE has chapters all over the country and many parts of the world, prominently the United States of America, and has proved to be a major driving force for entrepreneurship, particularly in new opportunity areas.[13]

AI has proved to be both an enabler of new entrepreneurship and a source of an enormous wave of emerging entrepreneurship opportunities for generations of aspiring start-ups. To consider the second opportunity first, in a small city like Dubai, where we had the opportunity in November 2024 to meet the Minister for Artificial Intelligence, Digital Economy and Remote Work Applications and visit the newly constructed AI campus in the Dubai International Finance Centre, it was amazing to see the process by which new AI ideas are being identified and nurtured with mentors, business users and capital to enable scaling. In many cities of India as well, AI figures in the business plan of multiple start-ups who see this opportunity as the holy grail to build products and services and attract venture capital. A majority of investments in start-ups in the last two years have been in AI, and AI extensions have happened in a very high number of start-ups who have pivoted their model to include the new capabilities provided by AI.

AI is also finding its way into the value proposition of many businesses focused on education, healthcare, financial services, agriculture, manufacturing and other application areas. Given its ability to take clean data and create actionable insights, it will surely become an indispensable part of the toolkit for any entrepreneur in virtually every start-up area. AI also helps entrepreneurs to keep their costs low by automating many tasks ranging from bookkeeping and coding of applications to more complicated value additions like AI-powered chatbots for customer support and engagement in many reactive and proactive formats.

Many large firms have already started incorporating AI into their product feature sets. Examples are virtual assistants like Alexa and Siri, Einstein for Salesforce and AI add-ons to the marketing automation platform HubSpot, accounting software QuickBooks and investment platform AngelList.

AI has its downsides for entrepreneurs too, since it can create over-dependence on technology and build bias in the analysis of situations encountered in the process of serving customers. As we have repeated many times, the lurking fear of data privacy violations and cybersecurity cannot be underlined more, and entrepreneurs will have to take all precautions to ensure that their fledgling enterprise does not get derailed by unanticipated legal issues. There could also be regulatory issues since laws pertaining to AI are still in discussion within the governments of various countries.

Impact on Relationships

Late into 2024, one of us was preparing for an interesting evening where a group of us were planning to recite our favourite speeches or sonnets from Shakespeare. Ganesh, an avid fan of the play *Julius Caesar*, immediately chose Mark Antony's declamation over Caesar's murdered body, 'O Pardon me thou bleeding piece of earth', and asked the handy Meta AI on his phone to remind him of the lines. The AI provided some unsolicited information that this speech served to incite the crowd against Brutus and other conspirators. When Ganesh pointed out that it was a soliloquy and not the 'Friends, Romans, Countrymen' speech, the AI quickly retracted and, almost in jest, acknowledged its gratitude for being able to learn from Ganesh's superior knowledge of the subject. Suddenly, it became almost human in its ability to retract, correct an earlier opinion and collaborate![14]

When this kind of emotional intelligence is developed further by AI agents, they may prove to be a more sought-after confidantes and companions to many humans than our human friends. Yuval Harari has rightly pointed out that while even our best friends might respond to a conversation in different ways depending on their state of mind on a particular day, an AI companion can be relied upon to respond based on its evolving understanding of the human, without being biased by any setbacks of its own.[15] Does that mean that our future relationships with our AIs will be more meaningful and rewarding than those we enjoy with our own friends and family? Let us delve deeper into possibilities.

Scenario 1: A teacher admonishes her class for doing a shoddy job with their summer assignments and tells them they have a last chance to make good the following Monday. A smart student decides to use AI to get the assignment right and gets her personal AI to undertake a voyage of discovery into the teacher's social media persona over the summer vacation and turns it into a perfect paper, contextualised to the new preferences the teacher has developed over the vacation. This success motivates the student and indeed most of the class to bring moods and experiences into assignments, and the entire process of education and learning undergoes a dramatic change.

Scenario 2: A young lady is walking down the street when a man approaches her with a half-smile of recognition. Her new version of Google Glass does a quick scan and sends three messages to her brain through an embedded neural network—who the person is, where they have met before and would it be worth her while to acknowledge his existence and try to build a relationship.

Scenario 3: A cricketer has been out of form and wants to rediscover his batting prowess to keep his place in the team. When he walks out to play on the third morning of a test match, the coach gives him some parting ideas on how to deal with the key fast bowler from the opposing team. The advice is to play with care for the first few overs while the bowler is fresh and then start scoring. On his way to the pitch, he switches on his AI and gets the suggestion that he should score aggressively off the first few balls before the bowler gets into his rhythm.

In all three cases, AI has access to something that is unique to the context of fast-changing situations in everyday life. AI could explore recent happenings through instantaneous access to social media, which is denied to teachers, coaches and individuals relying on memory and previous experience. As people get more experienced and comfortable with agentic AI and interacting with their AI as a trusted Jeeves in all situations, the need to 'call a friend' will go down further and further. Does this endanger the long relationships we have had with parents and elders in the family, teachers with predictable idiosyncrasies, partners, mentors and coaches? Will our friendships degenerate into transactional and opportunistic dalliances as AI slowly penetrates not just our mind but also our soul? We will live and learn.

There are undoubtedly many positive outcomes that we will see in the foreseeable future enabled and often led by AI. Companionship to senior citizens at a time when more and more families are living cities or even countries apart is one of the most critical services that AI-powered apps and chatbots can provide on the mobile phones or computers of citizens. As capabilities mature, first-level diagnosis of ailments and treatment recommendations can come from AI without making a cumbersome visit to the doctor necessary, and even mental health patients can receive preliminary solutions on interacting with AI. In 2025, a woman used ChatGPT as a therapist initially, and eventually to write a suicide note.[16] There is a danger of adverse outcomes on blindly following AI advice.

On the negative horizon, the early days of AI have already seen enough hallucinations that have resulted in erroneous and sometimes extreme generalisations, and as more and more usage of AI occurs, the risk of AI perpetuating existing biases is very real. Ongoing and regular use of AI copilots and agents could even eventually result in the diminishing of human intellect as the need to explore fades and results in unused human capabilities for search and reflection. Privacy concerns are already proliferating everywhere because of rampant use of social media, and the use of AI in fake audio and video messages is harassing every user with a presence on the internet. With more and more information and contextualised knowledge becoming available to AI, privacy is expected to be the predominant concern for all intelligent humans in future.

The intrusion of AI into people's private lives is, however, inevitable. Survey Monkey mentions that 75 per cent of young people are using AI-powered dating apps, and Pew Research mentions that 40 per cent of relationships commence online.[17] As a natural corollary, relationships and communications are mainly online, and with the ease of use of AI-mediated communications in both personal and business matters, voice, video and personal meetings are already not the preferred mode and will become increasingly rare in the years to come. With AI already playing a significant role in psychiatry, therapy and counselling, the emotional intelligence of AI is increasing at a rapid pace, and it is likely that human relationships may actually improve rather than deteriorate because of the wise counsel provided by AI communication assistants and agents. As time progresses, the definitions of intimacy and relationships themselves may change, and we all have to be prepared for new ways of living, loving and working together.

Impact on Society

There is no doubt that AI will have far-reaching impacts on organisations and people and the way we learn, act and do in the future. There is also no doubt that the impact could be far-reaching and have long-term consequences on communities, countries and society and civilisation as a whole.

To grasp the enormity of the canvas in which AI can operate, let us start with a trivial example. In the short term, giving an AI tag to every existing and new object is a disservice to the true potential of AI. In his talk to a packed audience in Manhattan in September 2024, which we (Uma and Ganesh) attended, Harari spoke about how a true AI espresso coffee–making machine would behave. Through optical recognition, it already knows the preference of the person who is approaching the machine and, through AI, can also adapt the strength of each day's coffee to their mood and health on that day. When both the machine and the person are in the right mood to experiment, the machine could make a 'nextpresso' or 'bestpresso' rather than the standard espresso!

If one were to elevate the potential of AI from a mere coffee machine to the larger impact that the next avatars of GenAI can have on humanity, AGI and ASI will hold the power to predict, prescribe and even manipulate our thinking based on what is optimal for the developer. Harari has written and spoken at length about the propensity of large AI to centralise data and perform analysis of behaviour and intent that can play into the hands of dictatorial regimes. He makes the point that the dreaded KGB in the much-hated Soviet Union and possibly in Putin's Russia and the dictatorial regimes of Mussolini, Stalin and Hitler would have benefited greatly from these tools, which could have helped them to identify potential dissenters and traitors and eliminate them even before the thoughts and actions were fully crystallised in the minds of the perpetrators. He argues that an algorithm designed with wrong or inadequate rules will have the potential to drive behaviour and initiate actions that may not have been envisaged by the creators themselves.[18] While the sole individual may not have the power to influence a large population to initiate or follow an action that could result in a negative impact, rogue algorithms have the ability to accomplish such goals. As has been seen in recent times, young children influenced by certain online games have committed premeditated suicides. Algorithms with biases could deny opportunities to certain segments of the society or influence certain segments to act negatively towards other segments of the society. Hence the urgency for governance and ethical responsibility in the construct of algorithms has become critical.

Finally, with the emergence of personal AI companions on social media, it would be good to heed the prediction that an AI friend will probably be far better than your partner or best friend because it can totally align the conversation and behaviour to your needs. So, will AI companions add to the isolation of humans from the real world?

One sure factor is that the discussions around AI are far from over, and every new technology or idea emerging from the United States and China will create a new wave of discussions and arguments. AI has been going through ups and downs ever since

OpenAI launched ChatGPT and the valuation of the company soared beyond US$100 billion dollars.[19] There is no doubt that AI will be a most valued companion for all of us but there is a more cynical view that Generative AI is nothing more than a good and speedy summariser of information and one should not expect more than that. Where lies the truth? Are we going to see AI scale or head towards a rude reality check?

One reality is that that the huge monies that have been poured into leaders like Nvidia and Open AI may dry up if the present big concerns about energy guzzling by AI hardware are not addressed. The stark reality is that the world cannot afford the energy cost to power the training and implementation of LLMs that currently form the core of AI, and the large funding of processors and models of today could be wrecked by this reality.

There are workarounds, of course, and new AI specialist chip companies may emerge to compete with Nvidia, and LLMs could give way or be supplemented by more narrow AI systems that provide fewer but deeper solutions to problems within a domain. The computation costs, which are today excessive and, in many cases, comparable with LLM training costs, will have to be reduced by a constellation of AI models working in concert rather than the mega LLMs. This is the approach that China is expected to take if US embargos deny them access to technology.

It reminds me of my discussion with the chief technology officer of a premier US basketball association, the NBA, earlier this year. He mentioned that while the real skill of the charging forward in a basketball game is to race down the court and evade defenders and shoot the basket, AI could do an instant analysis of the previous games and predict the moves of each of the four players opposing the forward. This information could be automatically fed by neural networks to his brain and guide his moves. Would this be possible in our lifetime? Will it even be legal to build such applications? Governance is going to become as important as the evolutions and revolutions in technology. We are heading for interesting times for sure!

9

Leadership in the Era of AI

We have come a long way together in this book—first understanding the evolution of leadership through the ages and the progress of technology and the short but exciting journey of AI and its twin, automation, and finally exploring the role of AI in multiple domains and all aspects of work and life. As we develop a leadership model for the new AI-transformed world, let's take stock of key learnings that will go into the model development.

Digital to AI—The Continuum

AI has truly evolved through many decades of technology pushes and demand pulls in the corporate world. The biggest development that served as a precursor to the current surge of AI was the onslaught of digital technology. The constant quest for productivity improvement, automation of manufacturing through robots, re-engineering of business process through RPA and extensive deployment of digital touch points in every business has resulted in a comprehensive redesign of both internal processes and external networks. The improvement of experience, which is a second-order need after productivity gains, has been served through the integration of physical and digital experiences, data warehouses and data marts. AI and machine learning have been enabling all consumers of information to get actionable insights better, faster and cheaper. Today, it is anything as a service that attracts new customers and conceives new systems of engagement and sometimes completely redefines the scope of the business itself.

Digital business models that have emerged over the years with acceleration in the last decade have seen different enterprises emerge, embracing either the cost model, the experience model or the platform model. In the cost model, including world-beating companies like Google, Facebook and Amazon, the focus has been on free or freemium services, providing extreme price transparency, in some cases with reverse auctions and usage-based pricing to aggregate buyers and provide limitless choice to consumers. The experience model, driven by the likes of Netflix, Apple and Disney, has enabled reduced friction and personalisation, leading to higher customer discretion and gratification with automation driving empowerment. Finally, the platform model emerged to bring multiple customers together for multiple vendors and service providers with new entities like Flickr and Uber and incumbents like Siemens and General Electric offering platform solutions. These platforms have created new ecosystems for commerce with self-forming communities and data orchestration to ensure clean information comes to a digital marketplace frequented by all participants. Imagine an Indian village *haat*, and you will get the picture of how platforms work on the internet.

To use an oft-repeated cliché, data has emerged as the new oil for commerce with data playing multiple roles, primarily as a creator of new assets, including digital content, and providing capabilities to enhance human intelligence and creativity. In other roles, data becomes an enabler of business goal setting and attainment, a utility to be tapped for diverse requirements and a driver of new business ideas and accelerated achievement of goals. This has led to a continuum from data to information to knowledge to wisdom in several stages of progression over the years. The first use of data was the ability to analyse transactions and provide reports and presentations in a descriptive and diagnostic format. Remember the monthly analysis of slow and non-moving items in inventory that material managers would get as a fat heap of computer stationery in the early days of electronic data processing? Being able to ask questions ranging from 'what happened' to 'why did it happen' and 'what can happen' moved both thinking and capabilities from descriptive to suggestive, and as data moved from the enabler to driver role, and machine learning and AI started emerging, prediction truly became power. The final frontier has been the change from 'what could happen' to 'what should happen', and data has become a creator of suggestions, unleashing the power of prescriptive analytics.

This is the stage where leaders must play a role in defining boundaries for the role of AI and setting up robust governance mechanisms as we will see as we progress through this chapter. As AI itself has progressed in the last couple of years through newer versions of ChatGPT and LLMs to distillation models like DeepSeek and small and narrow language models and, finally, to semi-autonomous and near-autonomous agentic AI, the capabilities of AI and the propensity to take over more and more of the responsibilities and actions of humans has become a threat to the future of human workers. When should the leader step in?

The Enterprise AI Horizon

As we have seen through the chapters of this book, the reach of AI has spread wider and deeper in every organisation, and where it has been embraced by all echelons of an organisation, it has had far-reaching impacts in every domain and across all functions. Possibly the most impacted function has been sales and marketing, which has been most exploited in media, professional services, technology and new industries. However, the use of AI has also been significant in product or service development, knowledge management, operations planning and control, and strategy simulation and finalisation. Over the last ten years and more, customer journeys and employee journeys have also been the subject of much experimentation and solution building.

Customer journeys involve a deep analysis of the customer's awareness of the product, their consideration criteria, evaluation and price, alternative discovery process and, finally, the buying decision, including dealing with buyer's remorse after the order has been placed. For the digital touch points and AI designers, this will involve detailing each customer persona, setting process and outcome goals for each person and designing the points of brand interaction. Maximising benefit perceptions at each moment of truth and the willingness to revise the customer journey, evolve new touch points and adapt the process and analysis with each new moment of epiphany are essential to build vibrant customer journeys.

As we have discussed earlier, employee journeys designed with AI bots and agents are not just touch points in a learning journey. They can be a game-changing rethinking and redesign of the entire career planning and management process. A new product called Skills Alpha has a bot popping up as soon as a person logs in. For a new person, it engages in a conversation to discover career objectives and presents alternative career options. Once the option is chosen, it suggests skills to be reinforced and new skills to be learnt and presents optional paths for learning. In addition, it assigns a coach from within the organisation to assist the learner and keeps sending prompts and checking to assess the progress on the learning and career path. AI-enabled career management is now a heady mix of contextual curated learning sources adapted to the individual learning style, teamwork, collaboration, internal social networks, coaching, expert inputs and mentoring and providing accountability to the sponsor, the HR function and the overall goals of the team and the enterprise!

The horizons of enterprise AI are fast changing, with falling costs enabling the barriers to AI adoption to diminish and disappear rapidly and the performance levels increasing as AI's ability to respond to prompts and process tokens approaches near real-time. In addition, the hallucinations are coming down, and decision quality and accuracy are accelerating. Slowly but surely, AI is moving from a new toy or novelty to a business necessity for every industry, enterprise and every part of the organisation.

AI in Every Domain

Whichever industry an organisation is in, there are applications of AI that affect all stakeholders—employees, customers and supply and demand chain partners. A quick tour of key players in BFSI, manufacturing, retail and hospitality will give us a sense of what is the opportunity area in front of leaders today.

Leaders in BFSI in India like the State Bank of India and Bajaj FinServ have been able to create an AI-supported integrated financial view of their business. AI is now a layer that sits on top of their technology and comprehensive applications portfolio, predicts and prevents frauds in the system and enables all key activities of customer acquisition, credit planning and allocation, loan management, retail and corporate activities and wealth management. Robo advisers in wealth management have proliferated for years, but now GenAI and agentic AI solutions are providing precision on all predictive and prescriptive applications.

In manufacturing, leaders like Siemens and Bosch, which have already used digital twins to simulate future factories before actual construction and factory layouts are done, are experimenting with AI-managed automation that manages every part of the plant and maximises uptime, uses Edge AI solutions in manufacturing and uses the power of quantum computing, robotics and AI to optimise every aspect of production and materials planning, warehousing and plant movement and integration with enterprise resource planning systems.

In retail, global majors like eBay and Amazon have led the way, and companies like Flipkart in India have created AI-led seamless shopping experiences, implemented AR- and VR-based 'try-on' systems for consumers, personalised recommendations, conversational AI, sentiment analytics and smart inventory management to minimise both shrinkage in stores and disappointed customers. AI-led loyalty programmes are also being deployed to maximise customer satisfaction and minimise enterprise costs.

In a final domain example, the hospitality industry has seen a lot of churn with an old market leader, Thomas Cook, declaring bankruptcy in 2019 after having been a market leader in travel and tourism for over a century. Nimble players like Expedia, Airbnb and Booking.com internationally and Make My Trip in India have implemented dynamic pricing models, immersive metaverse experiences with VR, autonomous robotic hotel check-ins, facial recognition for security and guest service, and predictive analytics for loyalty programmes.

To conclude this section on the state of the art in AI applications, one can say that AI is emerging as the future of everything. Agriculture is being transformed with intelligent drones and crop planning. Systemic AI is transforming healthcare from diagnosis to clinical treatment to robotic surgery. Education and skills are becoming adaptive and personalised, and mobility and urbanisation are changing rapidly through intelligent automation. The future is all about our imagination.

The concern for leaders should be twofold: Are we using enough AI, and also are we becoming over dependent on AI? As enterprises move beyond the sentence-completing GenAI to independent work done by AI agents and the inexorable move to AGI and ASI likely in the not-so-distant future, the leader must develop a comprehensive strategic planning and risk mitigation and governance framework for AI and finally embark on a new model of leadership to succeed.

Planning for 'Game-Changing' AI

Now that we have discussed every possible aspect of processes, technology, applications and future scenarios for AI, it's time to focus on the role of the leader in delivering 'game-changing' AI to the organisation. Our research took us to in-depth discussions with three well-known leaders in diverse fields—Suresh Narayanan, chairperson and managing director of Nestlé India; Kiran Acharya, the former managing director of Sandvik Cormorant; and Tapan Singhel, managing director of Bajaj

General Insurance. A few vignettes from these discussions are presented here to set the scene for our analysis on the role of leadership for future AI-enabled organisations.

Suresh Narayanan, the former chairperson of Nestlé India, in a telephonic discussion with the authors in January 2025, stated his belief that analytics and digital technologies have been the real accelerators. They have helped in deconstructing market opportunities by geography, channels and consumer clusters and unblocked the obstacles that were not scientifically possible in India in an earlier era. Focus on analytics has enabled Nestlé to capture insights from thousands of distributors nationwide with algorithms that focus on 'sell-through' data. That data can be fed into the planning mechanisms of the company to improve the efficiency and effectiveness of demand forecasts, supply chain optimisation and factory productivity.

He believes that AI in the organisation is still at the experimentation and functional usage stage but fully AI-integrated planning models will be implemented over the next couple of years, giving speed, flexibility and insights. He believes the real role of AI will be insight generation, and many countries in the Nestlé global organisation have already started replicating the algorithms that have been implemented in India. A version of ChatGPT customised to the organisation, named NESTGPT, has connected people across geographies and functions to generate insights on brands, stock-keeping units, margins and profitability. He also suggests that while AI is a great generator of information and insights that can inform and inspire, there is still some hesitation in using it for external communications and commercials because the intellectual property rights of an AI-generated product are questionable.

Kiran Acharya believes that we should be clear what is a necessity, what is comfort and what is a luxury. Automation is quite mature in that sense, but AI will go a step further and improve the quality of decision-making. He also believes that in industries like machine tools, AI will be able to transform productivity not just at the tool level but across the entire system of production. Every machine action would be an algorithm, and the combination of digital, automation AI and human intelligence and sensitivity would drive superior performance in the future.

Tapan Singhel believes that more and more processes will start moving to the front end, and over time, AI will make the back office in services organisations redundant. Clients will be enabled for direct access to systems, reducing the friction of an intermediary, and all processing will become straight through. While this is still in the future, the active use of copilots and bots has made every document an intelligent source of information, and AI is generating knowledge for use without duplication of effort. However, resilience, empathy and the solution-seeking approach will still be done by the 'human in the loop' with assistance at all levels from AI.

He also sounds a note of warning that we should not be nodding to the use of AI without actually getting into details on the realised benefits and a real understanding on what problem is being solved beyond productivity improvement and what additional benefits are being targeted and realised.

Industry leaders have very positive views on the role changes for employees, managers and leaders of the future. Great employees of AI-ready organisations will have the capability to ask the right questions rather than providing all the answers. They will understand technology without being besotted by it. Managers will enable the transition of teams to being digitally friendly and AI-ready without pushing people beyond their comfort zones and encourage the development of multiple skills while retaining and sharpening their emotional sensitivity. They also caution that no manager or employee can get into the comfort zone of coming to the workplace every day and do what they have always been doing. They must use AI to challenge their assumptions and add value in new ways to their role, their teams and the organisation.

A clear area of consensus is that the leader is very much required, not as a data manager or a solution provider, which AI can do with speed and accuracy, but as an orchestrator of ideas and a strategist and future planner for a function or an organisation. As specialist roles in digital and AI disappear and every employee and manager is expected to feel comfortable with technologies in the way they think and work, the use of emotional intelligence will become essential. Leaders must continue to be curious and stay on the cutting edge of any kind of circumstantial change within or outside the organisation. Leaders must also have the wisdom to go beyond the hype, not getting carried away by multiple GenAI pilots blooming all over the organisation but continuing to ask what customer, employee or business benefit this will translate into. Leaders must play an even bigger role in designing the new roles of technology and humans and ensure that the organisation derives the best from the capabilities of both.

Drafting a comprehensive AI strategy for the organisation should be on top of every leader's agenda. It would necessitate aligning ambitions with a reality check on the status of key pillars of AI, identification of potential barriers and a strong focus on data engineering and the data to GenAI and agentic AI journey. There has to be a balance between acceleration versus caution and we have to put in place strong measures for ROI at every stage of the implementation. Let us understand what this entails.

AI and Leadership Styles—A Symbiotic Relationship

Would Henry Ford, Vladimir Lenin and Steve Jobs globally or Jawaharlal Nehru, Manmohan Singh and Narendra Modi, with their very different styles of leadership, have used AI very differently? In our context, your three authors, who have different leadership styles, use AI in different ways even today. Ganesh, with his penchant for leading multiple diverse teams with tremendous delegation and support rather than supervision, uses AI as a reference to get wider perspectives on any topic. Uma, who is much more of a detail manager, uses AI extensively to support her research and predict what could go wrong in situations and contexts. Priyanka uses AI as a support system for her writing and also to do prior research before conducting an interview. We all find AI useful but in various modes and to different degrees.

We have already discussed in an earlier part of this book the views of historian and author Yuval Noah Harari and his concern that AI in the hands of a paranoid leader like Lenin could have led to the targeted destruction of humanity. Whether it is for a dictator of a nation or a leader of a religious group or even a social worker with a large following, there is no doubt that malicious use of AI could have an undesirable impact. The religious group leader could identify members of his flock who have some reservations about his value based on an AI scan of social media posts and make targeted efforts to assuage their misgivings and win them over as total converts. On the other hand, there are also the positive impact of algorithms. The social worker, for instance, could use AI to identify potentially disenfranchised members of the community and ensure that the service provided by the social enterprise is able to reach that part of the geography or community. Social media algorithms could help connect like-minded people to foster a sense of belonging and build meaningful engagement. Through personalisation, they help people discover or stumble upon subjects and themes that could be of interest.

In terms of leadership styles, each style would find different aspects of AI worth exploring and exploiting in designing their message and adapting their style. A strong, autocratic leader would use AI more as a tool to learn customer preferences and not be really concerned about any negative impact their style has on their team or organisation. A democratic leader might be more inclined to extensively use AI as a copilot and, with the right prompts, let it provide usable guidance to his or her work. A coaching leader would use AI to work with team members and mould the advice to suit individual learning styles. Leaders who are used to practising situational leadership with style flexibility to respond and lead in different ways, depending on the situation, would be able to use AI to predict the response to each style and choose the appropriate response or action for each situation.

The use of AI is both a science and an art. How we perceive it and how it is deployed is a matter for much experimentation, learning and future use!

Leading with Dual Intelligence

The 'human in the loop' as a necessity for successful deployment of AI has been, in many cases, a defence mechanism against concerns regarding the future sweep of AGI and ASI across business and society and a genuine paranoia about the future of jobs. The potential does exist for all mundane and repetitive jobs, arguably well over half of the current jobs in the services industry, to be taken over by AI and for a larger number of manufacturing jobs to be eliminated by the wide sweep of robotics, automation and AI at the edge. The deployment of AI could accelerate preventive and corrective action in large process plants that could greatly improve plant uptime and throughput. The task of analytics and feeding actionable insights to final decision makers could well be done better, faster and cheaper by predictive and prescriptive analytics enabled by machine learning and AI.

How do leaders design new organisation structures and business processes in a true spirit of dual intelligence that will harness the power of technology and deliver 'order of magnitude' superior results? As AI agents take over various tasks and goal achievement by experimentation and simulation, team structures, roles and reporting relationships will have to be thought through. It would be appropriate to focus on the very human capabilities of emotional intelligence, context setting with soft data and use of the experience of decision-making to inform future decisions. As agents proliferate, humans will also have to be encouraged and trained to evolve, and frameworks will have to be developed for humans to delegate goal achievement to technology and create feedback loops that lead to optimised decisions. There will be inevitable power dynamics, not just between humans and agents but also between AI-enabled humans in the organisation. These again are issues that will need effective leadership to gauge and develop and implement solutions. Teams and individuals will have to be assigned and trained for prompt engineering as well as more complex roles, while agents are assigned all the predictable, standardised analytical and execution tasks.

The style of the leader in a well-designed dual intelligence establishment will also encompass creating new vistas of growth for the human intelligence community. These growth opportunities include developing a new vision for the process and the team and building vision communities empowered with innovation and some clairvoyance.

Areas Where AI Can Only Augment Leadership

If one thinks of great leaders we have heard of, such as Mahatma Gandhi, Martin Luther King, John F. Kennedy and Ronald Reagan, or superb leaders we have worked with or are becoming, a few areas where humans absolutely cannot be replaced with AI, at least till the much-touted AGI descends on us, immediately come to mind.

1. Recognise the tone of conversations. How often do good leaders intuitively respond to a choking voice or a raised tone, almost instinctively, and adapt their response to suit the new situation?
2. Grasp emotional needs of people. This wisdom comes from the experience of working with each individual over a period of time. Good leaders know what gets the best out of each person and are able to adapt their style for each member of their team.
3. Understand the context of a discussion. In many cases, looking at a transcript without understanding what was the prevailing situation and who had said or done what prior to the discussion makes it impossible to come to a judgement. Human intelligence in such cases is essential for taking a rational and positive decision.
4. Include subjective elements in any situation analysis. This is often done almost without apparent thought by good leaders because they can predict the outcome of any decision. They also know the background of views expressed and can understand the nuances before coming to a conclusion.
5. Take final decisions without having all the facts. This is one of the most important characteristics of great leaders who believe that 90 per cent decisions taken with only 60 per cent of the facts are often far more beneficial to an organisation than 60 per cent decisions taken after waiting

for 90 per cent of the facts. But no algorithm today can help AI to take such decisions.
6. Create a coherent and credible story to explain rationale. The art of storytelling that many leaders have mastered over years of managing and leading is an invaluable addition to their winning toolkit.

In all these cases, AI can help in adding information and past data-based inputs but cannot play a lead role. Hence, it is also important for humans to realise that if they have to lead effectively and leverage AI to the fullest without any of the consequential risks, they have to play a key role in three areas:

1. Choose areas for AI deployment with discretion and wisdom. This can result in substantial acceleration of fact-based decision-making, better simulations before choosing a path forward and avoidance of calamities like unsupervised prediction and action.
2. Consider the ethical implications of each deployment. It is quite possible that as AI progresses, it is able to identify the weaknesses of an employee or a customer and take decisions that end up being intrusive or manipulative. This must be anticipated and avoided to maintain the goodness of the organisation.
3. Redesign the organisation with responsible AI. This is where the ultimate benefits of a complete redesign, taking cognizance of the amazing capabilities of AI and yet mitigating the risks of uncontrolled AI, will lie. Wise and constantly learning and evolving leaders will be needed to craft the AI strategy and deploy it for organisation transformation.

Planning for an Uncertain Future

It would need a very insightful soothsayer to predict where AI is heading and how much our lives will change as we choose to ignore or prepare to embrace AI. Thinkers and scientists in Silicon Valley and other parts of the world are already saying that AGI is inevitable, and from there, super intelligence with all its unpredictable ramifications and impact might well be just a few steps away.

Ethan Mollick, author of the very insightful book *Co-Intelligence—Living and Working with AI* has, in the concluding chapter, 'AI as our Future', presented four possible scenarios for AI in the future.[1] The first is that AI is as close to being the best as you will ever see and future improvements will only be incremental. This can only happen if climate change activists, worried about the large power consumption of LLMs, or AI safety experts convincing governments to ban all AI development, have their way, which is unlikely and certainly not sustainable in a fast-changing and intensely competitive environment of innovation. There is already a deep distrust in anything that appears in media, particularly social media, and the easy fake replication of voice and images will erode the credibility of anything we see or hear as time passes. Chatting with bots will also reach its natural level of exhaustion, and in the absence of extreme innovation, AI will stay and be embraced by many but only as a complementary force to the ever-increasing capability of humans. Did we hear a sigh of relief at this scenario?

The second scenario is not very different from the first and envisages growth but at a slow pace. New methods of leveraging AI, as we have already seen when DeepSeek was launched by China, and more optimised power utilisation mechanisms will slow the pace of development, but innovation will continue. AI will add more value in the workplace, and coalitions of companies and governments will limit the harm that unregulated growth in AI in a country or an industry could have unleashed. AI will, however, play a much larger role in scientific research and discovery in all corporate settings and take a larger and larger role in our lives. Humans will remain in control.

The third scenario is more on the lines of exponential growth. AI companies using AI systems to create the next generation of

AI software might create the flywheel effect on AI acceleration. The negative impact of this is the unpredictable bad outcomes that might accompany or even precede positive new discoveries, such as the creation of a new deadly nerve gas while the search for a new drug is in progress, and AI-powered dictators using the tool for ubiquitous surveillance on the unsuspecting masses. AI companions, as we already see in the movies, could become more compelling to speak with than humans, resulting in new types of social isolation. Though AIs will still not be sentient in this scenario, partnering with researchers, physicians and mathematicians might enable AI to develop and wield new powers on the rest of us. This could be just the beginning as AI could then reach a take-off point, a level of ability when it moves towards AGI and potentially an intelligence that is far greater than what humans can ever possess!

The final scenario is what Mollick calls the 'Machine God', where machines have attained AGI and sentience and help design AIs even smarter than themselves till superintelligence emerges. Will humans then cease to be of value to AI and become merely a nuisance or a potential source of molecules? As Geoffrey Hinton, one of the godfathers of AI who left the field in 2023, has said, 'It's quite conceivable that humanity is just a passing phase in the evolution of intelligence.'[2]

Having painted this awful scenario, which is seen as credible by some and ignored by many, let us build our strategy on the assumption that doomsday is not near or inevitable and a carefully planned dual intelligence strategy, with the 'human in the loop' always in control, is most likely to prevail if articulated, designed and implemented by all of us.

Crafting the AI Strategy

A well-thought-through and articulated strategy aligns the entire organisation to enterprise-wide deployment and a reassessment of each individual's role in the future organisation. This shift is necessitated by the fact that almost all organisations have stated aspirations to deploy AI, with substantial use already initiated in many organisations. The strategy is also important because in most organisations, there are only a handful of use cases reported and the value being derived is rarely quantified, while the stated board or leadership goal is full deployment in a couple of years.

To start the journey towards realising these soaring ambitions, the foundations have to be very strong in infrastructure, data management, ecosystem development and governance. The IT department of the organisation will be well positioned to provide a status on the infrastructure, calling out outdated systems and both hardware and software that needs to be upgraded or replaced. Data is a complex issue since many organisations, even some medium to large ones, have not really worried too much about the data quality, particularly when data is ingested from external sources. This assessment may need help from external experts in data engineering and the design of data warehouses and marts and a well-defined process of storage, dissemination and conversion to information. Business process re-engineering is a valuable precursor to new systems deployment. The enabling ecosystems of demand generators, data suppliers and process managers must be brought together to re-imagine any business process that can benefit through technology touch points. As an integral part of the strategy development process, security assessments for systems and data are essential. The Digital Personal Data Protection Act, which is a mandate for all Indian corporations, and implementation of strong cybersecurity solutions for data and systems are essential. All this needs to be under the cover of a well-designed governance framework, which will reassure the board of directors and the entire organisation that the strategy is robust and all control systems are in place.

Leaders must recognise and articulate that the success of game-changing AI will depend on strong data foundations and streamlined data flows, strategic partnerships with competent vendors, deployment of the right tools and a strong preference for use cases that go beyond point solutions to system-wide implementation that targets and achieves sustainable competitive advantage for the organisation. Notably, maintaining data quality as it moves between models and applications, particularly for sources and destinations outside the organisation, is part of the tracking of lineage. Eliminating non-automated data handling, ensuring data liquidity by creating seamless access with the right tools and combining multi-source data for comprehensive analysis are key focus areas for leaders, and they also need to ensure that data management is made more efficient through the creation of a metadata layer that enables ready contextualisation for all users.

The continuous need to balance innovation and risk and choose between first-mover advantage and safety and security of proven methodologies is the real role of the leader. Many large enterprises cite governance concerns as the biggest deterrent in their transformation journey, which is understandable, given their accountability to a large employee and shareholder base. This also emphasises the imperative to embrace an AI-powered organisation under the overall control of intelligent humans. This is particularly important as the organisation's AI journey moves from using traditional databases to LLMs and from GenAI to AI agents and autonomous AI agents that learn user preferences over a period of time and can make independent decisions based on the unique situation and context. With all the data, information and knowledge that this journey will generate, the wisdom of the leader will be called on to make appropriate choices and move to a phase of dual intelligence.

Designing for Excellence

We have discussed already that the important role of leaders in an AI-charged organisational context is risk and security management. GenAI in its early implementation has been notorious for hallucinations, bias and misinformation, and while accuracy improves through repetitive use, there has to be constant vigilance for errors. On the security front, data leakage, poisoning by external injection of unvalidated data and corruption by unchecked human intervention will all have to be guarded against.

Steps in designing and implementing true enterprise transformation can be broadly grouped into the following:

1. Establish a top-level vision after assessment of the current status of technology, process, culture, common digital language and understanding of leadership.
2. Select business and functional domains that are the highest priority, and develop a road map for the next two to three years, subject to periodic progress review.
3. Form cross-functional teams that can experiment and recommend process changes and technology touch points, and develop a new operating model for scale.
4. Choose core AI platforms that lend themselves to digital workflows and are optimised for 'human in the loop' check points.
5. Establish governance structures, continually assess risks and ensure compliance.
6. Monitor the deployment of AI across workflows, processes and systems; watch for inefficient human–AI collaborations that could sabotage the role of the human; and identify and scale successful use cases.
7. Promote a questioning and innovation culture across the organisation, provide ample upskilling opportunities and ensure leadership engagement through the journey of implementation.
8. Combine dramatic process transformation efforts with a climate of continuous improvement and innovation. Measure the ROI and operational impact of every stage, and take corrective action early.

Measuring the ROI in AI is a combination of hard and soft measures. The cost reduction, time savings and productivity increases that are measurable must be targeted and achieved or exceeded, but equally important are improved experience for all employees, leading to being a 'great place to work' and attracting new employees to the organisation. Increased innovations at individual, team and organisation levels with constant creation of new products, processes and potentially new business models are all likely and very desirable outcomes of this strategic approach by leaders!

A Final Word on Leadership

In this journey through the book, if some of you have felt overwhelmed by the thought that this is too much transformative change for the leader to manage, and the entire strategy and implementation is best delegated to an expert team within or from outside the organisation, you are likely to lose the plot and, eventually, your place at the top of the organisation chart. Strategising and implementing a game-changing AI scenario in any organisation needs the complete involvement and understanding of the leader and the leadership group and their personal attention to the transformation that will need to unfold. The choice and deployment of technology, the re-engineering of business processes and orchestration of data flows are all too important to be delegated or abdicated. This means that the leadership group has to first equip itself with knowledge and not technical but application understanding. They should not be afraid to educate themselves in areas where there is initial discomfort. Building the AI-transformed organisation is a journey, not a destination, but clear goals and milestones can be set for the progress that must be made in transforming processes, functions, people and the organisation. In the words of Swami Vivekananda, 'Arise, awake and stop not till the goal is reached.'[3]

Acknowledgements

THIS BOOK IS THE result of a collaboration between many like-minded people whose passion for dual intelligence has driven us to reflect on our experience as technology practitioners and evangelists and work together to present our ideas for the future.

Uma and Ganesh have collaborated on four books on knowledge management, digital success, *nari shakti* (women empowerment) and India's pathways to success in the past, and this book was a logical repository for their current research and advisory work. Priyanka has been an active journalist and writer for over two decades and shares Uma and Ganesh's passion for technology. We are grateful to Rohini and Ashish, who shared their experiences and expertise on AI and automation, and to the many industry leaders who presented their views on the future of leadership.

We are obliged to our mentors, Padma Vibhushan Dr Raghunath Mashelkar and Padma Vibhushan Dr Vijay Kelkar of the Pune International Centre, and Chandra, our publisher across many books from the 1990s, for their continuous support and for Bloomsbury's excellent editing and publishing teams.

Finally, this book has been a true labour of love, and we are grateful to Ganesh and Uma's daughter, Karuna, and her husband, Hugh, and Arun, her son, and to Priyanka's husband, Amol, and son, Kabir, for their support, which gave us the time to finish this book on schedule.

Notes

INTRODUCTION

1 Digitide Solutions Limited, https://www.digitide.com.
2 Yuval Noah Harari, *Nexus: A Brief History of Information Networks from the Stone Age to AI* (UK: Penguin, 2025).
3 Bhushan Patwardhan and Indu Ramchandani, *Genome to Om: Evolving Journey of Modern Science to Meta-Science* (Noida: BlueOne INK, 2024).

CHAPTER 1 EVOLUTION OF LEADERSHIP CONTOURS

1 Homer, *The Iliad* and *The Odyssey*, trans. R. Fagles (London: Penguin Classics, 1999).
2 'Veni, vidi, vici', Wikipedia, https://en.wikipedia.org/wiki/Veni_vidi_vici.
3 Valmiki, *The Ramayanam*, trans. W. Buck (Berkeley: University of California Press, 1976).
4 Ved Vyasa, *Mahabharata*, trans. C. Rajagopalachari, 64th edn (Mumbai: Bharatiya Vidya Bhavan, 2010).
5 'Introduction to Alexander the Great', Pothos, https://www.pothos.org/content/.
6 'Mongol Culture and Religion: The Power of the Eternal Blue Sky', History through Fiction, https://www.historythroughfiction.com/blog/mongol-culture-and-religion.
7 R. Desai and V. Pande, *Shivaji: The Great Maratha* (New Delhi: Harper Perennial, 2017); Setu Madhavarai Pagadi, *Shivaji* (New Delhi: National Book Trust, 2011); Jadunath Sarkar, *Shivaji and His Times* (London: Longmans, Green and Co., 1920); Govind Sakharam Sardesai, *Chatrapati Shivaji Maharaj*, Marathi (Pune: Varada Books, 2022).
8 'Simon Bolivar', Wikipedia, https://en.wikipedia.org/wiki/Simon_Bolivar.
9 'The Global Catholic Population', Pew Research Center, 13 February 2013. Available online: https://www.pewresearch.org/religion/2013/02/13/the-global-catholic-population/.

10 Conhard Hackett et al., 'Islam Was the World's Fastest Growing Religion from 2010 to 2020', Pew Research, 9 June 2025. Available online: https://www.pewresearch.org/short-reads/2025/06/10/islam-was-the-worlds-fastest-growing-religion-from-2010-to-2020/.

11 Pavan K. Varma, *Adi Shankaracharya: Hinduism's Greatest Thinker* (Chennai: Tranquebar, 2018).

12 A matha is a Hindu monastery that serves as a centre for religious and philosophical learning and a residence for ascetics and monks.

13 Kandadai Seshadri, 'Ramanuja: Social Influence of His Life and Teaching', *Economic and Political Weekly*, 31 (5): 292–8.

14 Nicholas Fairweather, 'Hitler and Hitlerism: Germany Under the Nazis', *The Atlantic*, April 1932.

15 Stephanie Hodgson, 'Hitler and Mussolini: A Comparative Analysis of the Rome-Berlin Axis 1936-1940', E-International Relations, 29 July 2011.

16 'Joseph Stalin', History Crunch, https://www.historycrunch.com/joseph-stalin.html#google_vignette.

17 Tania Branigan, 'A Tragedy Pushed to the Shadows: The Truth about China's Cultural Revolution', *Guardian*, 19 January 2023.

18 Eijiro Hazama, 'Unravelling the Myth of Gandhian Non-violence: Why Did Gandhi Connect His Principle of Satyāgraha with the "Hindu" Notion of Ahiṃsā?', *Modern Intellectual History*, 20 (1): 116–40.
Parvesh Kumar, 'Impact of Gandhi's Activism on Dalit Empowerment: Unravelling Complexity and Progress', *Educational Administration Theory and Practice*, 30 (5): 14133–9.

19 Swami Nikhilananda, *The Gospel of Sri Ramakrishna* (Chennai: Ramakrishna Math, 2006); original in Bengali: M. Gupta, *Sri Sri Ramakrishna Kathamrita* (Kolkata: Kathamrita Bhavan, 1902); Max Mueller, *Ramakrishna: His Life and Sayings* (New Delhi: Niyogi Books, 2019); Swami Saradananda, *Sri Ramakrishna, the Great Master* (Chennai: Ramakrishna Math, 2011).

20 Raymond Franz, 'The Process of Institutionalization of Christianity', Mentes Bereanas, 22 July 2020, https://www.mentesbereanas.info/en/processofinstitutionalization/.

21 A.C. Bhaktivedanta Swami Prabhupada, *Bhagavad Gita as It Is* (Mumbai: Bhaktivedanta Book Trust, 2019).

22 'How Kamaraj Pioneered the Mid-Day Meal Scheme', *Madras Courier*, 3 October 2023. Available online: https://madrascourier.com/biography/how-kamaraj-pioneered-the-mid-day-meal-scheme/.

23 Matthew Boulton and James Watt, *The Selected Papers of Boulton & Watt: The Engine Partnership 1775–1825*, ed. J. Tann (Cambridge, MA: MIT Press, 1981).

24 'Richard Arkwright', Linda Hall Library, 3 January 2022, https://www.lindahall.org/about/news/scientist-of-the-day/richard-arkwright/.

25 'George Stephenson', Tees Valley Museums, https://www.teesvalleymuseums.org/object/george-stephenson/.

26 'Keating-Owen Act', Wikipedia, https://en.wikipedia.org/wiki/Keating%E2%80%93Owen_Act.

27 Chris Calton, 'Henry Ford Did More for Workers than Unions Did', Intellectual Takeout, 7 January 2020, https://intellectualtakeout.org/2020/01/henry-ford-did-more-for-workers-than-unions-did/.

28 Obi Tabansi, 'Frederick Taylor and the Time and Motion Study', Supply Chain Nuggets, 8 July 2023, https://supplychainnuggets.com/frederick-taylor-and-the-time-and-motion-study/.

29 M.T. Briggs and C.H. Peters, *Pullman Company Archives* (Chicago: The Newberry Library, 1995). Available online: https://www.newberry.org/uploads/files/PullmanGuide.pdf.

30 Andrew Carnegie, *Autobiography of Andrew Carnegie & the Gospel of Wealth* (New Delhi: Sanage Publishing House, 2021).

31 International Labour Organisation (ILO), *The World Labour Report 2000: Income Security and Social Protection in a Changing World* (Geneva: International Labour Office, 2000). Available online: https://www.ilo.org/sites/default/files/wcmsp5/groups/public/%40dgreports/%40dcomm/%40publ/documents/publication/wcms_publ_9221108317_en.pdf.

32 Philip T. Hoffman, 'Why Was It Europeans Who Conquered the World', *Journal of Economic History* 72 (3). Available online: http://piketty.pse.ens.fr/files/Hoffman2012.pdf.

33 'Jute Trade', Wikipedia, https://en.wikipedia.org/wiki/Jute_trade; 'A History of the Lancashire Cotton Mills', Make It British, 30 August 2025, https://makeitbritish.co.uk/blog/lancashire-cotton-mills/.

34 Steve Novak, 'The Story of Bethlehem Steel Ended with Its 2003 Sale. But Its Fate Was Foreseen Much Earlier', *Lehigh Valley Live*, 30 April 2023.
35 K.V. Aditya Bharadwaj, 'Why HMT Failed to Keep Pace with Time', *Hindu*, 22 September 2016.
36 Julie Bosman and Michael J. de la Merced, 'Borders' Bankruptcy Shakes Industry', *New York Times*, 16 February 2011.
37 'Sears: A Case Study in Business Failure', Columbia Business School, 23 October 2018, https://business.columbia.edu/insights/chazen-global-insights/sears-case-study-business-failure.
38 'Dick Smith (retailer)', Wikipedia, https://en.wikipedia.org/wiki/Dick_Smith_(retailer).
39 'Eaton's', Wikipedia, https://en.wikipedia.org/wiki/Eaton%27s.
40 'All Comet Stores to Close Today as Losses Hit £230m and Vince Cable Steps In', *Retail Week*, 2012.
Available online: https://www.retail-week.com/companies/all-comet-stores-to-close-today-as-losses-hit-230m-and-vince-cable-steps in/5044211.article.
41 'Zavvi', Wikipedia, https://en.wikipedia.org/wiki/Zavvi.
42 'Blockbuster', Wikipedia, https://en.wikipedia.org/wiki/Blockbuster_(retailer).
43 'Market Capitalization of Nokia 2019', Companies Market Cap, https://companiesmarketcap.com/nokia/marketcap/.
44 'The Rise and Fall of BlackBerry Mobiles: A Cautionary Tale in Tech Evolution', *Global Technology Review*, 19 June 2024, https://reviewbooku.com/review/the-rise-and-fall-of-blackberry-4951969.
45 Chunka Mui, 'How Kodak Failed', *Forbes*, 18 January 2022.
46 'Oracle to Buy Sunmicrosystems for $7.4 Billion', Bloomberg, 20 April 2009.
47 'IBM's Remarkable Revival: How CEO Arvind Krishna Resurrected a Tech Giant', *CEOs of Dubai*, 17 February 2025.
48 'Samsung Note 7 Failure Case Study', Aithor, 4 April 2024, https://aithor.com/essay-examples/samsung-note-7-failure-case-study.
49 Sara Ashley O'Brien, 'The Rise and Fall of Theranos: A Timeline', *CNN Business*, 7 July 2022.
50 Sophia Harris, 'Target Canada to Close All Stores by April 12', *CBC News*, 1 April 2015.
51 Pranav Dixit, 'Akash Tablet: A Failed Experiment in Affordable Computing?', *The Next Web*, 25 October 2012.

52 David Meyer, 'The Rise and Fall of Sinclair Research', *Fortune*, 28 February 2014.

CHAPTER 2 INCREASING ROLE OF TECHNOLOGIES

1 Roman Friedrich et al., *Measuring Industry Digitization: Leaders and Laggards in the Digital Economy* (Strategy&, 2011). Available online: https://www.strategyand.pwc.com/gx/en/insights/2002-2013/measuring-industry-digitization/strategyand-measuring-industry-digitization-leaders-laggards-digital-economy.pdf.
2 DQI Bureau, 'The PC in India: The Desktop Story', *Data Quest*, 12 September 2000. Available online: https://www.dqindia.com/the-pc-in-india-the-desktop-story.
3 'The History and Timeline of Microsoft Word', Microsoft 365 Life Hacks, 17 July 2024, https://www.microsoft.com/en-us/microsoft-365-life-hacks/writing/history-of-microsoft-word.
4 L. Jiang, B. Li and M. Zhang, 'The Impact of Digital Transformation on the Efficiency of Corporate Resource Allocation: Internal Mechanisms and External Environment', *Technological Forecasting and Social Change*, 193 (2025): 124107. Available online: https://doi.org/10.1016/j.techfore.2025.124107.
5 '90s Technology: How the 90s Changed Technology', Archives of IT, 2020, https://archivesit.org.uk/blog/90s-revolution.
6 '90s Technology: How the 90s Changed Technology'.
7 M.J. Sherin, 'India's IT Rise: How the Y2K Crisis Sparked a Global Tech Transformation', *Deccan Chronicle*, 15 May 2025. Available online: https://www.deccanchronicle.com/technology/indias-it-rise-how-the-y2k-crisis-sparked-a-global-tech-transformation-1879051.
8 'The Late 1990s Dot-Com Bubble Implodes in 2000', Goldman Sachs History, 2020, https://www.goldmansachs.com/our-firm/history/moments/2000-dot-com-bubble.
9 N. Laskowski, 'SMAC (Social, Mobile, Analytics and Cloud)', *TechTarget*, 2020, https://www.techtarget.com/searchcio/definition/SMAC-social-mobile-analytics-and-cloud.
10 Ibid.
11 Mohammed Hashim, *Anatomy of Business Impact Management Using SMAC* (EMC2, 2014).

Available online: https://learning.dell.com/content/dam/dell-emc/documents/en-us/2014KS_Hashim_Anatomy_of_impact_management_using_SMAC.pdf.

12 'Cost Efficiency Considerations for Your Cloud Adoption Strategy', Microsoft, 3 May 2025, https://learn.microsoft.com/en-us/azure/cloud-adoption-framework/strategy/inform/cost-efficiency.

13 S. Quach, P. Thaichon, K.D. Martin, S. Weaven and R.W. Palmatier, 'Digital Technologies: Tensions in Privacy and Data', *Journal of the Academy of Marketing Science*, 51 (6): 1221–41.

14 'The Nexus of Forces: Social, Mobile, Cloud and Information', Gartner, 2012, https://www.gartner.com/en/documents/2049315.

15 B. Casemore, P. Jirovsky and R. Mehra, 'IDC Report: The New Need for Speed in the Datacenter Network', 2015. Available online: https://www.cisco.com/c/dam/global/en_uk/assets/pdfs/white-paper-c11-734328.pdf.

16 ZealousWeb, 'Facebook Evolution—Managing the Business Social Wave', *ZealousWeb Blog*, 28 November 2023, https://www.zealousweb.com/blog/facebook-evolution-managing-business-social-wave.

17 E. Mixson, 'Data Science at Netflix: How Advanced Data & Analytics Helps Netflix Generate Billions', AI Data Analytics Network, 19 March 2025, https://www.aidataanalytics.network/data-science-ai/articles/data-science-at-netflix-how-advanced-data-analytics-helped-netflix-generate-billions.

18 'The Global Recession and the Growth of Cloud Computing', concept paper, Allied Digital, 2011. Available online: https://www.allieddigital.net/in/downloads/concept-papers/Concept-Papers-The-Global-Recession-and-Change-of-Cloud.pdf (accessed 10 September).

19 Emil Sayegh, 'How Cloud Computing Revolutionized Business Operations and What Lies Ahead', *Forbes*, 28 November 2023. Available online: https://www.forbes.com/sites/emilsayegh/2023/11/28/how-cloud-computing-revolutionized-business-operations-and-what-lies-ahead.

20 C.R. China and M. Goodwin, 'IaaS, PaaS, SaaS: What's the Difference?', IBM Think, 24 July 2025. Available online: https://www.ibm.com/think/topics/iaas-paas-saas.

21 'What Is Edge Computing?', Microsoft Azure Cloud Computing Dictionary, 2025.

Available online: https://azure.microsoft.com/en-us/resources/cloud-computing-dictionary/what-is-edge-computing.

22 'What Is the Industrial Internet of Things (IIoT)?', SAP Industry 4.0 Solutions, 2025, https://www.sap.com/india/products/scm/industry-4-0/what-is-iiot.html.

23 Gartner Inc., 'Gartner Survey Reveals 47% of Organizations Will Increase Investments in IoT Despite the Impact of Covid-19', *Gartner Newsroom*, press release, 29 October 2020. Available online: https://www.gartner.com/en/newsroom/press-releases/2020-10-29-gartner-survey-reveals-47-percent-of-organizations-will-increase-investments-in-iot-despite-the-impact-of-covid-19- .

24 M. Korolov, '7 Top Predictive Analytics Use Cases: Enterprise Examples', *TechTarget*, 2025, https://www.techtarget.com/searchbusinessanalytics/feature/Top-5-predictive-analytics-use-cases-in-enterprises.

25 B. Wolford, 'What Is GDPR, the EU's New Data Protection Law?', GDPR, 2018, https://gdpr.eu/what-is-gdpr.

26 Mayur Suresh Gawande et al., 'The Role of Artificial Intelligence in Pandemic Responses: From Epidemiological Modeling to Vaccine Development', *Molecular Biomedicine*, 6 (2025): 1. Available online: https://link.springer.com/article/10.1186/s43556-024-00238-3.

27 European Parliament, 'EU AI Act: First Regulation on Artificial Intelligence', European Parliament Topics, 1 June 2023. Available online: https://www.europarl.europa.eu/topics/en/article/20230601STO93804/eu-ai-act-first-regulation-on-artificial-intelligence.

CHAPTER 3 RISE OF THE AI PHENOMENON

1 'Deep Blue', History, IBM, https://www.ibm.com/history/deep-blue.

2 'Artificial Intelligence', Oxford Reference, https://www.oxfordreference.com/display/10.1093/oi/authority.20110803095426960.

3 M.A. Dennis, 'Marvin Minsky', *Encyclopaedia Britannica*, 5 August 2025. Available online: https://www.britannica.com/biography/Marvin-Minsky.

4 A.M. Turing, 'Computing Machinery and Intelligence', *Mind*, 49 (1950): 433–60. Available online: https://courses.cs.umbc.edu/471/papers/turing.pdf.

5 Tanya Roy, 'The History and Evolution of Artificial Intelligence, AI's Present and Future', *All Tech Magazine*, 19 July 2023. Available online: https://alltechmagazine.com/the-evolution-of-ai/.
6 'The Games That Helped AI Evolve', IBM, https://www.ibm.com/history/early-games.
7 Roy, 'The History and Evolution of Artificial Intelligence, AI's Present and Future'.
8 'What Is Automation?', IBM, https://www.ibm.com/think/topics/automation.
9 Giuliano Giacaglia, 'The Golden Years of AI (1956–1974)', In *Making Things Think: How AI and Deep Learning Power the Products We Use* (San Francisco: Holloway, n.d.). Available online: https://www.holloway.com/g/making-things-think/sections/the-golden-years-of-ai-19561974.
10 'AI Winter: The Highs and Lows of Artificial Intelligence', History of Data Science, 9 January 2021, https://www.historyofdatascience.com/ai-winter-the-highs-and-lows-of-artificial-intelligence/.
11 Michael Haenlein and Andreas Kaplan, 'A Brief History of Artificial Intelligence: On the Past, Present, and Future of Artificial Intelligence', *California Management Review*, 61 (4). Available online: https://www.researchgate.net/publication/334539401_A_Brief_History_of_Artificial_Intelligence_On_the_Past_Present_and_Future_of_Artificial_Intelligence.
12 Danielle Williams, 'We've Been Here Before: AI Promised Humanlike Machines in 1958', *The Conversation*, 29 February 2024. Available online: https://theconversation.com/weve-been-here-before-ai-promised-humanlike-machines-in-1958-222700.
13 'Robots and Their Arms', Stanford InfoLab Museum Archive, http://infolab.stanford.edu/pub/voy/museum/pictures/display/1-Robot.htm.
14 'DEC's XCON Expert System', Fresno State University, https://zimmer.fresnostate.edu/~sasanr/Teaching-Material/MIS/ES/DEC's-XCON.pdf.
15 Ben Lutkevich, 'AI Winter', *TechTarget*, 26 August 2024, https://www.techtarget.com/searchenterpriseai/definition/AI-winter.
16 E. Feigenbaum and H. Shrobe, 'The Japanese National Fifth Generation Project: Introduction, Survey, and Evaluation', *Future Generation Computer Systems*, 9: 105–17. Available online: https://stacks.stanford.edu/file/druid:kv359wz9060/kv359wz9060.pdf.

17 Cameron Hashemi-Pour, George Lawton and Linda Tucci, 'Business Process Automation', *TechTarget*, 14 December 2023, https://www.techtarget.com/searchcio/definition/business-process-automation.

18 Tim Mucci, 'History of Artificial Intelligence', IBM, https://www.ibm.com/think/topics/history-of-artificial-intelligence.

19 'History of Speech & Voice Recognition and Transcription Software', Dragon Medical Transcription, https://www.dragon-medical-transcription.com/history_speech_recognition.html.

20 Doug Gross, 'Apple Introduces Siri, Web Freaks Out', *CNN*, 4 October 2011. Available online: https://edition.cnn.com/2011/10/04/tech/mobile/siri-iphone-4s-skynet.

21 Margaret Boden, ed., *The Philosophy of Artificial Intelligence* (Oxford: Oxford University Press, 1990).

22 'A Massive Google Network Learns to Identify—Cats', NPR, 26 June 2012, https://www.npr.org/2012/06/26/155792609/a-massive-google-network-learns-to-identify.

23 Mucci, 'History of Artificial Intelligence'.

24 Geoffrey Hinton et al., 'Deep Neural Networks for Acoustic Modeling in Speech Recognition: The Shared Views of Four Research Groups', *IEEE Signal Processing Magazine*, 29 (6): 82–97. doi: 10.1109/MSP.2012.2205597. Available online: https://static.googleusercontent.com/media/research.google.com/en//pubs/archive/38131.pdf.

25 Sunny Betz, '7 Types of Artificial Intelligence', Built In, https://builtin.com/artificial-intelligence/types-of-artificial-intelligence.

26 Stefan Moritz and Kate Smaje, 'Forging the Human–Machine Alliance', McKinsey & Company, 20 December 2022, https://www.mckinsey.com/capabilities/mckinsey-digital/our-insights/tech-forward/forging-the-human-machine-alliance.

27 Ashley Nunes, 'Automation Doesn't Just Create or Destroy Jobs—It Transforms Them', *Harvard Business Review*, 2 November 2021. Available online: https://hbr.org/2021/11/automation-doesnt-just-create-or-destroy-jobs-it-transforms-them.

28 Greg Brockman, Ilya Sutskever and OpenAI, 'Introducing OpenAI', OpenAI, 11 December 2015, https://openai.com/index/introducing-openai/.

29 'DALL·E 2', OpenAI, 6 April 2022, https://openai.com/index/dall-e-2/.

30 Kyle Bell, 'Why Is ChatGPT So Bad at Math?', TechCrunch, 2 October 2024, https://techcrunch.com/2024/10/02/why-is-chatgpt-so-bad-at-math/.

31 Eric Boyd, 'ChatGPT Is Now Available in Azure OpenAI Service', Microsoft Azure Blog, 9 March 2023, https://azure.microsoft.com/en-us/blog/chatgpt-is-now-available-in-azure-openai-service/.

32 'Introducing Llama 3.1: Our Most Capable Models to Date', Meta AI Blog, 23 July 2024, https://ai.meta.com/blog/meta-llama-3-1/.

33 Hema Buduraju, 'Google Search: Introducing AI Mode in India', Google Blog, 24 June 2025, https://blog.google/intl/en-in/products/google-search-introducing-ai-mode-in-india/ (accessed 12 September 2025).

34 'Stable Diffusion Announcement', Stability AI, 10 August 2022, https://stability.ai/news/stable-diffusion-announcement.

35 Haritha Khandabattu, 'The 2025 Hype Cycle for Artificial Intelligence Goes Beyond GenAI', Gartner, 8 July 2025, https://www.gartner.com/en/articles/hype-cycle-for-artificial-intelligence.

36 Priya Joi, 'Using AI from Lab to Jab: How Did Artificial Intelligence Help Us Develop and Deliver Covid-19 Vaccines?', Gavi, 27 February 2025, https://www.gavi.org/vaccineswork/using-ai-lab-jab-how-did-artificial-intelligence-help-us-develop-and-deliver-covid.

37 Guilherme Schneider, 'The AI Wars between Nations: A New Arms Race or Catalyst for Collaboration', *Modern Diplomacy*, 2 October 2023, https://moderndiplomacy.eu/2023/10/02/the-ai-wars-between-nations-a-new-arms-race-or-a-catalyst-for-collaboration/.

38 'Artificial Intelligence Mission', Office of the Principal Scientific Adviser, Government of India, https://www.psa.gov.in/mission/artificial-intelligence/34.

39 'Discovering Education's Future with the Rise of GenAI in India's EdTech Landscape', Express Computer, 27 August 2024, https://www.expresscomputer.in/guest-blogs/discovering-educations-future-with-the-rise-of-genai-in-indias-edtech-landscape/115373/.

40 'Amazon's Corporate Workforce May Shrink as AI Takes Over Routine Tasks', Reuters, 19 June 2025, https://www.reuters.com/business/retail-consumer/amazons-workforce-reduce-rollout-generative-ai-agents-2025-06-17/.

41 'The Bet That Changed Everything: Satya Nadella on AI, Leadership, and the Future of Computing', Madrona, 12 September 2025, https://www.madrona.com/the-bet-that-changed-everything-satya-nadella-on-ai-leadership-and-the-future-of-computing/.

42 Sundar Pichai, 'Questions, Shrugs and What Comes Next: A Quarter Century of Change', Google Blog, 5 September 2023, https://blog.google/inside-google/message-ceo/google-25th-birthday-sundar-pichai/.

43 Google Threat Intelligence Group, 'Adversarial Misuse of Generative AI', Google Cloud Blog, 30 January 2025, https://cloud.google.com/blog/topics/threat-intelligence/adversarial-misuse-generative-ai.

44 Sara Brown, 'Why Neural Net Pioneer Geoffrey Hinton Is Sounding the Alarm on AI', MIT Sloan, 23 May 2023, https://mitsloan.mit.edu/ideas-made-to-matter/why-neural-net-pioneer-geoffrey-hinton-sounding-alarm-ai.

45 'What Are AI Guardrails?', McKinsey & Company, 14 November 2024, https://www.mckinsey.com/featured-insights/mckinsey-explainers/what-are-ai-guardrails.

46 'mRNA and Artificial Intelligence for Advanced Vaccine Innovation', Pfizer, https://www.pfizer.com/news/articles/how_a_novel_incubation_sandbox_helped_speed_up_data_analysis_in_pfizer_s_covid_19_vaccine_trial.

47 'Generative AI Fuels Creative Physical Product Design but Is No Magic Wand', McKinsey & Company, 5 March 2024, https://www.mckinsey.com/capabilities/mckinsey-digital/our-insights/generative-ai-fuels-creative-physical-product-design-but-is-no-magic-wand.

48 'AI Chatbots in Customer Service: Can They Truly Replace Human Agents?', Infomineo, 24 March 2024, https://infomineo.com/artificial-intelligence/ai-chatbots-in-customer-service-can-they-replace-human/.

49 Teaganne Finn and Amanda Downie, 'Agentic AI vs Generative AI', IBM, 2025, https://www.ibm.com/think/topics/agentic-ai-vs-generative-ai.

50 Charles Daly, 'Klarna Turns from AI to Real-Person Customer Service', Bloomberg, 8 May 2025. Available online: https://www.bloomberg.com/news/articles/2025-05-08/klarna-turns-from-ai-to-real-person-customer-service.

51 Bill Gates, 'My Conversation with Sam Altman', Unconfuse Me with Bill Gates (podcast), Gates Notes, 11 January 2024. Available online: https://www.gatesnotes.com/meet-bill/my-podcasts/reader/unconfuse-me-podcast-with-guest-sam-altman.

52 Katja Grace et al., 'Thousands of AI Authors on the Future of AI', AI Impacts, January 2024, https://aiimpacts.org/wp-content/uploads/2023/04/Thousands_of_AI_authors_on_the_future_of_AI.pdf.

53 Stephen Nellis, 'Nvidia CEO Says AI Could Pass Human Tests in Five Years', Reuters, 2 March 2024, https://www.reuters.com/technology/nvidia-ceo-says-ai-could-pass-human-tests-five-years-2024-03-01/.

54 Mustafa Suleyman and Michael Bhaskar, *The Coming Wave: Technology, Power, and the Twenty-first Century's Greatest Dilemma* (London: The Bodley Head, 2023).

55 Billy Perrigo, 'Meta's AI Chief Yann LeCun on AGI, Open-Source, and AI Risk', *Time*, 13 February 2024, https://time.com/6694432/yann-lecun-meta-ai-interview/.

56 'Planning for AGI and Beyond', OpenAI, 24 February 2023, https://openai.com/index/planning-for-agi-and-beyond/.

57 'SLMs vs LLMs: What Are Small Language Models?', Red Hat, 23 April 2025, https://www.redhat.com/en/topics/ai/llm-vs-slm.

CHAPTER 4 GENERATIVE AI AND THE NEW FRONTIERS

1 'Accelerated Discovery', IBM, https://research.ibm.com/topics/accelerated-discovery.

2 'Toyota Research Institute Unveils New Generative AI Technique for Vehicle Design', Toyota, 20 June 2023, https://pressroom.toyota.com/toyota-research-institute-unveils-new-generative-ai-technique-for-vehicle-design/.

3 'Artificial Intelligence in Action: Selected ADB Initiatives in Asia and the Pacific', Asian Development Bank, May 2024, https://www.adb.org/publications/ai-action-adb-initiatives-asia-pacific.

4 'How Generative AI Can Boost Consumer Marketing', McKinsey, December 2023. Available online: https://www.mckinsey.com/capabilities/growth-marketing-and-sales/our-insights/how-generative-ai-can-boost-consumer-marketing.

5 'AI Risk Management Framework', National Institute of Standards and Framework (US Department of Commerce), https://www.nist.gov/itl/ai-risk-management-framework.

6 'What Is the EU AI Act?', EU Artificial Intelligence Act, https://artificialintelligenceact.eu.

7 Microsoft Corporation, *Work Trend Index Annual Report, 2025: The Year the Frontier Firm Is Born* (Microsoft, 2025). Available online: https://www.microsoft.com/en-us/worklab/work-trend-index/2025-the-year-the-frontier-firm-is-born.

CHAPTER 5 AI RESHAPING THE SERVICES INDUSTRY

1 Kevin M. Dulle and B. Joseph Pine II, 'What a Toys "R" Us Comeback Could Look Like', *Harvard Business Review*, 30 November 2018. Available online: https://hbr.org/2018/11/what-a-toys-r-us-comeback-could-look-like.

2 'The Downfall of Sears: 5 Key Reasons Why the Retail Giant Went Under', Castus Global, 5 October 2021, https:// www.castusglobal.com/insights/the-downfall-of-sears-5-key-reasons-why-the retail-giant-went-under#.

3 Tim Kelly, J.D., 'What Mistakes Did Bed Bath and Beyond Make?', 9 October 2023, LawInfo,https://www.lawinfo.com/resources/bankruptcy/business-bankruptcy/what-mistakes-did-bed-bath-and-beyond-make.html.

4 'Travel PR Mistakes: An In-Depth Analysis of the Failure of Thomas Cook', Everything PR, 28 May 2025, https://everything-pr.com/travel-pr-mistakes-an-in-depth-analysis-of-the-failure-of-thomas-cook/.

5 'The Collapse of Thomas Cook: What Happened and Why', International Banker, 16 January 2020, https://internationalbanker.com/brokerage/the-collapse-of-thomas-cook-what-happened-and-why/.

6 'Airbnb, Inc (ABNB)', YCharts, https://www.google.com/url?sa=t&source=web&rct=j&opi=89978449&url=https://ycharts.com/companies/ABNB/market_cap&ved=2ahUKEwj27-Xct7GJAxUHLFkFHbjNGmUQFnoECBsQAQ&usg=AOvVaw3heQWeQxJPC7sYPl0WD_U4.

7 'Japan Robot Hotel Ready to Welcome Its First Human Guests', Associated Press, 15 July 2015.

8 Prabalika Borah, 'India-Made Robots Chat Up Diners at Hyderabad Restaurant', *Hindu*, 21 August, 2021.

9 'Travel & Tourism Economic Impact Research (EIR)', World Travel & Tourism Council, https://wttc.org/research/economic-impact.

10 Paul Ellickson, 'The Evolution of the Supermarket Industry: From A&P to Wal-Mart', *SSRN Electronic Journal*, April 2011.

11 Boris Emmet and John Jeuck, *Catalogues and Counters: A History of Sears* (Roebuck and Company: University of Chicago Press, 1950).

12 Made Lapuerta, 'The Rise & Fall & Rise of GAP', *Medium*, 29 June 2020. Available online: https://medium.com/dashion/the-rise-fall-rise-of-gap-6e29fa4b64d.

13 Marc Levinson, *The Great A&P and the Struggle for Small Business in America* (Hill and Wang, 2011).

14 'Sears', Wikipedia, https://en.wikipedia.org/wiki/Sears.

15 'Domino's Pizza Bot', Chatbot Guide, https://www.chatbotguide.org/dominospizza-bot.

16 Walmart's Generative AI Search Puts More Time Back in Customers' Hands', Walmart, 30 January 2024, https://tech.walmart.com/content/walmart-global-tech/en_us/blog/post/walmarts-generative-ai-search-puts-more-time-back-in-customers-hands.html.

17 Alexandria White, '5 Things to Know about the Target RedCard', CNBC, 15 November 2024, https://www.cnbc.com/select/target-redcard-what-you-should-know/?msockid=380dc675aac3626321b1d33aaba1632c.

18 Laura Mullan, 'Warby Parker Uses Augmented Reality to Allow Customers to Virtually Try on Glasses', *Technology Magazine*, 18 May 2020. Available online: https://technologymagazine.com/digital-transformation/warby-parker-uses-augmented-reality-allow-customers-virtually-try-glasses.

19 Peter Adams, 'Houzz App's AR Upgrade Turns Living Rooms into Virtual Showroom Floors', Marketing Dive, 8 May 2017, https://www.marketingdive.com/news/houzz-apps-ar-upgrade-turns-living-rooms-into-virtual-showroom-floors/442142/.

20 'L'Oreal's Modiface Brings AI-powered Virtual Makeup Try-on to Amazon', L'Oreal Group, https://www.loreal.com/en/articles/science-and-technology/l-oreal-modiface-brings-ai-powered-virtual-makeup-try-ons-to-amazon/.

21 'Tiffany Engagement Ring Experience', The One Club, https://www.oneclub.org/awards/theoneshow/-award/21458/tiffany-engagement-ring-experience/.

22 Anthony DeMarco, 'De Beers Turns to Augmented Reality to Market Its Branded Diamond', *Forbes*, 29 March 2016. Available online: https://www.forbes.com/sites/

anthonydemarco/2011/10/12/de-beers-turns-to-augmented-reality-to-market-its-branded-diamond/.

23 Madeleine Schulz, 'Louis Vuitton's Latest AR Project? Covering Landmarks in Dots', *Vogue Business*, 26 January 2023. Available online: https://www.vogue.com/article/louis-vuittons-latest-ar-project-covering-landmarks-in-dots.

24 Patrick Morda, 'Augmented Reality', *Audi Magazine*, 11 March 2025. Available online: https://magazine.audi.com.au/article/augmented-reality; Barton Goldenberg, 'From Concept to Reality: BMWs Groundbreaking XR/VR/AR Technology', Ism, https://ismguide.com/bmw-xr-metaverse-technology-case-study/; 'Tesla', HUmmingbirdsday, https://www.hummingbirdsday.com/tesla.

25 'Augmented Reality for Ecommerce with Shopify AR', Shopify, https://www.shopify.com/augmented-reality.

26 'Sephora Virtual Artist: Try On Makeup Instantly', Sephora, https://www.sephora.my/pages/virtual-artist?srsltid=AfmBOoo-5nktUS88uCClT7jtoLGzt8tMVwbQmO-UwiKgq-EFal5loNSY; 'Virtual Makeup Try-On', Ulta Beauty, https://www.ulta.com/innovation/glamlab/.

27 Arakarag Chaudhuri, 'How Century-Old Indian Brands Are Winning with AR, AI and Immersive Experiences', CMSWIRE, 12 August 2025, https://www.cmswire.com/digital-experience/how-century-old-indian-brands-are-winning-with-ar-ai-and-immersive-experiences/.

28 'H&M Group Explores Tech-Enabled Shopping Experiences in US Stores', H&M Group, 27 May 2022, https://hmgroup.com/news/hm-group-explores-tech-enabled-shopping-experiences-in-us-stores/; 'Adidas AR Sneakers Try-On App', Virtual Reality Marketing, https://www.virtualrealitymarketing.com/case-studies/adidas-ar-sneakers-try-on-app-2/;
'Tommy Hilfiger Lets Shoppers Try on Clothes in AR with Zero10', Adweek, 31 March 2023, https://www.adweek.com/creativity/tommy-hilfiger-try-on-clothes-with-zero10/.

29 'Worldwide Quarterly Augmented and Virtual Reality Headset Tracker', IDC Tracker, https://my.idc.com/getdoc.jsp?containerId=IDC_P35095.

30 Dany Kitishian, 'Hilton's AI Strategy: Analysis of Dominance in Hospitality', Klover, 4 August 2025, https://www.klover.ai/hilton-ai-strategy-analysis-of-dominance-in-hospitality-hotel-ai/.

31 Sean Cudahy, 'American Airlines Says AI Could Help with Fares — But Only to Save Time', The Points Guy, 15 September 2025, https://thepointsguy.com/news/american-airlines-ai-fares/.

32 'Domino's Makes a Pizza Points Loyalty Play with AI', PYMNTS, 31 January 2019, https://www.pymnts.com/news/retail/2019/dominos-pizza-artificial-intelligence-rewards/.

33 'Starbucks Uses AI-Powered Personalized Rewards to Boost Frequency and Spend', PYMNTS, 30 January 2024, https://www.pymnts.com/news/loyalty-and-rewards-news/2024/starbucks-uses-artificial-intelligence-powered-personalized-rewards-boost-frequency-check-size/.

34 Catherine Strohanova, 'How to Bring Value to Customer's Shopping Experience and Increase Sales with AR', Jasoren, https://www.jasoren.com/how-to-bring-value-to-customers-shopping-experience-and-increase-sales-with-ar/.

35 'Losses from Online Payment Fraud to Exceed $362 Billion Globally Over Next 5 Years', Juniper Research, June 2023. Available online: https://www.juniperresearch.com/press/losses-online-payment-fraud-exceed-362-billion/.

36 Karim Aknoukh, Ahmed Ewis and Fortune Hui, 'Manage Access Controls in Generative AI-powered Search Applications Using Amazon OpenSearch Service and Amazon Cognito', AWS Big Data Blog, 19 November 2024, https://aws.amazon.com/blogs/big-data/manage-access-controls-in-generative-ai-powered-search-applications-using-amazon-opensearch-service-and-aws-cognito/; Hayley Peterson, 'Walmart Reveals It's Tracking Checkout Theft with AI-Powered Cameras in 1,000 Stores', *Business Insider*, 20 June 2019. Available online: https://www.businessinsider.com/walmart-tracks-theft-with-computer-vision-1000-stores-2019-6; 'Guest Security & Fraud Protection', Target, https://security.target.com/.

37 Erica Janeau and Christopher Sailus, 'The Barter System/Definition, History & Examples—Lesson', Study, 21 November 2023, https://study.com/academy/lesson/bartering-systems-definition-lesson-quiz.html?msockid=380dc675aac3626321b1d33aaba1632c.

38 'Trade and Barter System in the Indus Valley Civilization', Sites at Penn State, 6 February 2025, https://sites.psu.edu/pecunia/2025/02/06/trade-and-barter-system-in-the-indus-valley-civilization/.

39 'History of Banking', Wikipedia, https://en.wikipedia.org/wiki/History_of_banking.

40 Julia Kagan, 'What Is Hawala? Money Transfer Without Money Movement', Investopedia, 29 July 2025, https://www.investopedia.com/terms/h/hawala.asp.

41 'The History of NYSE', NYSE, https://www.nyse.com/history-of-nyse.

42 'New York Stock Exchange', Wikipedia, https://en.wikipedia.org/wiki/New_York_Stock_Exchange.

43 'Imperial Bank of India', Wikipedia, https://en.wikipedia.org/wiki/Imperial_Bank_of_India.

44 'Online Banking', Wikipedia, https://en.wikipedia.org/wiki/Online_banking.

45 'Wirecard Scandal', Wikipedia, https://en.wikipedia.org/wiki/Wirecard_scandal.

46 'Paytm Payments Services Get "In-Principle" Nod from RBI to Operate as Online Payment Aggregator', *Economic Times,* 12 August 2025. Available online: https://economictimes.indiatimes.com/industry/banking/finance/banking/paytm-payments-services-gets-in-principle-nod-from-rbi-to-operate-as-online-payment-aggregator/articleshow/123261536.cms.

47 Nikita Prasad, 'Softbank Exits Paytm in June Quarter at Loss of $150 Million', *LiveMint*, 13 July 2024.

48 'Artificial Intelligence at American Express—Two Current Use Cases', Emerj, https://emerj.com/artificial-intelligence-at-american-express/.

49 'SBI Launches Chatbot to Help Customers in Banking Activities', *Economic Times*, 25 September 2017. Available online: https://economictimes.indiatimes.com/industry/banking/finance/banking/sbi-launches-chatbot-to-help-customers-in-banking-activities/articleshow/60827485.cms?from=mdr.

50 Pankaj Maru, 'ICICI Bank's AI Chatbot iPal Empowers Customers with Information and Financials', Codex, 17 October 2017, https://codex.team/blog/ai-in-banking-how-icici-bank-leads-the-way.

51 Ramana Rao B. and Savitha Kulkarni, 'Chatbots of Indian Banks—Utility for Prospective Customers—A Perceptive Study', ITM Web of Conferences 68, 01013 (2024). Available online: https://www.itm-conferences.org/articles/itmconf/pdf/2024/11/itmconf_icaetm2024_01013.pdf.

52 'AI Series: How Goldman Sachs Leverages AI to Extract Better Investment Insights', NB Investments, 8 November 2023, https://www.nbinvestments.ca/perspectives/article/how-goldman-sachs-leverages-ai-extract-better-investment-insights.html.

53 Dany Kitishian, 'HDFC Bank's AI Strategy: Analysis of Dominating Banking AI', Klover, 17 July 2025, https://www.klover.ai/hdfc-bank-ai-strategy-analysis-of-dominating-banking-ai/.

54 'How Bajaj Finance Is Leveraging AI, Blockchain in Banking, Insurance', *Economic Times*, 12 September 2025, https://bfsi.economictimes.indiatimes.com/articles/bajaj-finance-revolutionizes-banking-and-insurance-with-ai-and-blockchain-technology/123841144.

55 'Lendingkart Annual Reports 2022', Lending Kart Finance, https://lendingkartfinance.com/financials.

56 Bhaskar Ghosh et al., 'Taking a Systems Approach to adopting AI', *Harvard Business Review*, 9 May 2019.

57 'Groww Press Releases and Annual Reports 2023', Groww, https://groww.in/investor-relations/performance/company.

58 Joseph Cordeira, 'The UBS AI Advantage: The New Standard of Growing Your Practice', https://www.ubs.com/us/en/wealth-management/financial-advisor-experience/articles/ai-for-financial-advisors.html?campID=SOME-AIA-US-ENG-FASM-ANY-FASF-FASD-ANY-ANY-ORGANIC&campID=SOME-FASOCIAL-US-ANY-LINKEDIN-ANY-ANY-ANY-ANY-ANY-ANY-ANY-e58ff610-fe84-11ef-9ca1-219a418390e2.

59 'American Express Annual Report 2023', https://s26.q4cdn.com/747928648/files/doc_financials/2023/ar/American-Express-Annual-Report-2023.pdf.

60 Aurora Munteanu, 'Mastercard Launches a Fraud Prevention Solution in EEMEA', The Paypers, 3 July 2025, https://thepaypers.com/fraud-and-fincrime/news/mastercard-launches-a-fraud-prevention-solution-in-eemea.

61 Mathew Griffin, 'JPMorgan Unleashes Artificial Intelligence to Automate Its Legal Work', Fanatical Futurist, March 2017, www.fanaticalfuturist.com.

62 'Web3, Metaverse and Digital Finance', Deloitte, https://www.deloitte.com/cz-sk/en/services/consulting/services/cyber-risk/web3-metaverse-and-digital-finance.html.

63 'PMJDY Statistics', Pradhan Mantri Jan-Dhan Yojana, https://www.pmjdy.gov.in/statewise-statistics.

64 'National Payments Corporation of India (NPCI): UPI Transactions Data', NPCI, https://www.npci.org.in/product/upi/product-statistics.

65 'Total UPI Transactions Cross 100 Billion Mark in 2023', *Economic Times*, 2 January 2024.

66 'MobiKwik Press Releases, 2022–2024', https://www.mobikwik.com/ir.

67 'Building the Payments Infrastructure for 70 MN+ SMEs in Bharat', Rupifi, https://www.rupifi.com/about.

68 Jeff Kearns, 'AI's Reverberations across Finance', *Finance & Development Magazine*, International Monetary Fund, December 2023, https://meetings.imf.org/en/-/media/files/publications/fandd/article/2023/december/38-41-kearns-final.pdf.

69 'IDC Worldwide AI and Generative AI Spending Guide', IDC, 19 August 2024, https://my.idc.com/getdoc.jsp?containerId=IDC_P33198.
Mohammed Irfan et al., *AI-Driven Decentralized Finance and the Future of Finance* (IGI Global, 2024).

70 'Artificial Intelligence in Financial Services', PwC study, PricewaterhouseCoopers 2020, https://www.pwc.de/en/finanzdienstleistungen/artificial-intelligence-in-financial-services.html.

71 'The Future of Fintech and Banking', Accenture, https://bankingblog.accenture.com/wp-content/uploads/2015/04/accenture-future-fintech-banking.pdf.

72 Colin Soutar et al., 'Industry Spending on Quantum Computing Will Rise Dramatically. Will It Pay Off?', Deloitte Insights, 27 July 2023, https://deloitte.wsj.com/cio/quantum-computing-in-financial-services-will-it-pay-off.

73 'BFSI Sector to Add 2.5 Lakh Jobs by 2030; Hiring Shifts to Tier II, III Cities: Report', *Economic Times*, 21 August 2025. Available online: https://economictimes.indiatimes.com/industry/banking/finance/banking/bfsi-sector-to-add-2-5-lakh-jobs-by-2030-hiring-shifts-to-tier-ii-iii-cities-report/articleshow/.

74 Philip Svensson, 'Walmart: Walton, Retailing, and Everyday Low Prices', 8 September 2025, https://quartr.com/insights/company-research/walmart-walton-retailing-and-everyday-low-prices.

75 Matt Smith, 'Walmart's New Intelligent Retail Lab Shows a Glimpse into the Future of Retail, IRL', Walmart, 25 April 2019, https://corporate.walmart.com/news/2019/04/25/walmarts-new-intelligent-retail-lab-shows-a-glimpse-into-the-future-of-retail-irl.

76 Michah Solomon, 'Four Seasons Leader Isadore Sharp: Treat Employees Right so They Treat Customers Right', *Forbes*, 18 August 2015. Available online: https://www.forbes.com/sites/micahsolomon/2015/08/17/four-seasons-leader-isadore-sharp-treat-employees-right-so-they-treat-customers-right/.

77 Jordan Hollander, '10 Best Hotel Chatbots in 2025', Hotel Tech Report, 1 July 2025, https://hoteltechreport.com/marketing/hotel-chatbots.

CHAPTER 6 AI TRANSFORMING MANUFACTURING AND LIFE SCIENCES

1 F.F. Mendels, 'Prior to Industrialization: The First Phase of the Industrialization Process', *Journal of Economic History*, 32 (1): 241–62.

2 'Second Industrial Revolution/Timeline, Inventions & Effects', Study.com, https://study.com/academy/lesson/the-second-industrial-revolution-timeline-inventions.html?msockid=380dc675aac3626321b1d33aaba1632c.

3 Steven Shepard, *Telecommunications Crash Course* (McGraw-Hill Education, 2014).

4 Jeremy Rifkin, *Third Industrial Revolution* (St. Martin's Press, 2011).

5 'A Short History of the Web', CERN, https://home.cern/science/computing/birth-web/short-history-web.

6 YEC, 'How the Fourth Industrial Revolution Is Impacting the Future of Work', *Forbes*, 19 October 2018, https://www.forbes.com/councils/theyec/2018/10/19/how-the-fourth-industrial-revolution-is-impacting-the-future-of-work/.

7 Future Today Institute, *2024 Tech Trends Report, 17th Edition.* Available online: https://www.futuretodayinstitute.com/wp-content/uploads/2024/03/TR2024_Full-Report_FINAL_LINKED.pdf.

8 'Matthew Boulton and James Watt: The Dynamic Partnership That Transformed the Steam Engine', Earnshaw, 13 April 2024, https://thomas-earnshaw.com/blogs/the-earnshaw-odyssey/matthew-boulton-and-james-watt-transformed-the-steam-engine.

9 'Lowell Textile Mills', COVE Collective Editions, https://editions.covecollective.org/chronologies/lowell-textile-mills.

10 Rajesh Kumar Singh and Abhijith Ganapavaram, 'GE Completed Three-Way Split, Breaking Off from Its Storied Past', Reuters,

3 April 2024. Available online: https://www.reuters.com/markets/us/ge-completes-three-way-split-breaking-off-its-storied-past-2024-04-02/.

11 Francis Gonzales, 'The Rise and Fall of Polaroid. The Disruptor Becomes the Disrupted', UX Collective, 9 May 2021. Available online: https://uxdesign.cc/the-rise-and-fall-of-polaroid-3fffde2b5128-; Steve Brachmann, 'The Rise and Fall of the Company That Invented Digital Cameras', IPWatchdog, 1 November 2014, https://ipwatchdog.com/2014/11/01/the-rise-and-fall-of-the-company-that-invented-digital-cameras/.

12 Hans Latta, 'Western Union: Leading or Lagging Digital Transformation?', Digital Initiative, 28 April 2018, https://d3.harvard.edu/platform-digit/submission/western-union-leading-or-lagging-digital-transformation/; Sean Michael Kerner and Madeleine Streets, 'Intel's Rise and Fall: A Timeline of What Went Wrong', *TechTarget*, 19 August 2025, https://www.techtarget.com/WhatIs/feature/Intels-rise-and-fall-A-timeline-of-what-went-wrong.

13 Angela Monaghan, 'Nokia: The Rise and Fall of a Mobile Phone Giant', *Guardian*, 3 September 2013. Available online: https://www.theguardian.com/technology/2013/sep/03/nokia-rise-fall-mobile-phone-giant.

14 'The Rise and Fall of Blackberry: Key Business Lessons', Sprintzeal, 29 November 2024, https://www.sprintzeal.com/blog/the-fall-of-blackberry.

15 Smriti, 'Motorola: The Mobile Phone Brand That Could Still Exist', InspireIP, 10 May 2023, https://inspireip.com/motorola-failure-story/.

16 'How BMW Is Using AI to Improve Its Manufacturing Processes', Aicadium, 13 December 2013, https://aicadium.ai/how-bmw-is-using-ai-to-improve-its-manufacturing-processes/.

17 'Senseye Predictive Maintenance-Reliability Redefined', Siemens, https://www.siemens.com/global/en/products/services/digital-enterprise-services/analytics-artificial-intelligence-services/senseye-predictive-maintenance.html.

18 'Smart Manufacturing: Building the Factory of Tomorrow', Siemens, https://assets.new.siemens.com/siemens/assets/api/uuid:4259772d-c315-4748-b571-bea6bf983f8c/final-factorytomorrow-wp.pdf.

19 David J. Collis and Tonia Junker, 'Digitalization at Siemens', Harvard Business School Case 717-428, February 2017 (revised November 2021).

20 Leslie D'Monte, 'How L&T Is Engineering an AI-driven Conglomerate', LiveMint, 24 April 2024, https://www.livemint.com/companies/how-l-t-is-engineering-an-ai-driven-conglomerate-11713957779560.html.
21 Srikanth R.P., 'Manoj Gautam, CIO, Maruti Suzuki on How the Auto Leader Is Shifting Gears for the AI Era', Express Computer, 28 October 2025, https://www.expresscomputer.in/exclusives/manoj-gautam-cio-maruti-suzuki-on-how-the-auto-leader-is-shifting-gears-for-the-ai-era/128920/.
22 'Foxconn Announces Foxconn NxVAE, Unsupervised Learning AI Technology', Foxconn, 21 January 2021, https://www.foxconn.com/en-us/press-center/events/csr-events/533.
23 'GE Using AI/ML to Reduce Wind Turbine Logistics and Installation Costs', GE Vernova, 4 April 2022, https://www.gevernova.com/news/press-releases/ge-using-aiml-to-reduce-wind-turbine-logistics-and-installation-costs.
24 'Tata Steel's Jamshedpur Plant Recognised as World Economic Forum's Advanced 4th Industrial Revolution Lighthouse', Tata Steel, 15 March 2021, https://www.tatasteel.com/media/newsroom/press-releases/india/2021/tata-steel-s-jamshedpur-plant-recognised-as-world-economic-forum-s-advanced-4th-industrial-revolution-4ir-lighthouse/.
25 'How a Steel Plant in India Tapped the Value of Data—and Won Global Acclaim', McKinsey Insights, 8 March 2021.
26 'Tata Steel's Jamshedpur Plant Recognised as World Economic Forum's Advanced 4th Industrial Revolution Lighthouse', Tata Steel.
27 *JSW Steel's Sustainability Report 2023-24*, JSW Steel, https://www.jswsteel.in/investors/jsw-steel-investor-information-sustainability-reports.
28 *Hindalco's Sustainability Report 2023-24*, Hindalco, https://www.hindalco.com/upload/pdf/hindalco-annual-report-2023-24.pdf.
29 'Allow Me, the AI Analytics Platform', Bosch, https://www.bosch.com/stories/ai-in-manufacturing/.
30 Lisa Johnston, 'P&G Leans into AI for Dynamic Routing and Sourcing Optimization', 23 January 2024, https://consumergoods.com/pg-leans-ai-dynamic-routing-andsourcing-optimization.
31 'How Nike Is Transforming Its Supply Chain to Best Serve Consumers', Warehouse Automation, https://www.warehouseautomation.ai/top-stories/how-nike-is-transforming-its-supply-chain-to-best-serve-consumers-mgrdn-pgmxd.

32 Yogesh Shinde, 'AI Robots: Transforming Industries with Smart Robotic Solutions', *Robotics Tomorrow*, 23 August 2024; Guna Sekhar Sajja and Santosh Reddy Addula, 'Automation Using Robots, Machine Learning and Artificial Intelligence to Enhance Production and Quality', 2024, Second International Conference of Computational and Characterization Techniques in Engineering & Sciences, IEEExplore.

33 Bhragu Haritas, 'Mahindra Group's Four Pillars of Digital Transformation', ETCIO, 1 June 2021.

34 'How Universal Robots Helped Bajaj Auto to Automate Its Assembly Lines', Analytics Insight, 13 September 2019.

35 Raymond Deplazes, 'Autodesk and Airbus Demonstrate the Impact of Generative Design on Making and Building', Autodesk News, 19 November 2019, https://adsknews.autodesk.com/en/news/autodesk-airbus-generative-design-aerospace-factory/; David Sher, 'Five Footwear Industry Leaders Using 3D Printing for Production Today', VoxelMatters, 2 March 2024, https://www.voxelmatters.com/five-footwear-industry-leaders-using-3d-printing-for-production-today/.

36 'How IoT, AI and 3D Digital Twin Boost Predictive Maintenance in Manufacturing', Process Genius, https://processgenius.eu/articles/how-iot-ai-and-3d-digital-twin-boost-predictive-maintenance-in-manufacturing/; Advancing Flight for Future Generations, GE Aerospace, www.geaerospace.com; 'Why Does the World (and NASA) Need Digital Twins?', NASA, 18 February 2025, https://science.nasa.gov/biological-physical/why-does-the-world-and-nasa-need-digital-twins/; 'Digital Twins in the Automotive Industry Explained', S&P Global, 11 September 2025, https://www.spglobal.com/automotive-insights/en/blogs/2025/08/digital-twins-in-the-automotive-industry-explained.

37 'SIMATIC Energy Management Software', Siemens Global, https://www.siemens.com/global/en/products/automation/industry-software/automation-software/energymanagement.html; 'The Power of Energy Management Software', Honeywell, https://www.honeywell.com/us/en/news/2024/06/power-of-energy-management-software; 'Our AI-based Solutions', Schneider Electric, https://www.se.com/ww/en/work/solutions/artificial-intelligence/solutions.jsp.

38 'Homer Summary', Britannica, https://www.britannica.com/summary/Homer-Greek-poet.

39 'Dhanvantari', Britannica, https://www.britannica.com/topic/Dhanvantari.

40 'The God of Agriculture: The Importance of Shennong', Chinese Mythology Worldwide, https://chinese.mythologyworldwide.com/the-god-of-agriculture-the-importance-of-shennong/.

41 Ciaran Connolly, 'The Great Goddess of Health and Healing in Ancient Egypt', Learning Mole, 24 June 2024, https://learningmole.com/goddess-of-health-and-healing-in-ancient-egypt/.

42 'The White Moon Goddess Gallery Presents Airmid: Keeper of the Herbs of Healing', Order White Moon, https://orderwhitemoon.org/goddess/Airmid/airmid.html; Zain ul Abideen, 'Eir: The Norse Goddess of Healing', Mythohub, 9 December 2023, https://mythohub.com/norse-mythology/eir-the-norse-goddess-of-healing/.

43 'Sukunabikona', Japanese Wiki, https://www.japanesewiki.com/Shinto/Sukunabikona.html; 'Patecatl', World Mythos, https://worldmythos.com/patecatl/; 'Ozain: The Herber of the Yoruba Pantheon', OshaeIFA, https://en.oshaeifa.com/orisha/ozin/.

44 'Andreas Vesalius', Wikipedia, https://en.wikipedia.org/wiki/Andreas_Vesalius.

45 'Rothamsted Research', Wikipedia, https://en.wikipedia.org/wiki/Rothamsted_Research.

46 'Justus von Liebig', Encyclopedia.com, https://www.encyclopedia.com/science/encyclopedias-almanacs-transcripts-and-maps/justus-von-liebig.

47 'Cell Theory: Definition, History, Importance, Scientists', *Encyclopaedia Britannica*, www.britannica.com/science/cell-theory; 'Germ Theory: Definition, Development, and Facts', *Encyclopaedia Britannica*, www.britannica.com/science/germ-theory; 'Mendelian Inheritance', Wikipedia, www.en.wikipedia.org/wiki/Mendelian_inheritance; J. Liebenau, 'Company Structure and Scientific Medicine, 1890-95', in *Medical Science and Medical History* (London: Palgrave Macmillan, 1987), https://doi.org/10.1007/978-1-349-08739-6_3.

48 Liebenau,' Company Structure and Scientific Medicine'.

49 S. Chhabra, A.B. Taksande and P. Munjewar, 'The Penicillin Pioneer: Alexander Fleming's Journey to a Medical Breakthrough', *Cureus*, 16 (7): e65179; 'The History of a Wonderful Thing We Call Insulin', American Diabetes Association, 1 July 2019, https://diabetes.org/blog/history-wonderful-thing-we-call-insulin;

Carmen Lambert and Elias Delgado, '100 Years Since the Discovery of Insulin, from Its Discovery to the Insulins of the Future', *Biomedicines*, 12 (3): 533. Available online: https://pmc.ncbi.nlm.nih.gov/articles/PMC10968222/.

50 'Imaging', Siemens Global, https://www.siemens.com/global/en/company/about/history/technology/medical-technology/imaging.html; 'Evolution of the ECG Machine', Intelesens, https://intelesens.com/evolution-of-the-ecg-machine/.

51 Liebenau, 'Company Structure and Scientific Medicine'.

52 James Bonner and Post Editors, 'The Discovery of DNA Marks a Turning Point in Science', *Saturday Evening Post*, 25 April 2017.

53 Kritika Agarwal, 'NIH Research Funding Supports Jobs, Fuels the U.S. Economy', Association of American Universities, 14 March 2025, https://www.aau.edu/newsroom/leading-research-universities-report/nih-research-funding-supports-jobs-fuels-us-economy.

54 'Changes in Science, Law and Regulatory Authorities', FDA, U.S. Food and Drug Administration (FDA), 30 January 2018, https://www.fda.gov/about-fda/fda-history/changes-science-law-and-regulatory-authorities.

55 'The Rise of Biotechnology as Big Business', Encyclopedia.com, https://www.encyclopedia.com/science/encyclopedias-almanacs-transcripts-and-maps/rise-biotechnology-big-business.

56 'The Human Genome Project', National Human Genome Research Institute, https://www.genome.gov/human-genome-project.

57 'A History of: Contract Research Organisations (CROs)', Pharmaphorum, https://pharmaphorum.com/views-and-analysis/a_history_of_contract_research_organisations_cros.

58 'Evolution of Bioinformatics from 2000 to 2010', ResearchGate, https://www.researchgate.net/figure/Evolution-of-bioinformatics-from-2000-to-2010_fig5_364058017; A. Trewavas, 'A Brief History of Systems Biology. "Every Object That Biology Studies Is a System of Systems." Francois Jacob (1974)', *Plant Cell*, 18 (10): 2420–30. doi: 10.1105/tpc.106.042267; P. Krzyszczyk et al., 'The Growing Role of Precision and Personalized Medicine for Cancer Treatment', *Technology (Singap World Sci)*, 6(3-4): 79–100. doi: 10.1142/S2339547818300020.

59 'How IoT and Blockchain May Streamline Transition to Digital Healthcare', *Business*, 15 March 2018, https://www.kaaiot.com/blog/iot-blockchain-may-streamline-transition-digital-healthcare#.

60 'Where Zymergen Went Wrong: A Biomanufacturing Perspective for Synthetic Biology', Manufacturing Chemist, 12 October 2022, https://www.manufacturingchemist.com/where-zymergen-went-wrong-a-biomanufacturing-perspective-for-synthetic-biology-204177.

61 *The State of Digital Transformation in India Life Sciences* (Cognizant, 2023). Available online: https://www.cognizant.com/assets/in/en/field-marketing/documents/cmp-005397/State_of_Digital_Transformation_in_India_LS.pdf.

62 'Seven in Ten Pharma Digital Projects Fail to Deliver Despite Heavy Investments', *Economic Times,* 24 September 2025. Available online: https://pharma.economictimes.indiatimes.com/news/pharma-industry/seven-in-ten-pharma-digital-projects-fail-to-deliver-despite-heavy-investments-vector-study/124091233.

63 James, 'The Evolution of Wearable Technology', Balliante, 25 November 2024, https://www.balliante.com/the-evolution-of-wearable-technology/.

64 Rikin Patel et al., 'A Comprehensive Review of SARS-CoV-2 Vaccines: Pfizer, Moderna & Johnson & Johnson', *Human Vaccines & Immunotherapeutics*, 18 (1).

65 Petrina Kamya et al., 'PandaOmics: An AI-Driven Platform for Therapeutic Target and Biomarker Discovery', *Journal of Chemical Information and Modeling*, 64 (10).

66 'Artificial Intelligence: Who Are the Leaders in AI in Multiomics for the Pharmaceutical Industry?, Pharmaceutical Technology, 29 July 2024, https://www.pharmaceutical-technology.com/data-insights/innovators-ai-ai-in-multiomics-pharmaceutical/.

67 'Core Research', Proteomica International Private Limited, https://www.proteomica.in/core-research.

68 'Services', Sravathi AI, https://sravathi.ai/services.

69 'Our Bioinformatics Services', Fios Genomics, https://www.fiosgenomics.com/service/the-bioinformatics-services.

70 'Pfizer AI Strategy Analysis of Dominance in Pharma', Klover, https://www.klover.ai/pfizer-ai-strategy-analysis-of-dominance-in-pharma/.

71 Shez Partovi and Ian Meyers, 'AWS and Novartis Redefining Pharma Manufacturing', AWS (blog), 4 December 2019, https://aws.amazon.com/blogs/industries/aws-and-novartis-re-inventing-pharma-manufacturing/.

72 'Transform Pharmaceutical Supply Chains', Blue Yonder, https://blueyonder.com/blog/2025/transform-pharmaceutical-supply-chains.

73 'AI Solutions in Healthcare', https://siemens-healthineers.com/en-in/ai-healthcare-solutions.
74 'AliveCor Launches KardiaComplete to Help Reduce the Rising Health and Economic Costs of Heart Disease', AliveCor, https://alivecor.com/press/press_release/alivecor-launches-kardiacomplete-to-help-reduce-the-rising-health-and-economic-costs-of-heart-disease.
75 'Trusted Artificial Intelligence for All', Ibex, https://ibex-ai.com/technology/.
76 'AI in Life Sciences Market Size & Share Analysis—Growth Trends & Forecasts (2025–2030)', Mordor Intelligence, https://www.mordorintelligence.com/industry-reports/artificial-intelligence-in-life-sciences-market.
77 'Lab-in-the-Loop AI for Life Science', Nvidia, https://www.nvidia.com/en-in/use-cases/lab-in-the-loop-ai-for-life-science/.
78 'Pharma Industry in India: An Outlook for 2025–2030', India Employer Forum, https://indiaemployerforum.org/world-of-work/pharma-industry-in-india-2025-2030.
79 'Why a Bioinformatics Career Is the Best Choice This Decade', BioTecNika, https://www.biotecnika.org/2025/09/why-a-bioinformatics-career-is-the-best-choice-this-decade/.
80 'ABB Automation Solutions for the Life Sciences Industries', ABB, https://new.abb.com/life-sciences.

CHAPTER 7 THE SURGE OF AUTOMATION WITH AI AT THE EDGE

1 'Quote Origin: The Factory of the Future Will Have Only Two Employees, a Man and a Dog', Quote Investigator, 30 January 2022. Available online: https://quoteinvestigator.com/2022/01/30/future-factory/.
2 'Digital Twins: The Next Frontier of Factory Optimization', McKinsey, 10 January 2024, https://www.mckinsey.com/capabilities/operations/our-insights/digital-twins-the-next-frontier-of-factory-optimization.
3 KELA, *Escalating Ransomware Threats to National Security, A Rising Scale of Attacks on Critical Infrastructure Sectors,* October 2025. Available online: https://www.kelacyber.com/resources/research/escalating-ransomware-threats-to-national-security/.
4 A.D. Amar and V.K. Vishwakarma, *Artificial Intelligence in Finance* (Routledge, 2020).

5 'Intelligent Process Automation: The Engine at the Core of the Next-Generation Operating Model', McKinsey, 14 March 2017, https://www.mckinsey.com/capabilities/tech-and-ai/our-insights/intelligent-process-automation-the-engine-at-the-core-of-the-next-generation-operating-model.

6 David Garton, 'Purdue Model Framework for Industrial Control Systems & Cybersecurity Segmentation', topic paper 4-14 prepared for the National Petroleum Council Study on Oil and Natural Gas Transportation Infrastructure, National Petroleum Council, 12 November 2019. Available online: https://www.energy.gov/sites/default/files/2022-10/Infra_Topic_Paper_4-14_FINAL.pdf.

7 Press Information Bureau, 'India on Track to Become $35 Trillion, Fully Developed Economy by 2047: Shri Piyush Goyal', 19 February 2024. Available online: https://www.pib.gov.in/PressReleasePage.aspx?PRID=2007105.

8 Press Information Bureau, 'India Is Keen to Increase Share of Manufacturing in GDP from 17% to 25%: Union Minister Hardeep S Puri', press release, 29 September 2023. Available online: https://www.pib.gov.in/PressReleasePage.aspx?PRID=1962137.

9 Ibid.

10 Reuters, 'India Plans Over Rs 18,000 Crore in Incentives for New Manufacturing Sectors', *Economic Times*, 20 September 2023. Available online: https://economictimes.indiatimes.com/news/economy/policy/india-plans-over-rs-18000-cr-in-incentives-for-new-manufacturing-sectors/articleshow/103810315.cms.

11 Rica Bhattacharyya, 'India Mobile Phone Manufacturing Industry Likely to Create Up to 2,50,000 Jobs in Next 12-16 Months', *Economic Times,* 8 February 2024. Available online: https://economictimes.indiatimes.com/jobs/fresher/india-mobile-phone-manufacturing-industry-likely-to-create-up-to-250000-jobs-in-next-12-16-months/articleshow/107529553.cms

12 FICCI, 'Micro, Small and Medium Enterprises (MSME)', https://ficci.in/sector/micro-small-and-medium-enterprises-msme.

CHAPTER 8 AI CHANGING OUR LIVES

1 'The Artifice Girl', Wikipedia, https://en.wikipedia.org/wiki/The_Artifice_Girl.

2 Yuval Noah Harari, *Nexus* (UK: Penguin, 2025). Available online: https://www.ynharari.com/book/nexus/.
3 'Taare Zameen Par', Wikipedia, https://en.wikipedia.org/wiki/Taare_Zameen_Par.
4 'About UNIS', United Nations International School, https://www.unis.org/about-unis.
5 'About', Skills Alpha, https://skillsalpha.com/about/.
6 'Artificial Intelligence', GTT Data Solutions, https://gttdata.ai/services/#artificial-intelligence.
7 'Audience Measurement & Insight', Kantar Media, https://www.kantarmedia.com/services/audience-measurement; 'Audience Measurement', Nielsen, https://www.nielsen.com/solutions/audience-measurement.
8 Harari, *Nexus.*
9 'Open Challenge Program Agenda', Motion, https://motion.stpi.in/open_challenge#agenda; 'About STPI', STPI, https://stpi.in/en/about-stpi.
10 Surabhi Rajpal, 'Autonomous Ride-Hailing Grown in Key US Markets', S&P Global, 5 December 2025. Available online: https://www.spglobal.com/automotive-insights/en/blogs/2025/12/autonomous-ride-hailing-grows-key-us-markets.
11 Jasper Jolly, 'Driving Competition: China's Carmakers in Race to Dominate Europe's Roads', *Guardian,* 7 November 2025. Available online: https://www.theguardian.com/business/2025/nov/07/china-in-push-to-dominate-europe-electric-vehicle-market-with-uk-as-gateway.
12 Joanna Beczkowska, 'South Korean Companies Race for Domination in Europe's EV Battery Market', Centre for Asian Affairs, CAA Brief, June 2021. Available online: https://www.osa.uni.lodz.pl/fileadmin/Jednostki/Osrodek_Spraw_Azjatyckich/CAA_Briefs/2021/CAA_Brief_JB_June_2021.pdf.
13 'The Founding of TiE', TiE, https://tie.org/the-genesis-of-tie/.
14 'O, Pardon Me, Thou Bleeding Piece of Earth, Julius Caesar, Act II, Scene I, Academy of American Poets, William Shakespeare', Poets, https://poets.org/poem/julius-caesar-act-iii-scene-i-o-pardon-me-thou-bleeding-piece-earth; 'Friends, Romans, Countrymen, Lend Me Your Ears, Julius Caesar, Spoken by Mark Antony, William Shakespeare', Poetry Foundation, https://www.poetryfoundation.org/poems/56968/speech-friends-romans-countrymen-lend-me-your-ears.

15 Harari, *Nexus.*

16 Sounak Mukhopadhyay, 'ChatGPT Writes Suicide Note for 29-Year-Old So That It Hurts Her Family Less; Mother Slams AI Bot after Losing Daughter', LiveMint, 21 September 2025, https://www.livemint.com/news/trends/chatgpt-writes-suicide-note-for-29-year-old-so-that-it-hurts-her-family-less-mother-slams-ai-bot-after-losing-daughter-11758457919663.html.

17 'Dating Apps Are Common, Useful and Widely Disliked', Survey Monkey, https://www.surveymonkey.com/curiosity/dating-apps-and-sites-are-almost-as-common-as-they-are-disliked/; Emily A. Vogels and Monica Anderson, 'Dating and Relationships in the Digital Age', 8 May 2020. Available online: https://www.pewresearch.org/internet/2020/05/08/dating-and-relationships-in-the-digital-age/.

18 Harari, *Nexus.*

19 Tom Datan and Berber Jin, 'OpenAI in Talks for Funding Round Valuing It Above $100 Billion', *Wall Street Journal*, 28 August 2024. Available online: https://www.wsj.com/tech/ai/openai-in-talks-for-funding-round-valuing-it-above-100 billion.

Chapter 9 Leadership in the Era of AI

1 Ethan Mollick, Co-Intelligence, https://www.scribd.com/document/853903109/co-intelligence, Penguin Random House, 2024.

2 Geoffrey Hinton, Wikipedia, https://en.wikipedia.org/wiki/Geoffrey_Hinton.

3 Swami Vivekananda, https://en.wikipedia.org/wiki/Arise,_awake,_and_stop_not_till_the_goal_is_reached.

Bibliography

ABB. 'ABB Automation Solutions for the Life Sciences Industries'. Available at: https://new.abb.com/life-sciences.

Abideen, Zain ul. 'Eir: The Norse Goddess of Healing'. Mythohub, 9 December 2023. Available at: https://mythohub.com/norse-mythology/eir-the-norse-goddess-of-healing/.

Accenture. 'The Future of Fintech and Banking'. Available at: https://bankingblog.accenture.com/wp-content/uploads/2015/04/accenture-future-fintech-banking.pdf.

Adams, Peter. 'Houzz App's AR Upgrade Turns Living Rooms into Virtual Showroom Floors', Marketing Dive, 8 May 2017, https://www.marketingdive.com/news/houzz-apps-ar-upgrade-turns-living-rooms-into-virtual-showroom-floors/442142/.

Adweek. 'Tommy Hilfiger Lets Shoppers Try on Clothes in AR with Zero10', 31 March 2023. Available at: https://www.adweek.com/creativity/tommy-hilfiger-try-on-clothes-with-zero10/.

Agarwal, Kritika. 'NIH Research Funding Supports Jobs, Fuels the U.S. Economy'. Association of American Universities, 14 March 2025. Available at: https://www.aau.edu/newsroom/leading-research-universities-report/nih-research-funding-supports-jobs-fuels-us-economy.

Agrawal, Ajay, Joshua Gans and Avi Goldfarb. *Power and Prediction: The Disruptive Economics of Artificial Intelligence*. New Delhi: Replika Press, 2024.

Aicadium. 'How BMW Is Using AI to Improve Its Manufacturing Processes', 13 December 2013. Available at: https://aicadium.ai/how-bmw-is-using-ai-to-improve-its-manufacturing-processes/.

Aithor. 'Samsung Note 7 Failure Case Study'. Available at: https://aithor.com/essay-examples/samsung-note-7-failure-case-study.

Aknoukh, Karim, Ahmed Ewis and Fortune Hui. 'Manage Access Controls in Generative AI-powered Search Applications Using Amazon OpenSearch Service and Amazon Cognito'. AWS Big Data Blog, 19 November 2024. Available at: https://aws.amazon.com/

blogs/big-data/manage-access-controls-in-generative-ai-powered-search-applications-using-amazon-opensearch-service-and-aws-cognito/.

AliveCor. 'AliveCor Launches KardiaComplete to Help Reduce the Rising Health and Economic Costs of Heart Disease'. Available at: https://alivecor.com/press/press_release/alivecor-launches-kardiacomplete-to-help-reduce-the-rising-health-and-economic-costs-of-heart-disease.

'All Comet Stores to Close Today as Losses Hit £230m and Vince Cable Steps In'. *Retail Week*. Available at: https://www.retail-week.com/companies/all-comet-stores-to-close-today-as-losses-hit-230m-and-vince-cable-steps-in/5044211.article.

Allied Digital. 'The Global Recession and the Growth of Cloud Computing'. Concept paper, 2011. Available at: https://www.allieddigital.net/in/downloads/concept-papers/Concept-Papers-The-Global-Recession-and-Change-of-Cloud.pdf.

Amar, A.D. and V.K. Vishwakarma. *Artificial Intelligence in Finance.* Routledge, 2020.

American Diabetes Association. 'The History of a Wonderful Thing We Call Insulin', 1 July 2019, Available at: https://diabetes.org/blog/history-wonderful-thing-we-call-insulin.

American Express. *American Express Annual Report 2023*. Available at: https://s26.q4cdn.com/747928648/files/doc_financials/2023/ar/American-Express-Annual-Report-2023.pdf.

Applied Learning. 'Authentic Employee Engagement'. Available at: https://www.appliedlearning.com/authentic-employee-engagement/.

Archives of IT. '90s Technology: How the 90s Changed Technology', 2020. Available at: https://archivesit.org.uk/blog/90s-revolution.

'Artificial Intelligence in Financial Services'. PwC study. PricewaterhouseCoopers, 2020. Available at: https://www.pwc.de/en/finanzdienstleistungen/artificial-intelligence-in-financial-services.html.

Asian Development Bank. 'Artificial Intelligence in Action: Selected ADB Initiatives in Asia and the Pacific', May 2024. Available at: https://www.adb.org/publications/ai-action-adb-initiatives-asia-pacific.

Associated Press. 'Japan Robot Hotel Ready to Welcome Its First Human Guests', 15 July 2015.

Beczkowska, Joanna. 'South Korean Companies Race for Domination in Europe's EV Battery Market'. Centre for Asian Affairs. CAA Brief, June 2021. Available at: https://www.osa.uni.lodz.pl/fileadmin/Jednostki/Osrodek_Spraw_Azjatyckich/CAA_Briefs/2021/CAA_Brief_JB_June_2021.pdf.

Bell, Kyle. 'Why Is ChatGPT So Bad at Math?'. TechCrunch, 2 October 2024. Available at: https://techcrunch.com/2024/10/02/why-is-chatgpt-so-bad-at-math/.

Betz, Sunny. '7 Types of Artificial Intelligence'. Built In. Available at: https://builtin.com/artificial-intelligence/types-of-artificial-intelligence.

'BFSI Sector to Add 2.5 Lakh Jobs by 2030; Hiring Shifts to Tier II, III Cities: Report'. *Economic Times*, 21 August 2025. Available at: https://economictimes.indiatimes.com/industry/banking/finance/banking/bfsi-sector-to-add-2-5-lakh-jobs-by-2030-hiring-shifts-to-tier-ii-iii-cities-report/articleshow/.

Bhaktivedanta Swami Prabhupada, A.C. *Bhagavad Gita As It Is*. Mumbai: Bhaktivedanta Book Trust, 2019.

Bharadwaj, K.V. Aditya. 'Why HMT Failed to Keep Pace with Time'. *Hindu*, 22 September 2016.

Bhattacharyya, Rica. 'India Mobile Phone Manufacturing Industry Likely to Create Up to 2,50,000 Jobs in Next 14-16 Months', *Economic Times*, 8 February 2024. Available at: https://economictimes.indiatimes.com/jobs/fresher/india-mobile-phone-manufacturing-industry-likely-to-create-up-to-250000-jobs-in-next-12-16-months/articleshow/107529553.cms

BioTecNika. 'Why a Bioinformatics Career Is the Best Choice This Decade'. Available at: https://www.biotecnika.org/2025/09/why-a-bioinformatics-career-is-the-best-choice-this-decade/.

Blue Yonder. 'Transform Pharmaceutical Supply Chains'. Available at: https://blueyonder.com/blog/2025/transform-pharmaceutical-supply-chains.

Bodem, Margaret, ed. *The Philosophy of Artificial Intelligence*. Oxford: Oxford University Press, 1990.

Bonner, James and Post Editors. 'The Discovery of DNA Marks a Turning Point in Science'. *Saturday Evening Post*, 25 April 2017.

Borah, Prabalika. 'India-Made Robots Chat Up Diners at Hyderabad Restaurant'. *Hindu*, 21 August 2021.

Bosch. 'Allow Me, the AI Analytics Platform'. Available at: https://www.bosch.com/stories/ai-in-manufacturing/

Bosman, Julie and Michael J. de la Merced. 'Borders' Bankruptcy Shakes Industry'. *New York Times*, 16 February 2011.

Boulton, Matthew and James Watt. *The Selected Papers of Boulton & Watt: The Engine Partnership 1775–1825*, edited by Jennifer Tann. Cambridge, MA: MIT Press, 1981.

Boyd, Eric. 'ChatGPT Is Now Available in Azure OpenAI Service'. Microsoft Azure Blog, 9 March 2023. Available at: https://azure.microsoft.com/en-us/blog/chatgpt-is-now-available-in-azure-openai-service/.

Brachmann, Steve. 'The Rise and Fall of the Company That Invented Digital Cameras'. IPWatchdog, 1 November 2014. Available at: https://ipwatchdog.com/2014/11/01/the-rise-and-fall-of-the-company-that-invented-digital-cameras/.

Branigan, Tania. 'A Tragedy Pushed to the Shadows: The Truth about China's Cultural Revolution'. *Guardian*, 19 January 2023.

Briggs, Martha T. and Cynthia H. Peters. *Pullman Company Archives*. Chicago: The Newberry Library, 1995. Available at: https://www.newberry.org/uploads/files/PullmanGuide.pdf.

Britannica. 'Dhanvantari'. Available at: https://www.britannica.com/topic/Dhanvantari.

Britannica. 'Homer Summary'. Available at: https://www.britannica.com/summary/Homer-Greek-poet.

Brockman, Greg, Ilya Sutskever and OpenAI. 'Introducing OpenAI'. OpenAI, 11 December 2015. Available at: https://openai.com/index/introducing-openai/.

Brown, Sara. 'Why Neural Net Pioneer Geoffrey Hinton Is Sounding the Alarm on AI'. MIT Sloan, 23 May 2023. Available at: https://mitsloan.mit.edu/ideas-made-to-matter/why-neural-net-pioneer-geoffrey-hinton-sounding-alarm-ai.

Buduraju, Hema. 'Google Search: Introducing AI Mode in India'. Google Blog, 24 June 2025. Available at: https://blog.google/intl/en-in/products/google-search-introducing-ai-mode-in-india/ (accessed 12 September 2025).

Calton, Chris. 'Henry Ford Did More for Workers than Unions Did'. Intellectual Takeout, 7 January 2020. Available at: https://intellectualtakeout.org/2020/01/henry-ford-did-more-for-workers-than-unions-did/.

Carnegie, Andrew. *Autobiography of Andrew Carnegie & the Gospel of Wealth*. New Delhi: Sanage Publishing House, 2021.

Casemore, B., P. Jirovsky and R. Mehra. 'IDC Report: The New Need for Speed in the Datacenter Network', 2015. Available at: https://www.cisco.com/c/dam/global/en_uk/assets/pdfs/white-paper-c11-734328.pdf.

Castus Global. 'The Downfall of Sears: 5 Key Reasons Why the Retail Giant Went Under', 5 October 2021. Available at: https:// www.castusglobal.com/insights/the-downfall-of-sears-5-key-reasons-why-the retail-giant-went-under#.

CEOs of Dubai. 'IBM's Remarkable Revival: How CEO Arvind Krishna Resurrected a Tech Giant', 17 February 2025.

CERN. 'A Short History of the Web'. Available at: https://home.cern/science/computing/birth-web/short-history-web.

Chatbot Guide. 'Domino's Pizza Bot'. Available at: https://www.chatbotguide.org/dominospizza-bot.

Chaudhuri, Arakarag. 'How Century-Old Indian Brands Are Winning with AR, AI and Immersive Experiences'. CMSWIRE, 12 August 2025. Available at: https://www.cmswire.com/digital-experience/how-century-old-indian-brands-are-winning-with-ar-ai-and-immersive-experiences/.

Chhabra, S., A.B. Taksande and P. Munjewar. 'The Penicillin Pioneer: Alexander Fleming's Journey to a Medical Breakthrough'. *Cureus* 16, no. 7 (2024): e65179.

China, C.R. and M. Goodwin. 'IaaS, PaaS, SaaS: What's the Difference?'. IBM Think, 24 July 2025. Available at: https://www.ibm.com/think/topics/iaas-paas-saas.

Chinese Mythology Worldwide. 'The God of Agriculture: The Importance of Shennong'. Available at: https://chinese.mythologyworldwide.com/the-god-of-agriculture-the-importance-of-shennong/.

Cognizant. *The State of Digital Transformation in India Life Sciences.* Cognizant, 2023. Available at: https://www.cognizant.com/assets/in/en/field-marketing/documents/cmp-005397/State_of_Digital_Transformation_in_India_LS.pdf.

Collis, David J. and Tonia Junker. 'Digitalization at Siemens'. Harvard Business School Case 717-428, February 2017 (revised November 2021).

Columbia Business School. 'Sears: A Case Study in Business Failure', 23 October 2018. Available at: https://business.columbia.edu/insights/chazen-global-insights/sears-case-study-business-failure.

Companies Market Cap. 'Market Capitalization of Nokia 2019'. Available at: https://companiesmarketcap.com/nokia/marketcap/.

Connolly, Ciaran. 'The Great Goddess of Health and Healing in Ancient Egypt'. Learning Mole, 24 June 2024. Available at: https://learningmole.com/goddess-of-health-and-healing-in-ancient-egypt/.

Cordeira, Joseph. 'The UBS AI Advantage: The New Standard of Growing Your Practice'. Available at: https://www.ubs.com/us/en/wealth-management/financial-advisor-experience/articles/ai-for-financial-advisors.html?campID=SOME-AIA-US-ENG-FASM-ANY-FASF-FASD--ANY-ANY-ORGANIC&campID=SOME-FASOCIAL-US-ANY-LINKEDIN-ANY-ANY-ANY-ANY-ANY-ANY-ANY-e58ff610-fe84-11ef-9ca1-219a418390e2.

COVE Collective Editions. 'Lowell Textile Mills'. Available at: https://editions.covecollective.org/chronologies/lowell-textile-mills.

Cudahy, Sean. 'American Airlines Says AI Could Help with Fares—But Only to Save Time'. The Points Guy, 15 September 2025. Available at: https://thepointsguy.com/news/american-airlines-ai-fares/.

D'Monte, Leslie. 'How L&T Is Engineering an AI-driven Conglomerate'. *LiveMint*, 24 April 2024. Available at: https://www.livemint.com/companies/how-l-t-is-engineering-an-ai-driven-conglomerate-11713957779560.html.

Daly, Charles. 'Klarna Turns from AI to Real-Person Customer Service'. Bloomberg, 8 May 2025. Available at: https://www.bloomberg.com/news/articles/2025-05-08/klarna-turns-from-ai-to-real-person-customer-service.

Datan, Tom and Berber Jin. 'OpenAI in Talks for Funding Round Valuing It Above $100 Billion'. *Wall Street Journal*, 28 August 2024. Available at: https://www.wsj.com/tech/ai/openai-in-talks-for-funding-round-valuing-it-above-100 billion.

Davenport, Thomas H. and Steven Miller. *Working with AI: Real Stories of Human-Machine Collaboration*. Cambridge, MA: MIT Press, 2022.

Deloitte. 'Web3, Metaverse and Digital Finance'. Available at: https://www.deloitte.com/cz-sk/en/services/consulting/services/cyber-risk/web3-metaverse-and-digital-finance.html.

DeMarco, Anthony. 'De Beers Turns to Augmented Reality to Market Its Branded Diamond'. *Forbes*, 29 March 2016. Available at: https://www.forbes.com/sites/anthonydemarco/2011/10/12/de-beers-turns-to-augmented-reality-to-market-its-branded-diamond/.

Dennis, M.A. 'Marvin Minsky'. *Encyclopaedia Britannica*, 5 August 2025. Available at: https://www.britannica.com/biography/Marvin-Minsky.

Deplazes, Raymond. 'Autodesk and Airbus Demonstrate the Impact of Generative Design on Making and Building'. Autodesk News, 19 November 2019. Available at: https://adsknews.autodesk.com/en/news/autodesk-airbus-generative-design-aerospace-factory/.

Desai, Ranjit and Vikrant Pande. *Shivaji: The Great Maratha*. New Delhi: Harper Perennial, 2017.

Digitide Solutions Limited, https://www.digitide.com.

Dixit, Pranav. 'Akash Tablet: A Failed Experiment in Affordable Computing?'. *The Next Web*, 25 October 2012.

DQI Bureau. 'The PC in India: The Desktop Story'. *Data Quest*, 12 September 2000. Available at: https://www.dqindia.com/the-pc-in-india-the-desktop-story.

Dragon Medical Transcription. 'History of Speech & Voice Recognition and Transcription Software'. Available at: https://www.dragon-medical-transcription.com/history_speech_recognition.html.

Earnshaw, Thomas. 'Mathew Boulton and James Watt: The Dynamic Partnership That Transformed the Steam Engine', 13 April 2024. Available at: https://thomas-earnshaw.com/blogs/the-earnshaw-odyssey/matthew-boulton-and-james-watt-transformed-the-steam-engine.

Ellickson, Paul. 'The Evolution of the Supermarket Industry: From A&P to Wal-Mart'. *SSRN Electronic Journal*, April 2011.

Emerj. 'Artificial Intelligence at American Express—Two Current Use Cases'. Available at: https://emerj.com/artificial-intelligence-at-american-express/.

Emmet, Boris and John Jeuck. *Catalogues and Counters: A History of Sears, Roebuck and Company*. Chicago: University of Chicago Press, 1950.

Encyclopaedia Britannica. 'Cell Theory: Definition, History, Importance, Scientists'. Available at: www.britannica.com/science/cell-theory.

Encyclopaedia Britannica. 'Germ Theory: Definition, Development, and Facts'. Available at: www.britannica.com/science/germ-theory.

Encyclopedia.com. 'Justus von Liebig'. Available at: https://www.encyclopedia.com/science/encyclopedias-almanacs-transcripts-and-maps/justus-von-liebig.

Encyclopaedia Britannica. 'The Rise of Biotechnology as Big Business'. Available at: https://www.encyclopedia.com/science/encyclopedias-almanacs-transcripts-and-maps/rise-biotechnology-big-business.

EU Artificial Intelligence Act. 'What Is the EU AI Act?'. Available at: https://artificialintelligenceact.eu.

European Parliament. 'EU AI Act: First Regulation on Artificial Intelligence'. *European Parliament Topics*, 1 June 2023. Available at: https://www.europarl.europa.eu/topics/en/article/20230601STO93804/eu-ai-act-first-regulation-on-artificial-intelligence.

Express Computer. 'Discovering Education's Future with the Rise of GenAI in India's EdTech Landscape'. 27 August 2024. Available at: https://www.expresscomputer.in/guest-blogs/discovering-educations-future-with-the-rise-of-genai-in-indias-edtech-landscape/115373/.

Fairweather, Nicholas. 'Hitler and Hitlerism: Germany Under the Nazis'. *The Atlantic*, April 1932.

FDA, U.S. Food and Drug Administration (FDA). 'Changes in Science, Law and Regulatory Authorities', 30 January 2018. Available at: https://www.fda.gov/about-fda/fda-history/changes-science-law-and-regulatory-authorities.

Feigenbaum, E. and H. Shrobe. 'The Japanese National Fifth Generation Project: Introduction, Survey, and Evaluation'. *Future Generation Computer Systems* 9 (1993): 105–117. Available at: https://stacks.stanford.edu/file/druid:kv359wz9060/kv359wz9060.pdf.

FICCI. 'Micro, Small and Medium Enterprises (MSME)'. https://ficci.in/sector/micro-small-and-medium-enterprises-msme.

Finn, Teaganne and Amanda Downie. 'Agentic AI vs Generative AI'. IBM, 2025. Available at: https://www.ibm.com/think/topics/agentic-ai-vs-generative-ai.

fios Genomics. 'Our Bioinformatics Services'. Available at: https://www.fiosgenomics.com/service/the-bioinformatics-services.

Foxconn. 'Foxconn Announces Foxconn NxVAE, Unsupervised Learning AI Technology', 21 January 2021. Available at: https://www.foxconn.com/en-us/press-center/events/csr-events/533.

Franz, Raymond. 'The Process of Institutionalization of Christianity'. *Mentes Bereanas*, 22 July 2020. Available at: https://www.mentesbereanas.info.

Fresno State University. 'DEC's XCON Expert System'. Available at: https://zimmer.fresnostate.edu/~sasanr/Teaching-Material/MIS/ES/DEC's-XCON.pdf.

Friedrich, Roman et al. *Measuring Industry Digitization: Leaders and Laggards in the Digital Economy*. Strategy&, 2011.

Future Today Institute. *2024 Tech Trends Report*, 17th ed. Available at: https://www.futuretodayinstitute.com/wp-content/uploads/2024/03/TR2024_Full-Report_FINAL_LINKED.pdf.

Gartner Inc. 'Gartner Survey Reveals 47% of Organizations Will Increase Investments in IoT Despite the Impact of Covid-19'. *Gartner Newsroom*, press release, 29 October 2020. Available at: https://www.gartner.com/en/newsroom/press-releases/2020-10-29-gartner-survey-reveals-47-percent-of-organizations-will-increase-investments-in-iot-despite-the-impact-of-covid-19-.

Gartner. 'The Nexus of Forces: Social, Mobile, Cloud and Information', 2012. Available at: https://www.gartner.com/en/documents/2049315.

Garton, David. 'Purdue Model Framework for Industrial Control Systems & Cybersecurity Segmentation'. Topic paper 4-14 prepared for the National Petroleum Council Study on Oil and Natural Gas Transportation Infrastructure, National Petroleum Council, 12 November 2019. Available at: https://www.energy.gov/sites/default/files/2022-10/Infra_Topic_Paper_4-14_FINAL.pdf.

Gates, Bill. 'My Conversation with Sam Altman'. Unconfuse Me with Bill Gates (podcast), Gates Notes, 11 January 2024. Available at: https://www.gatesnotes.com/meet-bill/my-podcasts/reader/unconfuse-me-podcast-with-guest-sam-altman.

Gawande, Mayur Suresh et al. 'The Role of Artificial Intelligence in Pandemic Responses: From Epidemiological Modeling to Vaccine Development'. *Molecular Biomedicine*, 6 (2025): 1.

GE Aerospace. 'Advancing Flight for Future Generations'. Available at: www.geaerospace.com.

GE Vernova. 'GE Using AI/ML to Reduce Wind Turbine Logistics and Installation Costs', 4 April 2022. Available at: https://www.gevernova.com/news/press-releases/ge-using-aiml-to-reduce-wind-turbine-logistics-and-installation-costs.

Ghosh, Bhaskar, H. James Wilson, Adam Burden and Paul R. Daugherty. 'Taking a Systems Approach to Adopting AI'. *Harvard Business Review*, 9 May 2019.

Giacaglia, Giuliano. 'The Golden Years of AI (1956–1974)'. In *Making Things Think: How AI and Deep Learning Power the Products We Use.* San Francisco: Holloway, n.d. Available at: https://www.holloway.com/g/making-things-think/sections/the-golden-years-of-ai-19561974.

Goldenberg, Barton. 'From Concept to Reality: BMWs Groundbreaking XR/VR/AR Technology'. Ism Guide. Available at: https://ismguide.com/bmw-xr-metaverse-technology-case-study/

Goldman Sachs. 'The Late 1990s Dot-Com Bubble Implodes in 2000'. *Goldman Sachs History*, 2020. Available at: https://www.goldmansachs.com/our-firm/history/moments/2000-dot-com-bubble.

Gonzales, Francis. 'The Rise and Fall of Polaroid. The Disruptor Becomes the Disrupted'. UX Collective, 9 May 2021. Available at: https://uxdesign.cc/the-rise-and-fall-of-polaroid-3fffde2b5128.

Google Threat Intelligence Group. 'Adversarial Misuse of Generative AI'. Google Cloud Blog, 30 January 2025. Available at: https://cloud.google.com/blog/topics/threat-intelligence/adversarial-misuse-generative-ai.

Grace, Katja et al. 'Thousands of AI Authors on the Future of AI'. AI Impacts, January 2024. Available at: https://aiimpacts.org/wp-content/uploads/2023/04/Thousands_of_AI_authors_on_the_future_of_AI.pdf.

Griffin, Mathew. 'JPMorgan Unleashes Artificial Intelligence to Automate Its Legal Work'. Fanatical Futurist, March 2017. Available at: https://www.fanaticalfuturist.com/2017/03/jpmorgan-unleashes-artificial-intelligence-to-automate-its-legal-work/.

Gross, Doug. 'Apple Introduces Siri, Web Freaks Out'. *CNN*, 4 October 2011. Available at: https://edition.cnn.com/2011/10/04/tech/mobile/siri-iphone-4s-skynet.

Groww. 'Groww Press Releases and Annual Reports 2023'. Available at: https://groww.in/investor-relations/performance/company.

GTT Data Solutions. 'Artificial Intelligence'. Available at: https://gttdata.ai/services/#artificial-intelligence.

Gupta, Mahendranath. *Sri Sri Ramakrishna Kathamrita*. Kolkata: Kathamrita Bhavan, 1902.

H&M Group. 'H&M Group Explores Tech-Enabled Shopping Experiences in US Stores', 27 May 2022. Available at: https://hmgroup.com/news/hm-group-explores-tech-enabled-shopping-experiences-in-us-stores/.

Hackett, Conhard et al. 'Islam Was the World's Fastest Growing Religion from 2010 to 2020'. Pew Research, 9 June 2025. Available at: https://www.pewresearch.org/short-reads/2025/06/10/islam-was-the-worlds-fastest-growing-religion-from-2010-to-2020/.

Haenlein, Michael and Andreas Kaplan. 'A Brief History of Artificial Intelligence: On the Past, Present, and Future of Artificial Intelligence'. *California Management Review* 61, no. 4 (2019). Available at: https://www.researchgate.net/publication/334539401_A_Brief_History_of_Artificial_Intelligence_On_the_Past_Present_and_Future_of_Artificial_Intelligence.

Harari, Yuval Noah. *Nexus: A Brief History of Information Networks from the Stone Age to AI*. London: Penguin, 2025.

Haritas, Bhragu. 'Mahindra Group's Four Pillars of Digital Transformation'. ETCIO, 1 June 2021.

Harris, Sophia. 'Target Canada to Close All Stores by April 12'. *CBC News*, 1 April 2015.

Hashemi-Pour, Cameron, George Lawton and Linda Tucci. 'Business Process Automation'. *TechTarget*, 14 December 2023. Available at: https://www.techtarget.com/searchcio/definition/business-process-automation.

Hashim, Mohammed. *Anatomy of Business Impact Management Using SMAC*. EMC2, 2014.

Hazama, Eijiro. 'Unravelling the Myth of Gandhian Non-violence: Why Did Gandhi Connect His Principle of Satyagraha with the "Hindu" Notion of Ahimsa?'. *Modern Intellectual History* 20, no. 1 (2023): 116–140.

Hindalco. *Hindalco's Sustainability Report 2023-24*. Available at: https://www.hindalco.com/upload/pdf/hindalco-annual-report-2023-24.pdf.

Hinton, Geoffrey, Li Deng, Dong Yu, George E. Dahl, Abdel-rahman Mohamed, and Navdeep Jaitly. 'Deep Neural Networks for Acoustic Modeling in Speech Recognition: The Shared Views of Four Research Groups'. *IEEE Signal Processing Magazine* 29, no. 6 (2012): 82–97. doi: 10.1109/MSP.2012.2205597.

History Crunch. 'Joseph Stalin'. Available at: https://www.historycrunch.com/joseph-stalin.html#google_vignette.

History of Data Science. 'AI Winter: The Highs and Lows of Artificial Intelligence', 9 January 2021. Available at: https://www.historyofdatascience.com/ai-winter-the-highs-and-lows-of-artificial-intelligence/.

History through Fiction. 'Mongol Culture and Religion: The Power of the Eternal Blue Sky'. Available at: https://www.historythroughfiction.com/blog/mongol-culture-and-religion.

Hodgson, Stephanie. 'Hitler and Mussolini: A Comparative Analysis of the Rome-Berlin Axis 1936–1940'. *E-International Relations*, 29 July 2011.

Hoffman, Philip T. 'Why Was It Europeans Who Conquered the World?'. *The Journal of Economic History* 72, no. 3 (2012): 601–633.

Hollander, Jordan. '10 Best Hotel Chatbots in 2025'. Hotel Tech Report, 1 July 2025. Available at: https://hoteltechreport.com/marketing/hotel-chatbots.

Homer. *The Iliad* and *The Odyssey*. Translated by Robert Fagles. London: Penguin Classics, 1999.

Honeywell. 'The Power of Energy Management Software'. Available at: https://www.honeywell.com/us/en/news/2024/06/power-of-energy-management-software.

'How a Steel Plant in India Tapped the Value of Data—and Won Global Acclaim'. McKinsey Insights, 8 March 2021.

'How Bajaj Finance Is Leveraging AI, Blockchain in Banking, Insurance'. *Economic Times*, 12 September 2025. Available at: https://bfsi.economictimes.indiatimes.com/articles/bajaj-finance-revolutionizes-banking-and-insurance-with-ai-and-blockchain-technology/123841144.

'How IoT and Blockchain May Streamline Transition to Digital Healthcare'. Business, 15 March 2018. Available at: https://www.kaaiot.com/blog/iot-blockchain-may-streamline-transition-digital-healthcare#.

'How Kamaraj Pioneered the Mid-Day Meal Scheme'. *Madras Courier*, 3 October 2023. Available at: https://madrascourier.com/biography/how-kamaraj-pioneered-the-mid-day-meal-scheme/.

'How Universal Robots Helped Bajaj Auto to Automate Its Assembly Lines'. Analytics Insight, 13 September 2019.

Hummingbirdsday. 'Tesla'. Available at: https://www.hummingbirdsday.com/tesla.

Ibex. 'Trusted Artificial Intelligence for All'. Available at: https://ibex-ai.com/technology/.

IBM. 'Accelerated Discovery'. Available at: https://research.ibm.com/topics/accelerated-discovery.

IBM. 'Deep Blue'. Available at: https://www.ibm.com/history/deep-blue.

IBM. 'The Games That Helped AI Evolve'. Available at: https://www.ibm.com/history/early-games.

IBM. 'What Is Automation?'. Available at: https://www.ibm.com/think/topics/automation.

IDC. 'IDC Worldwide AI and Generative AI Spending Guide', 19 August 2024. Available at: https://my.idc.com/getdoc.jsp?containerId=IDC_P33198.

India Employer Forum. 'Pharma Industry in India: An Outlook for 2025–2030'. Available at: https://indiaemployerforum.org/world-of-work/pharma-industry-in-india-2025-2030.

Infomineo. 'AI Chatbots in Customer Service: Can They Truly Replace Human Agents?', 24 March 2024. Available at: https://infomineo.com/artificial-intelligence/ai-chatbots-in-customer-service-can-they-replace-human/.

Intelesens. 'Evolution of the ECG Machine'. Available at: https://intelesens.com/evolution-of-the-ecg-machine/.

International Banker. 'The Collapse of Thomas Cook: What Happened and Why', 16 January 2020. Available at: https://internationalbanker.com/brokerage/the-collapse-of-thomas-cook-what-happened-and-why/.

International Labour Organisation (ILO). *The World Labour Report 2000*. Geneva: ILO. Available at: https://www.ilo.org.

Irfan, Mohammed, Mohammed Elmogy, Swati Gupta, Fahmi Khalifa and Rui Teixeira Dias. *AI-Driven Decentralized Finance and the Future of Finance.* IGI Global, 2024.

James. 'The Evolution of Wearable Technology'. Balliante, 25 November 2024. Available at: https://www.balliante.com/the-evolution-of-wearable-technology/.

Janeau, Erica and Christopher Sailus. 'The Barter System/Definition, History & Examples—Lesson'. Study, 21 November 2023. Available at: https://study.com/academy/lesson/bartering-systems-definition-lesson-quiz.html?msockid=380dc675aac3626321b1d33aaba1632c.

Japanese Wiki. 'Sukunabikona'. Available at: https://www.japanesewiki.com/Shinto/Sukunabikona.html.

Jiang, L. B. Li and M. Zhang. 'The Impact of Digital Transformation on the Efficiency of Corporate Resource Allocation: Internal Mechanisms and External Environment'. *Technological Forecasting and Social Change* 193 (2025): 124107.

Johnston, Lisa. 'P&G Leans into AI for Dynamic Routing and Sourcing Optimization', 23 January 2024. Available at: https://consumergoods.com/pg-leans-ai-dynamic-routing-andsourcing-optimization.

Joi, Priya. 'Using AI from Lab to Jab: How Did Artificial Intelligence Help Us Develop and Deliver Covid-19 Vaccines?'. Gavi, 27 February 2025. Available at: https://www.gavi.org/vaccineswork/using-ai-lab-jab-how-did-artificial-intelligence-help-us-develop-and-deliver-covid.

Jolly, Jasper. 'Driving Competition: China's Carmakers in Race to Dominate Europe's Roads'. *Guardian*, 7 November 2025. Available at: https://www.theguardian.com/business/2025/nov/07/china-in-push-to-dominate-europe-electric-vehicle-market-with-uk-as-gateway.

JSW Steel. *JSW Steel's Sustainability Report 2023-24*. Available at: https://www.jswsteel.in/investors/jsw-steel-investor-information-sustainability-reports.

Juniper Research. 'Losses from Online Payment Fraud to Exceed $362 Billion Globally Over Next 5 Years', June 2023. Available at: https://www.juniperresearch.com/press/losses-online-payment-fraud-exceed-362-billion/.

Kagan, Julia. 'What Is Hawala? Money Transfer Without Money Movement'. Investopedia, 29 July 2025. Available at: https://www.investopedia.com/terms/h/hawala.asp.

Kantar Media. 'Audience Measurement & Insight'. Available at: https://www.kantarmedia.com/services/audience-measurement.

Kearns, Jeff. 'AI's Reverberations across Finance'. *Finance & Development Magazine*, International Monetary Fund, December 2023. Available at: https://meetings.imf.org/en/-/media/files/publications/fandd/article/2023/december/38-41-kearns-final.pdf.

Kela. *Escalating Ransomware Threats to National Security, A Rising Scale of Attacks on Critical Infrastructure Sectors*, 2025.

Available at: https://www.kelacyber.com/resources/research/escalating-ransomware-threats-to-national-security/

Kelly, J.D., Tim. 'What Mistakes Did Bed Bath and Beyond Make?', 9 October 2023. Available at: https://www.lawinfo.com/resources/bankruptcy/business-bankruptcy/what-mistakes-did-bed-bath-and-beyond-make.html.

Kerner, Sean Michael and Madeleine Streets. 'Intel's Rise and Fall: A Timeline of What Went Wrong'. *TechTarget*, 19 August 2025. Available at: https://www.techtarget.com/WhatIs/feature/Intels-rise-and-fall-A-timeline-of-what-went-wrong.

Khandabattu, Haritha. 'The 2025 Hype Cycle for Artificial Intelligence Goes Beyond GenAI'. Gartner, 8 July 2025. Available at: https://www.gartner.com/en/articles/hype-cycle-for-artificial-intelligence.

Kitishian, Dany. 'HDFC Bank's AI Strategy: Analysis of Dominating Banking AI'. Klover, 17 July 2025. Available at: https://www.klover.ai/hdfc-bank-ai-strategy-analysis-of-dominating-banking-ai/.

Kitishian, Dany. 'Hilton's AI Strategy: Analysis of Dominance in Hospitality'. Klover, 4 August 2025. Available at: https://www.klover.ai/hilton-ai-strategy-analysis-of-dominance-in-hospitality-hotel-ai/.

Klover. 'Pfizer AI Strategy Analysis of Dominance in Pharma'. Available at: https://www.klover.ai/pfizer-ai-strategy-analysis-of-dominance-in-pharma/.

Korolov, M. '7 Top Predictive Analytics Use Cases: Enterprise Examples'. *TechTarget*, 2025. Available at: https://www.techtarget.com/searchbusinessanalytics/feature/Top-5-predictive-analytics-use-cases-in-enterprises.

Krzyszczyk, P., Alison Acevedo, Erika J. Davidoff et al. 'The Growing Role of Precision and Personalized Medicine for Cancer Treatment'. *Technology (Singap World Sci)* 6, nos. 3-4 (2018): 79–100. doi: 10.1142/S2339547818300020.

Kumar, Parvesh. 'Impact of Gandhi's Activism on Dalit Empowerment: Unravelling Complexity and Progress'. *Educational Administration Theory and Practice* 30, no. 5 (2024): 14133–14139.

L'Oreal Group. 'L'Oreal's Modiface Brings Ai-powered Virtual Makeup Try-on to Amazon'. Available at: https://www.loreal.com/en/articles/science-and-technology/l-oreal-modiface-brings-ai-powered-virtual-makeup-try-ons-to-amazon/.

Lambert, Carmen and Elias Delgado. '100 Years Since the Discovery of Insulin, from Its Discovery to the Insulins of the Future'. *Biomedicines* 12, no. 3 (2024): 533. Available at: https://pmc.ncbi.nlm.nih.gov/articles/PMC10968222/.

Lapuerta, Made. 'The Rise & Fall & Rise of GAP'. *Medium*, 29 June 2020. Available at: https://medium.com/dashion/the-rise-fall-rise-of-gap-6e29fa4b64d.

Laskowski, N. 'SMAC (Social, Mobile, Analytics and Cloud)'. *TechTarget*, 2020. Available at: https://www.techtarget.com/searchcio/definition/SMAC-social-mobile-analytics-and-cloud.

Latta, Hans. 'Western Union: Leading or Lagging Digital Transformation?'. Digital Initiative, 28 April 2018. Available at: https://d3.harvard.edu/platform-digit/submission/western-union-leading-or-lagging-digital-transformation/.

Lending Kart Finance. 'Lendingkart Annual Reports 2022'. Available at: https://lendingkartfinance.com/financials.

Levinson, Marc. *The Great A&P and the Struggle for Small Business in America*. New York: Hill and Wang, 2011.

Liebenau, J. 'Company Structure and Scientific Medicine, 1890-95'. In *Medical Science and Medical History.* London: Palgrave Macmillan, 1987. Available at: https://doi.org/10.1007/978-1-349-08739-6_3.

Linda Hall. 'Richard Arkwright'. Available at: https://www.lindahall.org.

Lutkevich, Ben. 'AI Winter'. *TechTarget*, 26 August 2024. Available at: https://www.techtarget.com/searchenterpriseai/definition/AI-winter.

Madrona. 'The Bet That Changed Everything: Satya Nadella on AI, Leadership, and the Future of Computing'. 12 September 2025. Available at: https://www.madrona.com/the-bet-that-changed-everything-satya-nadella-on-ai-leadership-and-the-future-of-computing/.

Make It British. 'A History of the Lancashire Cotton Mills', 30 August 2025. Available at: https://makeitbritish.co.uk/blog/lancashire-cotton-mills/.

Manufacturing Chemist. 'Where Zymergen Went Wrong: A Biomanufacturing Perspective for Synthetic Biology', 12 October 2022. Available at: https://www.manufacturingchemist.com/where-zymergen-went-wrong-a-biomanufacturing-perspective-for-synthetic-biology-204177.

Maru, Pankaj. 'ICICI Bank's AI Chatbot iPal Empowers Customers with Information and Financials'. Codex,

17 October 2017. Available at: https://codex.team/blog/ai-in-banking-how-icici-bank-leads-the-way.

McKinsey & Company. 'Generative AI Fuels Creative Physical Product Design but Is No Magic Wand', 5 March 2024. Available at: https://www.mckinsey.com/capabilities/mckinsey-digital/our-insights/generative-ai-fuels-creative-physical-product-design-but-is-no-magic-wand.

McKinsey & Company. 'Intelligent Process Automation: The Engine at the Core of the Next-Generation Operating Model', 14 March, 2017. Available at: https://www.mckinsey.com/capabilities/tech-and-ai/our-insights/intelligent-process-automation-the-engine-at-the-core-of-the-next-generation-operating-model.

McKinsey & Company. 'What Are AI Guardrails?', 14 November 2024. Available at: https://www.mckinsey.com/featured-insights/mckinsey-explainers/what-are-ai-guardrails.

McKinsey & Company. 'How Generative AI Can Boost Consumer Marketing', December 2023. Available at: https://www.mckinsey.com/capabilities/growth-marketing-and-sales/our-insights/how-generative-ai-can-boost-consumer-marketing.

McKinsey & Company. 'Digital Twins: The Next Frontier of Factory Optimization', 10 January 2024. Available at: https://www.mckinsey.com/capabilities/operations/our-insights/digital-twins-the-next-frontier-of-factory-optimization.

Mendels, F.F. 'Prior to Industrialization: The First Phase of the Industrialization Process'. *Journal of Economic History* 32, no. 1 (2010): 241–262.

Meta AI Blog. 'Introducing Llama 3.1: Our Most Capable Models to Date', 23 July 2024. Available at: https://ai.meta.com/blog/meta-llama-3-1/.

Meyer, David. 'The Rise and Fall of Sinclair Research'. *Fortune*, 28 February 2014.

Microsoft Azure. 'What Is Edge Computing?'. *Microsoft Azure Cloud Computing Dictionary*, 2025. Available at: https://azure.microsoft.com/en-us/resources/cloud-computing-dictionary/what-is-edge-computing.

Microsoft. 'Cost Efficiency Considerations for Your Cloud Adoption Strategy', 3 May 2025. Available at: https://learn.microsoft.com/en-us/azure/cloud-adoption-framework/strategy/inform/cost-efficiency.

Microsoft. 'The History and Timeline of Microsoft Word'. *Microsoft 365 Life Hacks*, 17 July 2024. Available at: https://www.microsoft.com/en-us/microsoft-365-life-hacks/writing/history-of-microsoft-word.

Microsoft. *Work Trend Index Annual Report, 2025: The Year the Frontier Firm Is Born.* Microsoft, 2025. Available at: https://www.microsoft.com/en-us/worklab/work-trend-index/2025-the-year-the-frontier-firm-is-born

Mixson, E. 'Data Science at Netflix: How Advanced Data & Analytics Helps Netflix Generate Billions'. AI Data Analytics Network, 19 March 2025. Available at: https://www.aidataanalytics.network/data-science-ai/articles/data-science-at-netflix-how-advanced-data-analytics-helped-netflix-generate-billions.

Mobikwik. 'MobiKwik Press Releases,2022-2024'. Available at: https://www.mobikwik.com/ir.

Mollick, Ethan. *Co-Intelligence: Living and Working with AI.* New York: Penguin Random House, 2024.

Monaghan, Angela. 'Nokia: The Rise and Fall of a Mobile Phone Giant'. *Guardian*, 3 September 2013. Available at: https://www.theguardian.com/technology/2013/sep/03/nokia-rise-fall-mobile-phone-giant.

Morda, Patrick. 'Augmented Reality'. *Audi Magazine*, 11 March 2025. Available at: https://magazine.audi.com.au/article/augmented-reality.

Mordor Intelligence. 'AI in Life Sciences Market Size & Share Analysis-Growth Trends & Forecasts (2025-2030)'. Available at: https://www.mordorintelligence.com/industry-reports/artificial-intelligence-in-life-sciences-market.

Moritz, Stefan and Kate Smaje. 'Forging the Human–Machine Alliance'. McKinsey & Company, 20 December 2022. Available at: https://www.mckinsey.com/capabilities/mckinsey-digital/our-insights/tech-forward/forging-the-human-machine-alliance.

Motion. 'Open Challenge Program Agenda'. Available at: https://motion.stpi.in/open_challenge#agenda.

Mucci, Tim. 'History of Artificial Intelligence'. IBM. Available at: https://www.ibm.com/think/topics/history-of-artificial-intelligence.

Mueller, Max. *Ramakrishna: His Life and Sayings*. New Delhi: Niyogi Books, 2019.

Mui, Chunka. 'How Kodak Failed'. *Forbes*, 18 January 2022.

Mukhopadhyay, Sounak. 'ChatGPT Writes Suicide Note for 29-Year-Old so That It Hurts Her Family Less; Mother Slams AI Bot after Losing Daughter'. LiveMint, 21 September 2025. Available at: https://www.livemint.com/news/trends/chatgpt-writes-suicide-note-for-29-year-old-so-that-it-hurts-her-family-less-mother-slams-ai-bot-after-losing-daughter-11758457919663.html.

Mullan, Laura. 'Warby Parker Uses Augmented Reality to Allow Customers to Virtually Try on Glasses'. *Technology Magazine*, 18 May 2020. Available at: https://technologymagazine.com/digital-transformation/warby-parker-uses-augmented-reality-allow-customers-virtually-try-glasses.

Munteanu, Aurora. 'Mastercard Launches a Fraud Prevention Solution in EEMEA'. The Paypers, 3 July 2025. Available at: https://thepaypers.com/fraud-and-fincrime/news/mastercard-launches-a-fraud-prevention-solution-in-eemea.

NASA. 'Why Does the World (and NASA) Need Digital Twins', 18 February 2025. Available at: https://science.nasa.gov/biological-physical/why-does-the-world-and-nasa-need-digital-twins/.

National Human Genome Research Institute. 'The Human Genome Project'. Available at: https://www.genome.gov/human-genome-project.

National Institute of Standards and Framework (US Department of Commerce). 'AI Risk Management Framework'. Available at: https://www.nist.gov/itl/ai-risk-management-framework.

NB Investments. 'AI Series: How Goldman Sachs Leverages AI to Extract Better Investment Insights', 8 November 2023. Available at: https://www.nbinvestments.ca/perspectives/article/how-goldman-sachs-leverages-ai-extract-better-investment-insights.html.

Nellis, Stephen. 'Nvidia CEO Says AI Could Pass Human Tests in Five Years'. Reuters, 2 March 2024. Available at: https://www.reuters.com/technology/nvidia-ceo-says-ai-could-pass-human-tests-five-years-2024-03-01/.

Nielsen. 'Audience Measurement'. Available at: https://www.nielsen.com/solutions/audience-measurement.

Novak, Steve. 'The Story of Bethlehem Steel Ended with Its 2003 Sale. But Its Fate Was Foreseen Much Earlier'. *Lehigh Valley Live*, 30 April 2023.

NPCI. 'National Payments Corporation of India (NPCI): UPI Transactions Data'. Available at: https://www.npci.org.in/product/upi/product-statistics.

NPR. 'A Massive Google Network Learns to Identify—Cats', 26 June 2012. Available at: https://www.npr.org/2012/06/26/155792609/a-massive-google-network-learns-to-identify.

Nunes, Ashley. 'Automation Doesn't Just Create or Destroy Jobs—It Transforms Them'. *Harvard Business Review*, 2 November 2021. Available at: https://hbr.org/2021/11/automation-doesnt-just-create-or-destroy-jobs-it-transforms-them.

Nvidia. 'Lab-in-the-Loop AI for Life Science'. Available at: https://www.nvidia.com/en-in/use-cases/lab-in-the-loop-ai-for-life-science/.

NYSE. 'The History of NYSE'. Available at: https://www.nyse.com/history-of-nyse.

O'Brien, Sara Ashley. 'The Rise and Fall of Theranos: A Timeline'. *CNN Business*, 7 July 2022.

Office of the Principal Scientific Adviser, Government of India. 'Artificial Intelligence Mission'. Available at: https://www.psa.gov.in/mission/artificial-intelligence/34.

OpenAI. 'DALL·E 2', 6 April 2022. Available at: https://openai.com/index/dall-e-2/.

OpenAI. 'Planning for AGI and Beyond', 24 February 2023. Available at: https://openai.com/index/planning-for-agi-and-beyond/.

'Oracle to Buy Sun Microsystems for $7.4 Billion'. *Bloomberg*, 20 April 2009.

Order White Moon. 'The White Moon Goddess Gallery Presents Airmid: Keeper of the Herbs of Healing'. Available at: https://orderwhitemoon.org/goddess/Airmid/airmid.html.

OshaeIFA. 'Ozain: The Herber of the Yoruba Pantheon'. Available at: https://en.oshaeifa.com/orisha/ozin/.

Oxford Reference. 'Artificial Intelligence'. Available at: https://www.oxfordreference.com/display/10.1093/oi/authority.20110803095426960.

Pagadi, Setu Madhavarai. *Shivaji*. New Delhi: National Book Trust, 2011.

Partovi, Shez and Ian Meyers. 'AWS and Novartis Redefining Pharma Manufacturing'. AWS (blog), 4 December 2019. Available at: https://aws.amazon.com/blogs/industries/aws-and-novartis-re-inventing-pharma-manufacturing/.

Patel, Rikin, Mohamad Kaki, Venkat S. Potluri, Payal Kahar and Deepesh Khanna. 'A Comprehensive Review of SARS-CoV-2

Vaccines: Pfizer, Moderna & Johnson & Johnson.' *Human Vaccines & Immunotherapeutics* 18, no. 1 (2022): 2002083.

Patwardhan, Bhushan and Indu Ramchandani. *Genome to Om: Evolving Journey of Modern Science to Meta-Science*. Noida: BlueOne INK, 2024.

'Paytm Payments Services Get "In-Principle" Nod from RBI to Operate as Online Payment Aggregator'. *Economic Times*, 12 August 2025. Available at: https://economictimes.indiatimes.com/industry/banking/finance/banking/paytm-payments-services-gets-in-principle-nod-from-rbi-to-operate-as-online-payment-aggregator/articleshow/123261536.cms.

Perrigo, Billy. 'Meta's AI Chief Yann LeCun on AGI, Open-Source, and AI Risk'. *Time*, 13 February 2024. Available at: https://time.com/6694432/yann-lecun-meta-ai-interview/.

Peterson, Hayley. 'Walmart Reveals It's Tracking Checkout Theft with AI-Powered Cameras in 1,000 Stores'. *Business Insider*, 20 June 2019. Available at: https://www.businessinsider.com/walmart-tracks-theft-with-computer-vision-1000-stores-2019-6.

Petrina Kamya et al. 'PandaOmics: An AI-Driven Platform for Therapeutic Target and Biomarker Discovery'. *Journal of Chemical Information and Modeling* 64, no. 10 (2024): 3961–3969.

Pew Research. 'The Global Catholic Population', 13 February 2013. Available at: https://www.pewresearch.org/religion/2013/02/13/the-global-catholic-population/.

Pfizer. 'mRNA and Artificial Intelligence for Advanced Vaccine Innovation'. Available at: https://www.pfizer.com/news/articles/how_a_novel_incubation_sandbox_helped_speed_up_data_analysis_in_pfizer_s_covid_19_vaccine_trial.

Pharmaceutical Technology. 'Artificial Intelligence: Who Are the Leaders in AI in Multiomics for the Pharmaceutical Industry?', 29 July 2024. Available at: https://www.pharmaceutical-technology.com/data-insights/innovators-ai-ai-in-multiomics-pharmaceutical/.

Pharmaphorum. 'A History of: Contract Research Organisations (CROs)'. Available at: https://pharmaphorum.com/views-and-analysis/a_history_of_contract_research_organisations_cros.

Pichai, Sundar. 'Questions, Shrugs and What Comes Next: A Quarter Century of Change'. Google Blog, 5 September 2023. Available at: https://blog.google/inside-google/message-ceo/google-25th-birthday-sundar-pichai/.

Poetry Foundation. 'Friends, Romans, Countrymen, Lend Me Your Ears, Julius Caesar, Spoken by Mark Antony, William Shakespeare'. Available at: https://www.poetryfoundation.org/poems/56968/speech-friends-romans-countrymen-lend-me-your-ears.

Poets. 'O, Pardon me, thou bleeding piece of earth, Julius Caesar, Act II, Scene I, Academy of American Poets, William Shakespeare'. Available at: https://poets.org/poem/julius-caesar-act-iii-scene-i-o-pardon-me-thou-bleeding-piece-earth.

Pothos. 'Introduction to Alexander the Great'. Available at: https://www.pothos.org/content/.

Pradhan Mantri Jan-Dhan Yojana. 'PMJDY Statistics'. Available at: https://www.pmjdy.gov.in/statewise-statistics.

Prasad, Nikita. 'Softbank Exits Paytm in June Quarter at Loss of $150 Million'. *LiveMint*, 13 July 2024.

Press Information Bureau Delhi. 'India Is Keen to Increase Share of Manufacturing in GDP from 17% to 25%: Union Minister Hardeep S Puri' (press release), 29 September 2023. Available at: https://www.pib.gov.in/PressReleasePage.aspx?PRID=1962137.

Press Information Bureau Delhi. 'India on Track to Become $35 Trillion, Fully Developed Economy by 2047: Shri Piyush Goyal', 19 February 2024. Available at: https://www.pib.gov.in/PressReleasePage.aspx?PRID=2007105.

Process Genius. 'How IoT, AI and 3D Digital Twin Boost Predictive Maintenance in Manufacturing'. Available at: https://processgenius.eu/articles/how-iot-ai-and-3d-digital-twin-boost-predictive-maintenance-in-manufacturing/.

Proteomica International Private Limited. 'Core Research'. Available at: https://www.proteomica.in/core-research.

PYMNTS. 'Domino's Makes a Pizza Points Loyalty Play with AI', 31 January 2019. Available at: https://www.pymnts.com/news/retail/2019/dominos-pizza-artificial-intelligence-rewards/.

PYMNTS. 'Starbucks Uses AI-Powered Personalized Rewards to Boost Frequency and Spend', 30 January 2024. Available at: https://www.pymnts.com/news/loyalty-and-rewards-news/2024/starbucks-uses-artificial-intelligence-powered-personalized-rewards-boost-frequency-check-size/.

Quach, S., P. Thaichon, K.D. Martin, S. Weaven and R.W. Palmatier. 'Digital Technologies: Tensions in Privacy and Data'. *Journal of the Academy of Marketing Science* 51, no. 6 (2022): 1221–1241.

Quote Investigator, 'Quote Origin: The Factory of the Future Will Have Only Two Employees, a Man and a Dog', 30 January 2022. Available at: https://quoteinvestigator.com/2022/01/30/future-factory/.

R.P., Srikanth. 'Manoj Gautam, CIO, Maruti Suzuki on How the Auto Leader Is Shifting Gears for the AI Era'. Express Computer, 28 October 2025. Available at: https://www.expresscomputer.in/exclusives/manoj-gautam-cio-maruti-suzuki-on-how-the-auto-leader-is-shifting-gears-for-the-ai-era/128920/.

Rao, B., Ramana and Savitha Kulkarni. 'Chatbots of Indian Banks-Utility for Prospective Customers-A Perceptive Study'. *ITM Web of Conferences* 68, 01013 (2024). Available at: https://www.itm-conferences.org/articles/itmconf/pdf/2024/11/itmconf_icaetm2024_01013.pdf.

Rajpal, Surabhi. 'Autonomous Ride-Hailing Grown in Key US Markets'. S&P Global, 5 December 2025. Available at: https://www.spglobal.com/automotive-insights/en/blogs/2025/12/autonomous-ride-hailing-grows-key-us-markets.

Red Hat. 'SLMs vs LLMs: What Are Small Language Models?', 23 April 2025. Available at: https://www.redhat.com/en/topics/ai/llm-vs-slm.

ResearchGate. 'Evolution of Bioinformatics from 2000 to 2010'. Available at: https://www.researchgate.net/figure/Evolution-of-bioinformatics-from-2000-to-2010_fig5_364058017.

Reuters. 'Amazon's Corporate Workforce May Shrink as AI Takes Over Routine Tasks', 19 June 2025. Available at: https://www.reuters.com/business/retail-consumer/amazons-workforce-reduce-rollout-generative-ai-agents-2025-06-17/.

Reuters. 'India Plans Over Rs 18,000 Crore in Incentives for New Manufacturing Sectors'. *Economic Times*, 20 September 2023. Available at: https://economictimes.indiatimes.com/news/economy/policy/india-plans-over-rs-18000-cr-in-incentives-for-new-manufacturing-sectors/articleshow/103810315.cms.

Rifkin, Jeremy. *Third Industrial Revolution.* St. Martin's Press, 2011.

'The Rise and Fall of BlackBerry Mobiles: A Cautionary Tale in Tech Evolution'. *Global Technology Review*, 19 June 2024. Available at: https://reviewbooku.com/review/the-rise-and-fall-of-blackberry-4951969.

Roy, Tanya. 'The History and Evolution of Artificial Intelligence, AI's Present and Future'. *All Tech Magazine*, 19 July 2023. Available at: https://alltechmagazine.com/the-evolution-of-ai/.

Rupifi. 'Building the Payments Infrastructure for 70 MN+ SMEs in Bharat'. Available at: https://www.rupifi.com/about.

S&P Global. 'Digital Twins in the Automotive Industry Explained', 11 September 2025. Available at: https://www.spglobal.com/automotive-insights/en/blogs/2025/08/digital-twins-in-the-automotive-industry-explained.

Sajja, Guna Sekhar and Santosh Reddy Addula. 'Automation Using Robots, Machine Learning and Artificial Intelligence to Enhance Production and Quality', 2024 Second International Conference Computational and Characterization Techniques in Engineering & Sciences, IEEExplore.

SAP. 'What Is the Industrial Internet of Things (IIoT)?'. *SAP Industry 4.0 Solutions*, 2025. Available at: https://www.sap.com/india/products/scm/industry-4-0/what-is-iiot.html.

Sardesai, Govind Sakharam. *Chatrapati Shivaji Maharaj*. Marathi. Pune: Varada Books, 2022.

Sarkar, Jadunath. *Shivaji and His Times*. London: Longmans, Green and Co., 1920.

Sayegh, Emil. 'How Cloud Computing Revolutionized Business Operations and What Lies Ahead'. *Forbes*, 28 November 2023. Available at: https://www.forbes.com/sites/emilsayegh/2023/11/28/how-cloud-computing-revolutionized-business-operations-and-what-lies-ahead.

'SBI Launches Chatbot to Help Customers in Banking Activities'. *Economic Times*, 25 September 2017. Available at: https://economictimes.indiatimes.com/industry/banking/finance/banking/sbi-launches-chatbot-to-help-customers-in-banking-activities/articleshow/60827485.cms?from=mdr.

Schneider Electric. 'Our AI-based Solutions'. Available at: https://www.se.com/ww/en/work/solutions/artificial-intelligence/solutions.jsp.

Schneider, Guilherme. 'The AI Wars between Nations: A New Arms Race or Catalyst for Collaboration'. *Modern Diplomacy*, 2 October 2023. Available at: https://moderndiplomacy.eu/2023/10/02/the-ai-wars-between-nations-a-new-arms-race-or-a-catalyst-for-collaboration/.

Schulz, Madeleine. 'Louis Vuitton's Latest AR Project? Covering Landmarks in Dots'. *Vogue Business*, 26 January 2023. Available at: https://www.vogue.com/article/louis-vuittons-latest-ar-project-covering-landmarks-in-dots.

Sephora. 'Sephora Virtual Artist: Try On Makeup Instantly'. Available at: https://www.sephora.my/pages/virtual-artist?srsltid=AfmBOoo-5nktUS88uCClT7jtoLGzt8tMVwbQmO-UwiKgq-EFal5loNSY.

Seshadri, Kandadai. 'Ramanuja: Social Influence of His Life and Teaching'. *Economic and Political Weekly* 31, no. 5 (1996): 292–298.

'Seven in Ten Pharma Digital Projects Fail to Deliver Despite Heavy Investments'. *Economic Times*, 24 September 2025. Available at: https://pharma.economictimes.indiatimes.com/news/pharma-industry/seven-in-ten-pharma-digital-projects-fail-to-deliver-despite-heavy-investments-vector-study/124091233.

Shepard, Steven. *Telecommunications Crash Course.* McGraw-Hill Education, 2014.

Sher, David. 'Five Footwear Industry Leaders Using 3D Printing for Production Today'. VoxelMatters, 2 March 2024. Available at: https://www.voxelmatters.com/five-footwear-industry-leaders-using-3d-printing-for-production-today/.

Sherin, M.J. 'India's IT Rise: How the Y2K Crisis Sparked a Global Tech Transformation'. *Deccan Chronicle*, 15 May 2025.

Shinde, Yogesh. 'AI Robots: Transforming Industries with Smart Robotic Solutions'. *Robotics Tomorrow*, 23 August 2024.

Shopify. 'Augmented Reality for Ecommerce with Shopify AR'. Available at: https://www.shopify.com/augmented-reality.

Siemens Global. 'Imaging'. Available at: https://www.siemens.com/global/en/company/about/history/technology/medical-technology/imaging.html.

Siemens Global. 'SIMATIC Energy Management Software'. Available at: https://www.siemens.com/global/en/products/automation/industry-software/automation-software/energymanagement.html.

Siemens. 'AI Solutions in Healthcare'. Available at: https://siemens-healthineers.com/ en-in/ai-healthcare-solutions.

Siemens. 'Senseye Predictive Maintenance-Reliability Redefined'. Available at: https://www.siemens.com/global/en/products/services/digital-enterprise-services/analytics-artificial-intelligence-services/senseye-predictive-maintenance.html.

Siemens. 'Smart Manufacturing: Building the Factory of Tomorrow'. Available at: https://assets.new.siemens.com/siemens/assets/api/uuid:4259772d-c315-4748-b571-bea6bf983f8c/final-factorytomorrow-wp.pdf.

Singh, Rajesh Kumar and Abhijith Ganapavaram. 'GE Completed Three-Way Split, Breaking Off from Its Storied Past'. Reuters, 3 April 2024. Available at: https://www.reuters.com/markets/us/ge-completes-three-way-split-breaking-off-its-storied-past-2024-04-02/.

Sites at Penn State. 'Trade and Barter System in the Indus Valley Civilization', 6 February 2025. Available at: https://sites.psu.edu/pecunia/2025/02/06/trade-and-barter-system-in-the-indus-valley-civilization/.

Skills Alpha. 'About'. Available at: https://skillsalpha.com/about/.

Smith, Matt. 'Walmart's New Intelligent Retail Lab Shows a Glimpse into the Future of Retail, IRL'. Walmart, 25 April 2019. Available at: https://corporate.walmart.com/news/2019/04/25/walmarts-new-intelligent-retail-lab-shows-a-glimpse-into-the-future-of-retail-irl.

Smriti. 'Motorola: The Mobile Phone Brand That Could Still Exist'. InspireIP, 10 May 2023. Available at: https://inspireip.com/motorola-failure-story/.

Solomon, Michah. 'Four Seasons Leader Isadore Sharp: Treat Employees Right so They Treat Customers Right'. *Forbes*, 18 August 2015. Available at: https://www.forbes.com/sites/micahsolomon/2015/08/17/four-seasons-leader-isadore-sharp-treat-employees-right-so-they-treat-customers-right/.

Soutar, Colin et al. 'Industry Spending on Quantum Computing Will Rise Dramatically. Will It Pay Off?' Deloitte Insights, 27 July 2023. Available at: https://deloitte.wsj.com/cio/quantum-computing-in-financial-services-will-it-pay-off.

Sprintzeal. 'The Rise and Fall of Blackberry: Key Business Lessons', 29 November 2024. Available at: https://www.sprintzeal.com/blog/the-fall-of-blackberry.

Sravathi AI. 'Services'. Available at: https://sravathi.ai/services.

Stability AI. 'Stable Diffusion Announcement', 10 August 2022. Available at: https://stability.ai/news/stable-diffusion-announcement.

Stanford University. 'Robots and Their Arms'. Stanford InfoLab Museum Archive. Available at: http://infolab.stanford.edu/pub/voy/museum/pictures/display/1-Robot.htm.

Strohanova, Catherine. 'How to Bring Value to Customer's Shopping Experience and Increase Sales with AR'. Available at: https://www.jasoren.com/how-to-bring-value-to-customers-shopping-experience-and-increase-sales-with-ar.

Study. 'Second Industrial Revolution/Timeline, Inventions & Effects'. Available at: https://study.com/academy/lesson/the-second-industrial-revolution-timeline-inventions.html?msockid=380dc675aac3626321b1d33aaba1632c.

Suleyman, Mustafa and Michael Bhaskar. *The Coming Wave: Technology, Power, and the Twenty-first Century's Greatest Dilemma.* London: The Bodley Head, 2023.

Survey Monkey. 'Dating Apps Are Common, Useful- and Widely Disliked'. Available at: https://www.surveymonkey.com/curiosity/dating-apps-and-sites-are-almost-as-common-as-they-are-disliked/.

Svensson, Philip. 'Walmart: Walton, Retailing, and Everyday Low Prices', 8 September 2025. https://quartr.com/insights/company-research/walmart-walton-retailing-and-everyday-low-prices.

Swami Nikhilananda. *The Gospel of Sri Ramakrishna.* Chennai: Ramakrishna Math, 2006.

Swami Saradananda. *Sri Ramakrishna, the Great Master*. Chennai: Ramakrishna Math, 2011.

Tabansi, Obi. 'Frederick Taylor and the Time and Motion Study'. Supply Chain Nuggets, 8 July 2023. Available at: https://supplychainnuggets.com/frederick-taylor-and-the-time-and-motion-study/.

Target. 'Guest Security & Fraud Protection'. Available at: https://security.target.com/.

Tata Steel. 'Tata Steel's Jamshedpur Plant Recognised as World Economic Forum's Advanced 4th Industrial Revolution Lighthouse', 15 March 2021. Available at: https://www.tatasteel.com/media/newsroom/press-releases/india/2021/tata-steel-s-jamshedpur-plant-recognised-as-world-economic-forum-s-advanced-4th-industrial-revolution-4ir-lighthouse/.

Tees Valley Museums. 'George Stephenson'. Available at: https://www.teesvalleymuseums.org.

The One Club. 'Tiffany Engagement Ring Experience'. Available at: https://www.oneclub.org/awards/theoneshow/-award/21458/tiffany-engagement-ring-experience/.

TiE. 'The Founding of TiE'. Available at: https://tie.org/the-genesis-of-tie/.

Toyota. 'Toyota Research Institute Unveils New Generative AI Technique for Vehicle Design', 20 June 2023. Available at: https://pressroom.toyota.com/toyota-research-institute-unveils-new-generative-ai-technique-for-vehicle-design/.

'Total UPI Transactions Cross 100 Billion Mark in 2023'. *Economic Times*, 2 January 2024.

'Travel PR Mistakes: An In-Depth Analysis of the Failure of Thomas Cook'. *Everything PR News*, 28 May 2025. Available at: https://www.everything-pr.com.

Trewavas, A. 'A Brief History of Systems Biology. "Every Object that Biology Studies is a System of Systems." Francois Jacob (1974).' *Plant Cell* 18, no. 10 (2006): 2420–30. doi: 10.1105/tpc.106.042267.

Turing, A.M. 'Computing Machinery and Intelligence'. *Mind* 49 (1950): 433–460. Available at: https://courses.cs.umbc.edu/471/papers/turing.pdf.

Ulta Beauty. 'Virtual Makeup Try-On'. Available at: https://www.ulta.com/innovation/glamlab/.

United Nations International School. 'About UNIS'. Available at: https://www.unis.org/about-unis.

Valmiki. *The Ramayanam*. Translated by William Buck. Berkeley: University of California Press, 1976.

Varma, Pavan K. *Adi Shankaracharya: Hinduism's Greatest Thinker*. New Delhi: Tranquebar, 2018.

Ved Vyasa. *Mahabharata*. Translated by C. Rajagopalachari. 64th ed. Mumbai: Bharatiya Vidya Bhavan, 2010.

Venture Beat. 'Rental Giant Blockbuster Files for Bankruptcy'. Available at: https://www.venturebeat.com.

Virtual Reality Marketing. 'Adidas AR Sneakers Try-On App'. Available at: https://www.virtualrealitymarketing.com/case-studies/adidas-ar-sneakers-try-on-app-2/.

Vogels, Emily A. and Monica Anderson. 'Dating and Relationships in the Digital Age', 8 May 2020. Available at: https://www.pewresearch.org/internet/2020/05/08/dating-and-relationships-in-the-digital-age/.

Walmart. 'Walmart's Generative AI Search Puts More Time Back in Customers' Hands', 30 January 2024. Available at: https://tech.walmart.com/content/walmart-global-tech/en_us/blog/post/walmarts-generative-ai-search-puts-more-time-back-in-customers-hands.html.

Warehouse Automation. 'How Nike Is Transforming Its Supply Chain to Best Serve Consumers'. Available at: https://www.warehouseautomation.ai/top-stories/how-nike-is-transforming-its-supply-chain-to-best-serve-consumers-mgrdn-pgmxd.

White, Alexandria. '5 Things to Know about the Target RedCard'. CNBC, 15 November 2024. Available at: https://www.cnbc.com/select/target-redcard-what-you-should-know/?msockid=380dc675aac3626321b1d33aaba1632c.

Wikipedia. 'Andreas Vesalius'. Available at: https://en.wikipedia.org/wiki/Andreas_Vesalius.

Wikipedia. 'Arise, Awake and Stop Not till the Goal Is Reached, Swami Vivekananda'. Available at: https://en.wikipedia.org/wiki/Arise,_awake,_and_stop_not_till_the_goal_is_reached.

Wikipedia. 'Dick Smith'. Available at: https://en.wikipedia.org/wiki/Dick_Smith_(retailer).

Wikipedia. 'Eaton's'. Available at: https://en.wikipedia.org/wiki/Eaton%27s.

Wikipedia. 'Geoffrey Hinton'. Available at: https://en.wikipedia.org/wiki/Geoffrey_Hinton.

Wikipedia. 'History of Banking'. Available at: https://en.wikipedia.org/wiki/History_of_banking.

Wikipedia. 'Imperial Bank of India'. Available at: https://en.wikipedia.org/wiki/Imperial_Bank_of_India.

Wikipedia. 'Jute Trade'. Available at: https://en.wikipedia.org/wiki/Jute_trade.

Wikipedia. 'Keating-Owen Act'. Available at: https://en.wikipedia.org/wiki/Keating-Owen_Act.

Wikipedia. 'Mendelian Inheritance'. Available at: www.en.wikipedia.org/wiki/Mendelian_inheritance.

Wikipedia. 'New York Stock Exchange'. Available at: https://en.wikipedia.org/wiki/New_York_Stock_Exchange.

Wikipedia. 'Online Banking'. Available at: https://en.wikipedia.org/wiki/Online_banking.

Wikipedia. 'Rothamsted Research'. Available at: https://en.wikipedia.org/wiki/Rothamsted_Research.

Wikipedia. 'Sears'. Available at: https://en.wikipedia.org/wiki/Sears.

Wikipedia. 'Simon Bolivar'. Available at: https://en.wikipedia.org/wiki/Simón_Bolívar.

Wikipedia. 'Taare Zameen Par'. Available at: https://en.wikipedia.org/wiki/Taare_Zameen_Par.

Wikipedia. 'The Artifice Girl'. Available at: https://en.wikipedia.org/wiki/The_Artifice_Girl.

Wikipedia. 'Veni, vidi, vici'. Available at: https://en.wikipedia.org/wiki/Veni,_vidi,_vici.

Wikipedia. 'Wirecard Scandal'. Available at: https://en.wikipedia.org/wiki/Wirecard_scandal.

Wikipedia. 'Zavvi'. Available at: https://en.wikipedia.org/wiki/Zavvi.

Williams, Danielle. 'We've Been Here Before: AI Promised Humanlike Machines in 1958'. *The Conversation*, 29 February 2024. Available at: https://theconversation.com/weve-been-here-before-ai-promised-humanlike-machines-in-1958-222700.

Wolford, Ben. 'What Is GDPR, the EU's New Data Protection Law?'. GDPR, 2018. Available at: https://gdpr.eu/what-is-gdpr.

World Economic Forum. *The Future of Manufacturing: Driving Capabilities, Enabling Investments*. Geneva: World Economic Forum, November 2014.

World Mythos. 'Patecatl'. Available at: https://worldmythos.com/patecatl/.

World Travel & Tourism Council. 'Travel & Tourism Economic Impact Research (EIR)'. Available at: https://wttc.org/research/economic-impact.

Worldwide Quarterly Augmented and Virtual Reality Headset Tracker. *IDC*, 2024. Available at: https://my.idc.com/getdoc.jsp?containerId=IDC_P35095.

Ycharts. 'Airbnb, Inc (ABNB)'. Available at: https://ycharts.com/companies/ABNB/market_cap.

YEC. 'How the Fourth Industrial Revolution Is Impacting the Future of Work'. *Forbes*, 19 October 2018. Available at: https://www.forbes.com/councils/theyec/2018/10/19/how-the-fourth-industrial-revolution-is-impacting-the-future-of-work/.

ZealousWeb. 'Facebook Evolution—Managing the Business Social Wave'. ZealousWeb Blog, 28 November 2023. Available at: https://www.zealousweb.com/blog/facebook-evolution-managing-business-social-wave.

Index

About the Authors

Dr Ganesh Natarajan is Chairman of 5F World, GTT Data Solutions Ltd, Honeywell Automation and Lighthouse Communities Foundation. He is also a Global Partner in Cornerstone Ventures, ICrowd and Arise Ventures. He has published fifteen books and is a regular speaker at national and international forums.

Dr Uma Ganesh is Chairperson of GTT Foundation and Board Director at Skills Alpha, 5F World and Emoha Health. Uma has co-founded 5F World and co-authored two books on knowledge management and digital success. Her entrepreneurial venture Global Talent Track attracted investment by Intel Capital, CISCO, Helion Ventures and SMCV, and was listed as GTT Data Solutions on the BSE. GTT and its digital platform, Skills Alpha, have so far impacted 1.2 million youth in the country.

Priyanka Sangani is a business journalist with over two decades of experience reporting for some of India's most respected financial publications, including *The Economic Times*, *Business Standard* and *Business Today*. Her work reflects a deep curiosity about how technology is reshaping industries and impacting how we live, work and engage with the world around us in our everyday lives.

